MORE
South African
Insults

Also by Sarah Britten:
The Worst Year of My Life—So Far (2000)
The Martin Tudhope Show (2002)
The Art of the South African Insult (2006)
McBride of Frankenmanto: The Return of the South African Insult (2007)

Published in 2009 by 30° South Publishers (Pty) Ltd.
3 Ajax Place, 120 Caroline Street, Brixton
Johannesburg 2092, South Africa
www.30degreessouth.co.za
info@30degreessouth.co.za

Design and origination by 30° South Publishers (Pty) Ltd.
Cartoon sketches by Sarah Britten

Printed and bound by Pinetown Printers, Durban

ISBN 978-0-9584890-8-9

MORE
South African
Insults

Sarah Britten

30° South Publishers

Sarah Britten has been described by Barry Ronge as "Hitler with tits". Her first piece of comic reportage, on the wonders of kugels and buying a Matric dance dress in Sandton City, appeared in *Style* magazine in 1991 when she was 17.

She has won Sanlam Prizes for Youth Literature for *The Worst Year of My Life—So Far* (2000) and *The Martin Tudhope Show* (2002). She wrote her Master's research report on South African humour (with a focus on Madam & Eve) and has a doctorate in Applied English Language Studies, the title of her thesis being 'One nation, one beer: the mythology of the new South Africa in advertising'.

Her area of academic interest relates to national identity and comedy, and the concept of 'National Intimacy', as defined by the anthropologist Michael Herzfeld. The good citizens of Mooinooi once tried to send her death threats after she quoted a man who described them as being like ropes—thick, hairy and twisted—but they couldn't find her number in the phone book. David Bullard's fans, who resemble a pack of escaped Labradors gone bad after a week without Bob Martins and Eukanuba, were mightily offended when she pointed out a punctuation error in one of his articles. She already has an active 'hate club' of ex-pat whingers in Perth, Australia.

Sarah enjoys birdwatching, wildlife, painting with lipstick (and pastels). She plays the piano, her favourite composer is Bach and she plans to write a fugue in four parts based on the Nokia ring tone. She can also do a mean Australian accent for anyone who asks.

Contents

Chapter 1

State of the Nation

"South Africans are masters of craziness, and natural geniuses when it comes to insults." Chris Roper

"I love South Africans," Fred Khumalo declares.

"I love them because they are creative. We are denialists (we learnt from the best, of course). We are racists. We are tribalists. But, hell, we can laugh at ourselves ... when we feel like doing it."

This book has been written in the interests of helping the nation along with that task in mind.

"For the eternal optimists among us." Dedication in Zapiro's collection, *Pirates of Polokwane*

Laughing at ourselves is not always easy. In fact, a lot of the time, it's tempting to get really depressed. Many South Africans would agree with News24 user Sello Molekwa, who said he was going to stop watching TV because he was tired of all the bad news. "I really wish I can sleep for a year and wake up when all this nonsense is over!" he wrote. "After this lengthy dose of scandals and bad news, South Africans have no reason to be inspired and motivated. Morale is low and all we do is accuse and blame one another and go on bickering."

David Bullard understands. He writes: "The truth is that SA Inc has been so badly managed over the years by a combination of dickheads and incompetents that it's hardly any wonder we all feel gloomy. Would you let Alec Erwin rewire your house? Maybe the next lot will bring some much needed cheer."

"We are a nation of bedwetters and also-rans and it's all thanks to the ANC policy of constantly droning on about the struggle, racism, colonialism etc etc." David Bullard, post axing by the *Sunday Times*

Based on pronouncements by Zuma, Malema, Vavi et al, that seems unlikely. As David Kau has observed, "After calls to nationalize Bafana Bafana, hasn't it become clear that if you want to completely destroy something and lose money on anything — hand it over to the government?"

He points out: "If you still don't have an idea of what it would be like to have the national soccer team run by the government, look no further than home affairs, Eskom, the department of health, the department of lack of safety and security, roads and public works, housing, transport — anywhere in government except in the tender-giving department."

"It was as big as the Reserve Bank Governor, softer than the Presidency's policy towards Zimbabwe and smelt worse than my fridge after two days of Eskom folly." Kevin McCallum describes the pile of dog poo into which he stepped at a Springbok training session

So, ja hey, life in South Africa is one long emotional roller coaster. Except maybe with fewer highs.

South Africans are bipolar, says Jared Cinman, who's one of the few staunch patriots left. "Put some bleeding guy with an oblong-shaped ball on a patch of grass and the entire country clings to one another like chewing gum to an economy-class table. But raise the topics of crime or politics and we're ready to go to war with one another within the first few phrases of the debate."

Heidi Holland, Robert Mugabe's biographer, argues that South Africa is in need of extensive therapy.[1] "Far from being a society in the advanced stages of recovery from our terrible history," she writes, "South Africa is a gigantic psychiatric unit. With so many of us, whites as well as blacks, failing to acknowledge, let alone wrestle with, our wounded psyches, we are not so much a nation in decline following great expectations, but a traumatized people hovering between depression and delusion."

---

[1] Let's hope it's covered by medical aid.

Anyone who makes the mistake of embracing optimism is reminded by Sipho Seepe: "We have become prisoners of hope. The sooner we disabuse ourselves of the notion that changes will occur miraculously, the better."

> "I'm very involved and participating in what happens in this country because I love this bloody fucked-up place." Steve Hofmeyr

Breyten Breytenbach is in no danger of making that mistake: "If a young South African were to ask me whether he or she should stay or leave, my bitter advice would be to go," he wrote in *Harper's* magazine.

In response, the satirical website Hayibo.com—a South African equivalent of The Onion—quoted a couple of confused young South Africans: "I thought Breyten Breytenbach was the Latin name for a yeast infection," said Luckystrike Xaba, 18, of Soweto. And Chrizanlimarie Brits, 16, of Welkom posed the question: "But why would anyone ask him anything when we don't know who he is?"

As it turned out, many South Africans came back. 2008 might have been a crappy year, but did give many of their compatriots who were planning to emigrate a very good reason to stay. The global financial crisis meant that there were no jobs for them overseas. Under a heading that would have provoked more than a little schadenfreude— "Broke expats return home"—the *Sunday Times* reported that expats who had lost their jobs in the global financial bloodbath were being forced to return.

Perhaps they will learn to change their ways. As Jarred Cinman argues, "Saying negative, depressing, pessimistic stuff about South Africa is of absolutely no help to anyone. It's a cynical form of entertainment that lubricates the otherwise dull days of middle-class life. It's so obscenely ingrained in our culture that it's become a social disease ... Basically I'm saying this: Get over your crap, South Africa. I'm excited and happy to be here. Come join me in the light."

And he's right: the sun will shine tomorrow. In South Africa, it usually does.

> "If we get it right, we'll project ourselves as the warm, passionate, creative and funny nation that we are—a people who still share a stubborn spirit of hope and courage." Carlos Amato on the 2010 World Cup

Chapter 2

Malemaphobia:
Julius Malema and the Actual Imbeciles

"Oh, how I love Julius Malema. I can't help it. I'm besotted with his chubby little face, his gimlet eyes, his petulant lips. He's like a cross between an unshaven Britney Spears and crack cocaine, except with half the talent and twice as addictive." Chris Roper

Zapiro depicted him as a baby in a nappy farting at his audience. The Freedom Front Plus said he was an example of what happened when corporal punishment was banned. David Bullard suggested that South Africa buy Iceland and send him there to cool off. He was described, variously, as "obdurately gormless", a "contumelious nincompoop", the "jelly tsotsi", an "Msholozi Mini-Me", the "Paris Hilton of South African politics".

At the beginning of 2008, nobody had heard of Julius Malema. By the end of the year, everybody wished they hadn't.

"We cannot allow Malema's mouth to ruin this country." Khaya Dlanga

The days when Fikile Mbalula was president of the ANC Youth League are now but a distant, happy memory. Many South Africans were initially worried that the departure for cabinet of the man famous for saying there were too many Indians at the University of KwaZulu-Natal would reduce the steady supply of material from what Hogarth referred to as Brett Kebble Single Malt-Tasting Academy.

After all, under Mbalula's tenure, the ANCYL-biters, as Chris Roper lovingly described them, issued such gems as "The ANC Youth League calls on the Deputy Chief Justice of the Constitutional Court, Dikgang Moseneke, to apologize. During the solemn occasion of his 60th birthday, Deputy Chief Justice discussed the ANC in the company of his friends including the former Head [of the National Prosecuting Authority] Bulelani Ngcuka, who led a crusade of suicide bombers against Cde Jacob Zuma."

"Language like that," reflected Andrew Donaldson, the leading chronicler of the Youth League's wit and wisdom, "always conjures up images of small people on podiums screeching away at dull-eyed children and teenagers in drab uniforms.

"It could be the Hitler Youth, it could be Mao's Red Guards, it could be those poor brainwashed grubs in red neckerchiefs in North Korea singing along to Kim Jong-il, and it could even be Robert Mugabe's so-called Green Bombers, the ZANU-PF youth brigadiers currently engaged in the obliteration of the forces that threaten the Zimbabwean 'democracy'."

> "Register to vote on 8 and 9 November and vote in the 2009 election. If you don't bother, Julius Malema might become a cabinet minister!" Evita Bezuidenhout

Political arses

If Donaldson and other collectors of ANCYL *bon mots* were concerned about a decline in output, they needn't have worried. When Julius Malema supporters dropped their broeks and exposed their well-rounded bums to their opponents at a chaotic ANCYL shindig in Bloemfontein—at which Mbalula himself was not welcome—it was a sign of things to come. Julius explained, "This is not your youth league, Mbalula; you led a different youth league. You did not have to deal with naked people at your congress. Our youth league congress had naked people all over the place, yours didn't!"

"The thing is that you could laugh at Fikile," one Vinny the Saffer would reflect ruefully in a letter to news24 some months later, "but you grimace in horror at Julius."

> "My opinion is that Mr Malema is a criminal—a real scoundrel and a buffoon."
> Letter to the *Sunday Times*

All of these exposed arses prompted Fred Khumalo to reflect on a subject he baptized "the Philosophical Nuances of Bums in African Political Discourse and Society in General". The incident reminded him of how, back in the '80s, Chief Buthelezi complained that the

IFP was a genuine political movement, whereas the UDF activists were followed only by their backsides. David Kau said that he'd always suspected that the members of the Youth League were a bit old, and now that he had seen their bums he was convinced of it. Still, somebody should have been sent to babysit them. "This is kak we definitely can't blame on apartheid," he said.

The precise purpose of all those naked backsides was never clear, but perhaps it was some sort of symbolic reference to the fact that ANCYL sounds like a brand of hemorrhoid cream available from your local Dischem. Andrew Donaldson apologized for bringing up the subject again, "but there are enough arses—figuratively speaking—in our public life. We don't need to see the other ones".

Despite such an auspicious beginning, Julius started his tenure at the head of the country's leading think tank for preschoolers sounding worryingly sensible. When South Africa was ripped apart by xenophobic violence in May, Julius said, "We call on government to unleash every resource at its disposal to nip this anarchy in the bud, including deployment of the military if the need arises." He added that those responsible for the violence should be apprehended and the criminal justice system "must ensure that they rot in jail".

All of which sounded reasonable enough under the circumstances.

"We are prepared to take up arms and kill for Zuma"

Soon enough, however, everyone's fears were allayed and the Youth League was in top form once more. In June, Julius announced, "We are prepared to take up arms and kill for Zuma." (For good measure, he also told the crowd in Thaba N'chu not to beat up foreigners, leaving the question about what to do with foreigners who were not Jacob Zuma supporters something of a grey area.)

Not entirely unexpectedly, some took exception to these remarks. Indeed, Julius demonstrated a truly heartwarming ability to bring political opponents together by identifying a common enemy. The IFP called him a "thug". The DA's Sandra Botha said Jacob Zuma should condemn the "Mugabe-style" rhetoric. Kgalema Motlanthe of the pro-Zuma wing of the ANC cautioned that it was "intemperate and reckless for anyone to say any such thing, especially after the recent [xenophobic] killings". The Azanian Youth Organization criticized Julius's "empty-headed utterances" while even SASCO, hardly known for its commitment to the rule of law, said it was "extremely shocked and disappointed" by the "inciting" words.

Julius remained defiant in the face of the storm, declaring that his remarks were in "the interest of freedom and democracy" and that they were blown out of proportion. The ANCYL, he said, was prepared to "kill these tendencies that manifest themselves in the form of trying to undermine the leadership of the black majority". In a truly stunning display of originality, he spoke of "forces of darkness" and "counter-revolutionary forces".

Julius had his defenders. "There is no need for our Comrade Pres Julius Malema to apologize, since he was exercising his Freedom of Speech," wrote one DJ Mokonyane to *The Citizen*. "Besides, the Malema phrase usage was overanalyzed, especially by the media. They should note the word 'kill' is broad in context; it is useful to comprehend the difference between literal and figurative meanings. Aluta Continua."

(Clearly, crowds in Thaba N'chu are well-versed in the quirks of English idiom, and understand that "We are prepared to take up arms and kill for Zuma" is much the same as "I could kill for a double espresso right now".)

"Perhaps it is opportune to educate the armchair critics that the nature of politics is such that players on the political terrain consistently eliminate each other through political manoeuvres. It is for this specific reason that parties come and go," intoned a press release which, in a vintage example of ANCYL style, managed to combine patronizing self-righteousness, contempt *and* paranoia. "Recent media articles and statements attributed to certain politicians suggesting that the word 'eliminate' in this context necessary means 'kill' is rather mischievous and demonstrate the level of desperation in portraying the President of the ANCYL as an imbecile, while they are the actual imbeciles."

Read that again and see if it makes any more sense than it did the first time.

"Julius Malema should learn to shut the fuck up." Khaya Dlanga

It was a mere formality that this "jumped-up Msholozi Mini-Me" would be crowned Mampara of the Week. Hogarth noted, "He opens his mouth and great clods of dung are splattered far and wide," and expressed the assumption that "chances are the fool will be silenced soon enough by adroitly stuffing both his feet in his mouth."

If only.

Julius promised the Human Rights Commission that he would never use the word 'kill' again, but, as it turned out, that did not mean he would not raid the thesaurus for words favoured by such luminaries as Adriaan Vlok. In July, he told a crowd in Vredefort that ANC members who got involved in crime were, somewhat confusingly, "rotten apples" who "carried sour grapes". He also said that the ANC must "intensify the struggle to eliminate the remnants of counter-revolution, which include the DA and a loose coalition of those who want to use state power to block the ANC President's ascendancy to the highest office of the land".

Demonstrating touching naiveté, the DA complained to the HRC. Argued Sandra Botha: "In the context of Mr Malema's previous exhortation for people to 'kill in support of Jacob Zuma', it is not unreasonable to assume that Malema is calling for the killing of members of the DA or those who are earnestly working in our judicial institutions to ensure that justice is dispensed without fear of favour. Malema may have adjusted his vocabulary, but his intentions clearly remain the same."

"There is no one in the ANC that can tell us what to do." Julius Malema

Then Julius further irritated the DA by declaring that Jacob Zuma would rule the country, even from a prison cell. "We can't imagine the courts finding [Zuma] guilty because if you arrest him, he will lead us from prison," he said. At a meeting during which he was introduced to the crowd as "the blockbuster", he told them that Mbeki was a "coward": "He's dealing with his own comrades. And these people in their ties and suits, they want us to keep quiet and not tell you that Mbeki is the problem."

It is not clear which blockbuster the ANC had in mind. *Dumb and Dumber?*, *The Attack of the Killer Tomatoes?*, *Shrek II?* Perhaps the thieves that broke into Julius's Mercedes Benz at his Sandton home, stealing a handbag[1] containing his passport, identity document and bank cards, were merely over-excited Julius fans. The ANCYL was highly offended. "We condemn this act of cowardice in the strongest possible terms," said spokesperson Vuyiswa Tulelo. "An attack on leaders of the ANCYL is an attack on the ANCYL itself."

Hayibo.com had its own take on the incident. "According to Tetanus Zwane, the league's

---

[1] A handbag? Julius carries a *handbag*? There is something he is not telling us.

deputy treasurer and interim Head of Book-Burning, the revelation about Malema's choice of car has shaken cadres to the core," read the report. "He said that Malema was a 'brilliant but humble scholar of ANC history' and would be acutely aware that driving a Mercedes instead of a BMW went against the founding principles of the liberation movement."

> "[He] is dumber than a box of rocks and his is a face wholly uncluttered by any form of intelligence whatsoever." Andrew Donaldson

Julius again trotted out his theory about a conspiracy against Jacob Zuma (somewhat unexpectedly; the colonizers and Thabo Mbeki had apparently made common cause, which would have surprised Ronald Suresh Roberts) and said that Zuma's supporters were ready: "Our people are going to be mobilized. The JZ issue is equally going to be used to mobilize people for the election because we need to educate our people and show them that the imperialists, the colonizers, still exist and the colonizer is attacking you through your own leadership."

Max du Preez reminded "scared whiteys" worried about these sorts of threats that the Youth League "couldn't even organize its own congress, never mind get it together to paralyze the country". He wasn't worried about Julius, who was "just an immature, attention-seeking clown".

At the same time, no less a sage than Trevor Manuel defended young Julius against the depredations of the media, saying, "Young people behave sometimes in an outrageous fashion," he opined. "Young people do and say these kinds of things. The key is not to get hooked on [it]."

Perhaps he was simply trying to prevent the rand from crashing.

> "There is a part of Oxford Road, in Rosebank, that so strongly calls to mind the contents of his skull that we may as well give it to the ANC Youth League president at once: the Julius Malema Sinkhole." Andrew Donaldson

"The ANC has descended into anti-intellectualism and ideological incoherence with the likes of Julius Malema," Khaya Dlanga wrote in a mixture of anger and despair. "Every single young person in this country ought to be embarrassed by him."

What could be the explanation for all of this outrageous behaviour?

Fred Khumalo had his theories about Julius. "Where I come from," he explained, "we have a nice little word that can be used to describe Julius Malema: *ihlongandlebe*. There is no English equivalent for this Zulu word, but many choose to translate it to mean 'a contumelious nincompoop'."

Khumalo felt that to call Julius a rude fool was to be dismissive of the finer qualities of rude fools. "Whereas a rude fool is very much in charge of his faculties—knowing when to reach full tilt in his rudeness, and when to step back and gather steam so he can pounce again— he, 27-year-old Malema, knows no such subtleties. He reacts to controversy like a shark drawn to blood—and like a shark, he can only move forward."

Khumalo also wondered why Julius insisted on speaking English in public settings, "a language that clearly defies his intellect". Still, he concluded, we should be grateful that he was a bit backward at school: "Imagine a highly educated Malema. He would be going all over the place like one Ronald Suresh Roberts, insulting everyone who disagrees with his notion of what makes a good intellectual, or a good analyst, or a good politician, or a good human being, for that matter. Now, there's a real ihlongandlebe."

"If Julius Malema can breed without a licence, I don't see why I shouldn't be able to drive without one." Ben Trovato

Naturally, the education of Julius Malema was a topic of intense interest. There were rumours that he did not actually have a matric, though these were quashed when his results were leaked onto the internet. He had scored an H for mathematics and a G for woodwork on standard grade but some of his other results, notably the D for Afrikaans, were surprising. One radio listener wondered whether Julius was the carpenter who made the chair that famously collapsed under finance committee chairman Nhlanhla Nene during a live TV interview on SABC2. Comedian Nick Rabinowitz quipped, "If he got a G for woodwork, how can we expect him to form a cabinet?"

The Freedom Front Plus Youth thought that the matric results were his personal business, although leader Cornelius Jansen van Rensburg did allow that "Mr Malema's grade 12 marks are just as radical as the statements he regularly makes".

Julius once explained his dismal school record, saying, "I got excited after joining COSAS and failed grade 8. In 1997, I was expelled for political activities and pleaded to be taken back, and I repeated grade 9 in 1998." Andrew Donaldson speculated whether Julius got much out of "a dozen or so years of rolling plasticine worms at the ANC". Doubtless they were wasted, though one could "easily imagine his buxom teachers having to wipe the drool from his chin, particularly during story-time sessions, when young Julius would fall out of his chair thrilling to the tales of Msholozi's exploits in the trouser department".

Hayibo.com reported that the ANCYL had dismissed the significance of the results, declaring that "Malema's mark for Woodwork was a revolutionary rejection of racism. In a statement released this morning the league said that one of the founding tenets of racism was that blacks were consigned to being 'hewers of wood and carriers of water'". The Hayibo report also noted that political commentators were alarmed by Julius's H for mathematics. "According to one, who wished to remain anonymous because he wished to remain alive, getting an H on the standard grade meant that Malema was 'counting using his fingers and toes, and running into trouble after one hand'."

But not everyone was convinced the Julius was stupid. "Do not let this buttcrack fool you: Julius Malema is a very intelligent man," wrote zenbiscuit, a blogger student at UNISA, something that Julius himself never managed.[2] "He's learned that idiocy is the best way to say anything you want, because invariably smart people don't take you too seriously. It's only the people just as dumb as you are that pay you any attention. Cleverly, these dumb people constitute 'the masses', and therein lies Mr Malema's hat trick: who needs the scholars, the academics, the witty peanut gallery, when you have the masses? … I doff my hat, Jules, you've got the smart 'uns by the short and curlies."

"This is an insult to kindergarten children worldwide." A Hogarth reader objects to the ANCYL being described as the "kindergarten"

By September, Julius was even bolder. The 'Malema generation' would ensure that whatever the judgment in Zuma's corruption trial, Zuma would be president in 2009. "Any force on our way we will eliminate. We are on a mission here. We will crush you. It doesn't matter who you are, even if you are in the ANC," he said to enthusiastic applause.

---

[2] She is also an ordained minister, something she may or may not have in common with Jacob Zuma.

The question of the sobriety of the judge who was to rule in the matter was a cause for some concern. Presumably Julius was thinking of our good friend Judge Motata, when he quipped, "You know these days you can't even say people are sober like judges as some of them get drunk and bump into walls ... so they have discredited the good image of the judiciary." Julius, however, was confident that this judge, who looked "very sober" would find in Zuma's favour and, as it turns out, he was right.

In the mean time, AfriForum Youth delivered a copy of *Politics for Dummies* to Luthuli House, as they felt that Julius Malema and his fellow actual imbeciles could benefit from studying its contents. The Youth League was furious. "I think they are a group of crazy, racist people. They're not in the pursuit of democracy; they're in the pursuit of regressive regimes. Since when does AfriForum know about democracy?" said spokesperson Floyd Shivambu. "If they want to speak to us, they must not come through backdoors, so we're not even going to entertain that thing [the book]."

Soon afterwards, at a conference including the clotted cream of the country's youth, Julius said he was convinced that he would succeed in his bid to oust Mbeki. He had spoken to the majority of the National Executive Committee, and they agreed with the Youth League. He joked that he would have lobbied Mbeki if he was an NEC member: "That you can agree, Mbeki, that you must go."

He said the National Prosecuting Authority's desire to prosecute Zuma was a "racist agenda" which carried "the aspirations and interests of the apartheid regime". He also dismissed Mbeki as a "dictator". As for Zuma's description of the president of the country as a "dead snake", "We are no longer beating it and we are burying this snake this weekend."

> "Julius Malema is a stirrer. Just what he's stirring in his bubbling, foul-smelling cauldron, I'll leave up to your imagination, but it isn't pretty, chaps." Vinny the Saffer

"Mr Malema is a great comedian, but a mediocre democrat. The fate of our country should not be determined by the likes of him," responded the UDM Youth Vanguard spokesperson Velile Yayi. Disagreement, he said, should not mean being disrespectful and insulting.

Vinny the Saffer thought that Julius was disrespectful in the extreme: "Like him or not,

Mbeki is the President of the country, and the fact that an upstart like Malema sees his way clear to show blatant disrespect for that office and indicates the poor breeding, lack of proper judgment, and insight of the man ... Malema's baleful glare and remorseless words, coupled with his obvious chip-on-the-shoulder attitude, reeks of vengeance, hatred and racism."

(Yes, folks, in South Africa, everybody's a racist.)

Naturally, comparisons were made to famously stupid politicians elsewhere in the world. Brandon Faber compared the ANC Youth League favorably to the "King of village idiots" George Bush. "I fear not even Econo-sized boxes of Ritalin, constant prayer, isolation, electro-shock-therapy or—heaven forbid—momentary lapses of common sense will help the kindergarten pick itself up from the floor," he wrote.

Chris Roper was irritated when an American suggested that Sarah Palin was crazier than Julius Malema. "Why do these capitalist dogs always have to run down the Third World every time they have a drink?" he complained. "Can't these racists bring themselves to believe that Africa is as capable of producing a world-class twit as their beloved United States of America?"

> "What Malema really needs is a big fat bowl of 'Shut the hell up' for breakfast, lunch and dinner and to go back to school and get good grades!" Letter to *The Citizen*

Eventually, as the history books will record, Julius got his way and, as he would have put it, the snake was indeed buried. Thabo Mbeki was forced out on September 20; half of his cabinet followed him, though—much to everyone's disappointment—not Manto.

Zola Skweyiya was deeply troubled. The Minister of Social Development—who was not so loyal to the man formerly known as President Mbeki that he was prepared to resign in solidarity—said that Julius's behaviour was un-African. "We are Africans and an elderly person is an elderly person," he complained in an interview with the *Sunday Independent*. "We say: you shall not dishonour your parents." Julius, he said, was an "embarrassment" to the ANC: "People ... call me every night complaining 'What are you doing about this child?'"

The league leapt to the defence of its brave leader. "We condemn the uncomradely act of Skweyiya attacking Malema in public and without firm base," said Sicelo Mdletshe,

ANCYL North Coast spokesman. "We expect senior people like Skweyiya to correct, not attack us." Julius should be left alone because he was "merely expressing the views of the Young Lions, not his own".

"We urge all comrades who are in the leadership positions to respect each other, if not so we shall take them head on," Mdletshe warned. "People who want to distract us will bear the consequences."

Some of his supporters did come to regret their lack of foresight. The Western Cape branch of the league wished it could take it all back. Julius, they said, was "a political comedian and a despot in the making" and he posed "a real danger to the future of young people of this country".

Too late, they cried.

"Malema can't fix my broken tublu woordwork" and "Julius please go back to study". Placards displayed at the convention to discuss the launch of Lekota's and Shilowa's new political movement, which would eventually be named Congress of the People

In October, the man with the most vowels in politics, Mosiuoa Lekota,[3] added grist to Julius's mill by announcing plans to form a breakaway movement that would contest the elections in 2009. "The possible formation of the political party by Ntate Lekota and Mluleki George, who think they are anointed born leaders, will represent nothing but narrow right-wing opportunism of people who want to express bitterness, self-enrichment and disrespect of organization principles," the jelly tsotsi told the media.

When the Congress of the People, soon dubbed COPE, was launched, Julius dismissed their leaders as "blue-light revolutionaries who can't imagine their life without bodyguards and had forgotten how to drive, but are faced with the reality to do so". Lekota, he said, wanted to hang onto power. He was a "factory fault who behaved like he has never been to the ANC's political school".

Say what you like, but Julius has a way with words.

---

[3] Hayibo.com reported that Lekota was planning to add more vowels to his name in order to enhance his appeal: "According to Lekota aides, he is likely to rename himself Moiiuoaieiosiouaeuuoia Lekota, although pundits agree it will make little difference as his name will still be unpronounceable."

Anele Mda, leader of COPE's youth wing that she did not spend a lot of her time thinking about Julius, but thought his behaviour was as simple as that of a wild animal. "There isn't any domestic animal I liken Malema's behaviour to because I'm going to do injustice to those animals," she said.

> "For Europeans who haven't visited the jungles of Cape Town, young lions are the ones who lie around exposing their buttocks while the females hunt, and who then take the choice bits for themselves." Chris Roper on the "militant young lions" of the ANC Youth League

After Lekota took to talking about Julius at COPE meetings, the ANCYL said that Lekota violated their integrity every time he made a reference to the "kill for Zuma" remarks. "We believe that the continued allegations and utterances by Mr Lekota that the ANCYL or any of its members are potential murderers and/or assassins violate our rights to integrity as individual members of the ANCYL and as an organization," the league said, in a statement which was predicated on the rather curious assumption that ANCYL members have any integrity to begin with.

They declared that they were tired of being defamed and they were going to complain to the Human Rights Commission. Lekota, said Floyd Shivambu, was "in essence accusing the ANCYL of an intention to literally kill people and he is violating our rights and freedoms as an organization".

"We have no regrets, none whatsoever, to march with you to the Union Buildings come 2009." Julius said of Zuma. He said that the youth were impatient. "This lot of noise by these shenanigans, the Mickey Mouse organization, makes us to want to go now to elections so that the ANC could teach them a lesson."

> "He would be better suited to lead an English football mob during a clash with Serbia." Mondli Makhanya

The leaders of the new political movement would soon find out that they were only popular among editors and journalists, said Julius. "Under Mbeki, the resources of the country were distributed to certain individuals and a certain tribe," he said, alluding to Mbeki's

Xhosa heritage. "Not everyone benefited. But under [ANC president Jacob] Zuma we expect everyone to benefit."

Khaya Dlanga was disgusted. "The problem with listening to some of the things that he says leaves one even stupider for having heard them," he wrote of Julius. "For that, he should not be forgiven. The things he says not only defy logic, but stupidity too. He overcompensates for his lack of intellectual curiosity with his bellicose statements, which he mistakes for coherence."

> "I give up on this young man. He must just learn to keep his mouth shut. He is really making the rest of us black youngsters seem like idiots." Email to *The Citizen*

Hayibo.com announced that Julius Malema was going to dress up as himself for Halloween. "Asked if it was true that Julius Malema was going to Trick or Treat disguised as a pair of lips fixed to Jacob Zuma's bottom, [spokesperson] Tshabalala said that while the ANCYL leader did admire Mr Zuma's bottom and had considered the disguise, he had decided to dress up as himself instead," reported the site. "'Halloween is all about frightening people,' said Tshabalala, adding that research had shown that Malema was terrifying to most whites, many Sesothos, all Xhosas, and most of his extended family."

The fact that a lot of people find Julius quite off-putting was not lost on the ANC.

When the SABC was asked not to portray Kgalema Motlanthe as *quite* so presidential compared to Jacob Zuma the pop star, the report was officially denied. But a source acknowledged that a request was made that Julius not be shown with Zuma. "They say where he is seen with Malema, the young man must be edited out—but Malema sits really very close to Zuma," said the source.

The Media Monitoring Project was asked to analyze SABC news broadcasts to see if there was any truth in these rumours. "Zuma is mostly shown speaking positively on a variety of issues, except where there is Julius Malema, because almost everything Malema says is negative," said William Bird.

> "… just a special-needs child who needs a little time before his own special love light comes shining through …" Andrew Donaldson

MORE South African Insults

In November, Zuma announced that Julius was a changed man, though this did not prevent the latter from saying that Dipuo Peters, the premier of the Northern Cape, had been "bought" by business, and calling Mbhazima Shilowa a "security guard" who defaulted on child-support payments. Nonetheless, as if to demonstrate the validity of JZ's assertions, the Msholozi Mini-Me said sorry. In an interview on 702, he said, "If we did sound like we're inciting violence, we are very sorry. That was not our intention; we'll never incite violence. We will never do anything unconstitutional. We are law-abiding citizens of this country and we will protect the Constitution of this republic."

How many of 702's listeners believed a word of this is hard to say.

> "This ANC has gone through difficult times, but we will never be defeated by a group of clowns." Julius Malema

In November 2008, it seemed that Julius might have a rival as the name that inspires the most Google searches for "immigration New Zealand". His name is Jason Mkhwane, which suggests that his parents were hoping that he would attend a model C school and become an accountant in a fast-track graduate program at KPMG. Instead, he joined the ANC Youth League, became chairperson of the Sedibeng region and told Al Jazeera that members of COPE were "cockroaches" and, quite logically, cockroaches should be killed. When the *Mail & Guardian* queried this statement, he refused to back down. "All these people in COPE are behaving like cockroaches and cockroaches should be killed," he reiterated.

Did he mean this literally? Was this a metaphor? A complex allusion to the profound alienation experienced by modern man in his quest for ideological perfection? Perhaps Jason has been reading too much Kafka.

At least Julius apologized, eventually. Chris Roper thinks we should be grateful for him. "Without his rantings, misstatements, and general all-round craziness," he argues, "our political scene would be a poorer place, a place where knives get inserted into backs silently and clandestinely, rather than out in the open for everyone to laugh at."

Not everyone is so sanguine. *The Times* warned in an editorial in July, "The dogs of populism are loose and their bark is, as yet, worse than their bite. But, as they smash their way into the highest offices in the land, make no mistake—their bite will come."

Still, as Julius himself said when he was campaigning for Mbeki to be shafted, "Politicians are the easiest to replace. We will move forward and they will carry on with the programmes which are there."

Many South Africans can't wait to see him regret those words.

> "It was the ANC who taught them the simple things, like drinking red wine, about forks and knives." Julius Malema criticizes COPE's rejection of affirmative action

To absolutely nobody's surprise, Julius—"the young man with verbal cholera"—was honoured as Mampara of the Year by Hogarth, who explained, "One remarkable thing about this mampara is his zest for the absurd, his boundless energy at creating endless pieces of verbal twaddle, and his inability to appreciate just what a flibbertigibbet he is. Being a nincompoop is second nature to him. Imbecile is his middle name."

This was after a momentous week in which, not only was he pranked by Darren 'Whackhead' Simpson who called him pretending to be Barack Obama, but Malema told students at Cape Peninsula University of Technology that Jacob Zuma's rape accuser had had a "nice time" with him because she had "requested breakfast and taxi money". These were the hallmarks, apparently, of women that have had enjoyed the sexual encounter. To cheers and applause, he added, ""You can't ask for money from somebody who raped you."

> "Having Malema campaign for you is like bonking for chastity." Comment, news24.com

At another event, he told his audience that Zuma's relationship with Schabir Shaik was not corrupt. "How many of you have helped wash a comrade's car or pay their children's school fees? That's how the ANC taught us. It then means we are all corrupt, because that's how we live." Julius also defended Zuma's lack of education. "[Zuma] was taught by people on the ground," he said. "He is the most educated president. Economics is simple—put bread on the table." Also in the putative next president's favour was the fact that after being fired from his job as deputy president, he understood the plight of the unemployed. "He does not wait for Markinor studies to understand poverty," said Julius. "He understands as he is part of society."

Then there was a very entertaining spat over the right of the ANC to campaign in an IFP stronghold notorious for political violence. "We will go back to Nongoma," declared Julius. "No amount of intimidation will stop us, not even [Mangosuthu] Buthelezi. We will campaign even in his backyard or his house and recruit his children to join the ANC."

The IFP was not charmed. "Julius Malema must come," said their deputy national spokesperson, Thulasizwe Buthelezi. "We are waiting for him. He will arrive at Nongoma and find boys his own age who will teach him what happens to a loud-mouthed chatterbox imbecile like him."

Displaying a penchant for insults worthy of honorary membership of the ANCYL, Buthelezi continued, "We are tired of this imbecile. He has become a cluster bomb and we are not going to allow him to explode on us. We will teach him a lesson by force, since we have seen that education is his core deficiency."

He said that what the ANC had seen so far in Nongoma would be a "Sunday-school picnic" compared to what they could expect if they continued to "provoke, insult and harass" the IFP.

Mangosuthu Buthelezi himself was roused from hibernation to criticize Julius for not understanding "the unspoken rules of politics", pointing out that he had been in politics for longer than Julius had been alive.

> "Not any time soon. I think Parliament is for old people, don't you agree? It's not my favourite place." Julius explains why he turned down an ANC nomination to become an MP

Buti Manamela of the Youth Communist League defended Julius against Thulasizwe Buthelezi. "It is an admission that the IFP is guilty of what happened in Nongoma. This man who wrote the statement must be arrested and rot in jail. We don't need this barbarism, not now."

Mangosuthu Buthelezi[4] then issued a long and involved press release discussing the problem of Julius. "Julius Malema is no more than an ill-bred brat whose behaviour is not only un-African, but crude by the standards of any culture in the world," was his assessment. "What worries one is that the ruling Party uses him to denigrate those they

---

[4] Yes, all these Buthelezis are confusing

have targeted for denigration and insults. So Mr Malema is the ANC's spoilt brat," he concluded, "and he thinks he can take on me because he did what he did to President Mbeki."

> "I am willing to sponsor a flight for Malema to Timbuktu until after the elections." Eastern Cape MEC for public works—and ANC member—Christian Martin. He also described Julius as a "genuine 24-carat disgrace to our youth"

Later in February 2009, IFP MP Koos van der Merwe described Julius as the "grand hero" of opposition parties, and expressed his gratitude for his "unstinting efforts to win votes for the opposition".

Julius dismissed rumours that the ANC was going to send him to an American university to study leadership to prevent him from scoring more votes for the opposition. "I don't need any political training. I have learnt politics through structures of the ANC. Why would I go overseas? I would rather go back to Limpopo than go and be trained by imperialists."

"Ja *buti*," reflected the *Mail & Guardian*'s political gossip columnist, "but then you'd have to sell that house you bought in Sandton in the same gated community as those other imperialists—and it's not a seller's market right now, even for a *khaya* as nice as yours."

> "There's also our man Julius who seems to be an enraged fusion of a rabid dog and a confused child whose disenchanted parents have dropped him off at the adoption centre." David Mosely

"Malema reminds me of Robert Mugabe. He used to say that about his opponents," Helen Zille laughed after Julius described her as "racist", "colonialist" and "imperialist", while her deputy Joe Seremane's role was to "smile at the madam". Julius also said that Zille was using "Michael Jackson tactics". ANCYL spokesperson Floyd Shivambu clarified the remarks, explaining that Julius meant that Zille was "being dramatic about everything", was guilty of displaying "flamboyant flagrancies".

DA youth leader Khume Ramulifho then challenged Julius to a debate. Julius refused, saying he would not debate with "Zille's garden boys".

"No amount of insulting rhetoric and pathetic name-calling should detract from the fact that Malema is afraid that his vast intellectual shortcomings will be exposed," Ramulifho retorted, describing Julius as "a petty little man who is unable to engage in meaningful debate, and capable only of resorting to the basest form of gutter politics to make his point". He also said that Julius would do "no better than a garden gnome" in a debate with the DA.

For her part, Helen Zille told a gathering that Julius was an *inkwenkwe*, literally an uncircumcised boy. The ANC was deeply offended, but Zille was unrepentant. As she pointed out: "If Malema hands out insults, he must be prepared to take a *klap* back." His behaviour was "unacceptable in politics," she said. "He is full of gratuitous insults, he never debates issues and the only argument he has is the race card."

Later she wrote in her weekly newsletter that Julius would "fall hard". "Poor Julius. He thinks he has reached the top rung of the ladder; he doesn't anticipate how soon it will be knocked out from under him." She described him as "a man who opens his mouth only to change feet" and said it was tempting to dismiss him as "a political lightweight; a harmless buffoon prone to delivering crass sound bites".

> "At least his carpentry skills permit him to acknowledge being 'as thick as two short planks'." Comment, *The Times*

Crass though those soundbites may have been, they generated column inches, adoring crowds of Zuma supporters and even an ad campaign. Shortly before the elections, Nando's featured a puppet that bore an uncanny resemblance to Julius and told the interviewer: "We demand change."

The ANC Youth League was not amused, describing the ad as "disgusting" and "racist" and threatened to "mobilize the people of South Africa to take militant action" against Nando's. Presumably they planned to boycott peri-peri flame-grilled chicken in favour of the eleven herbs and spices of KFC.

Nando's assured the public that it would not "chicken out" and brought the campaign back, this time pixellating the puppet so that its identity was obscured. Later the puppet used in the campaign was sold for R100,000.

> "It's time to bury Julius, not to praise him." Njabulo Ndebele

Barney Mthombothi could not understand why Julius enjoyed so much media coverage. "There's a simple way to deal with him: ignore him," he argued. "Deny him the oxygen of publicity, and he'll fade into the obscurity that he richly deserves.

In contrast, Mondli Makhanya felt that Julius was a symbol of where South African society was going wrong. He reflected that "in laughing at Malema, we mask the peril that he is to our society ... We are at a point where, at the behest of our leaders, we are beginning to accept the normality of the abnormal and the morality of the immoral".

In January 2009, Hogarth predicted that, at the rate he was going, Julius wouldn't just be the 2008 Mampara of the Year, but keep his title in 2009. "We'd laugh," said Hogarth reflecting on his latest pronouncements, "but we're too scared."

Ray Hartley wondered whether the country would eventually get bored with Julius, who would, he predicted, eventually want to be part of the establishment he criticized at every opportunity. "And somewhere in the youth league, there are other wannabe demagogues awaiting their turn. They will push, government will pull and with a loud pop, Malema will escape the bottle of populism to find himself in the ranks of the establishment.

"But, until then, the South African psyche is in for a rough ride."

"We need to ask will we produce leaders like Nelson Mandela?" Julius Malema speculates on the future of the ANC Youth League

Chapter 3

Snakes, Dogs, Donkeys and Cockroaches:
ANC vs COPE

"The fight between the ANC and COPE will not lead us anywhere … ANC and COPE politicians must stop this barbaric behaviour. It casts a shadow on our hard-won democracy." Ntshengedzeni Ramugondo, Ngudza Village, letter to the *Daily Sun*

"Our leaders call each other nasty names, insult and undermine our judicial system, appoint criminals to positions of power, neglect their duties, threaten to kill their political opponents and too often push their grubby little fingers into the nation's till," Max du Preez wrote as the inauguration of Barack Obama in November 2008 captured the attention of the world. "Petty grievances, false promises, recriminations and worn-out dogmas are standard fare in our political life nowadays."

It was a bit of an unfair comparison, pitting the charismatic leader of the free world, the father of Obamamania, against South Africa's uninspiring lot. Du Preez was right about the nasty names, though. It was a year in which politicians likened each other to snakes, dogs, donkeys and cockroaches. Occasionally old snakeskin, too … and the odd baboon.

It could get a bit confusing at times.

"… there are hundreds—including most of our existing ruling elite, the Cabinet, the ANCYL, ANCWL, NEC, NWC, SACP, PAC, COSATU and any number of their cronies—who owe the human gene pool big time." Llewellyn Kriel reflects on the Darwin Awards

Following a chicken through the gates of hell

So it's best to go back to where it all started, in Polokwane. Ndumiso Ngcobo reported that proceedings involved lots of singing of Umshini Wami, rude gestures[1] and a very long and boring speech by Thabo Mbeki. "Suicide is starting to become an attractive option," he SMSed his wife when the president reached page 29 of 42. Describing a media briefing by Smuts Ngonyama, he reported, "Afterwards, I conducted a snap survey among the media personnel. Ninety-seven percent said they'd rather have spent those 45 minutes being given a pineapple enema than listening to Smuts talk."

The most entertaining aspect of Polokwane involved insurrection by Jacob Zuma supporters, who sang Umshini Wam' at every opportunity, refused to keep quiet when asked, and voted for all their favourite Zumbies. Later Mosioua aka Terror Lekota would say of Polokwane that it was a "place where I was surrounded by rude, drunk and hostile elements".

Watching the process, one reader of *Thought Leader* observed, "Now we see the monumental buffoonery that passes for leadership in SA. If you want intelligent, mature, compelling debate check out Animal Planet. There's a thrilling episode on the role of pheromones in the mating habits of the Western Patagonian aardvark. I'd follow a headless chicken through the Gates of Hell before pledging allegiance to that weird agglomeration of carbon-based metabolism in Polokwane."

A kangaroo court

After Polokwane, the dust settled, for a little while. In January, an article did appear in the *Cape Times* declaring "Cape Town is being invaded by cockroaches", which was surprising because Parliament wasn't due to open for another month. It turned out that this was a reference to the insects rather than their human equivalents. According to the South African Pest Control Association (SAPCA), the causes included poor sanitation and global warming. Little did they know that, as the year progressed, cockroaches of a different sort would scuttle back and forth across the land.

Just when South Africans had become used to the new political order of things, Julius Malema made his "kill for Zuma" statement. Then Zwelanzima Vavi said it was a disgrace

---

[1] Ngcobo reported, "I sense some serious venom towards Lekota. The delegates are emulating that arm-roll motion that disgruntled Bafana fans (Whoever says 'Is there any other kind?', please grow up) use to communicate that they want a particular player substituted."

that the Human Rights Commission, in the form of a kangaroo court, had called on Malema to retract his statement. Then protests by Zuma supporters outside the court in Pietermaritzburg were matched with the kind of rhetoric that sent even calmer types to flysaa.com to look for special offers. To anywhere.

Max du Preez was bitterly disappointed. "I was all for the New ANC after Polokwane," he wrote, "but if this is the leadership that is going to surround President Jacob Zuma after next year's election, then we were better off with the Essop Pahads and Manto Tshabalala-Msimangs.

"I think I need a drink."

Dead snakes and divorces

When Judge Chris Nicolson ruled that the decision to prosecute Jacob Zuma was invalid, Zuma told his supporters: "This time, in particular, you have an opportunity ... there's an administration coming to an end, so if you do so [continue attacking the administration that's going] *unjengomuntu oshaya inyoka esifile, ubhizi uyayishaya inyoka ife kudala, uyayishaya kodwa* [it is like you are beating a snake that is long dead. You are wasting your energy]." ("Why equate the poor, hapless snake with a powerful administration that had failed to deliver on its mandate?" wondered Fred Khumalo.)

Inspired by the dead snake reference, Julius Malema told a conference involving COSAS, SASCO and ANCYL and the Youth Communist League—the combined intellectual power in that room must have been truly awe-inspiring—that the dead snake would be buried that weekend. "This one we won't lose," he said. "We'll have Mbeki removed. We don't fight to lose ... even now you must sense something. He is going. It doesn't matter who says what. Mbeki will not be president of this country when we go to elections."

"The Young Communist League notes the cowardly media briefing convened by political mercenaries and aprons of the naked emperor, Terror Lekota and Mluleki George, today 08 October 2008, at Hyde Park, Johannesburg ... But currently this is a joke and that is why we say it is a farce." YCL statement

Mbeki's supporters were not happy. Soon enough, Mosioua Lekota was threatening to issue divorce papers to the ANC. Mathews Phosa urged calm. A house was built with many bricks, he said. They were not going to throw stones at Lekota, or "fire a bullet" at its members. "We are more interested in uniting ANC members so a member who feels a need to throw stones needs to reflect," he said, sounding like a marriage counsellor with consulting rooms in Sandton.[2]

All to no avail. Lekota went ahead with the divorce anyway, announcing the planned formation of a new party live on eNews. "Let it be the people of South Africa to choose whether they want to go with the Malemas of this world," he said.

Fred Khumalo was not impressed with Lekota's vitriol and lack of detail. He read the press conference as a "gimmick to gauge public sentiment" and an "emotional ego trip". "For a moment," he said, "I thought I was listening to an older, more rotund version of Malema." This from a man whom he had admired. "We know Lekota's conquests," he wrote. "He earned his stripes as a leader when Malema was still a (bad?) dream in his father's mind.

"The country is starving for common decency. So, please, Uncle Terror, feed me not another Malemaesque sound bite. Feed me respect and common decency."

Xolela Mangcu also had his doubts about Lekota. "Surely, there is something wrong with the violence and militarism of the new ANC," he said. "I am just not sure if a highly compromised Lekota is the person to swing the ANC against it."

Similarly, Ahmed Motala was not convinced by the notion that the as-yet-unnamed new party was an alternative to the ANC. "They seem to think that South Africans are suffering from amnesia and do not remember that they have until recently been senior members of the ANC. The very same party that has sought to enrich itself through the setting up of Chancellor House, and subsidiaries, that have been awarded government contracts. Under their leadership the ANC has also ensured that a few black business people who are either senior members of the ANC or closely associated with it have been enriched through the black economic empowerment programme. More importantly, it is the same ANC that has presided over increasing poverty in our country."

In contrast, Michael Trapido was excited by all the change in the air. "While Terror Lekota and the dissidents (there's the name for a rock group right there) kick off their national convention in Sandton, the ANC continues to refer to them unapologetically as

---

[2] Perhaps, after his foray into Afrikaans poetry, he is planning to become the Dr Phil of South African politics.

dogs and a bunch of poisonous snakes; seemingly upgraded from the dead snake of a few weeks ago. Indeed there can no longer be any doubt that the ruling party is concerned about the damage that all of this is doing. In my humble opinion this is the best thing that could ever have happened to the ANC and South Africa."

Fred Khumalo said he was getting tired of all the stories of the split in the ANC. "Which is why I love all these refreshing takes on our rotting body politic. More air fresheners or deodorant, please, to chase away the pungency of the Terrorderant, Duarterant and Zumaderant that is clogging our breathing space."

"Zuma you are a dead snake." Placard held up by disgruntled ANC member from KwaZulu-Natal, at a convention to discuss the launch of Lekota and Shilowa's new movement

The dogs bark but the caravan moves on

After snakes, it was dogs—although why ANC dissidents should be confused with an animal famous for its loyalty was never clear.

"Now that the dogs are leaving, there will be peace and we will be stronger. The dogs arrived in the ANC and they have left," said ANC Women's League president Angie Motshekga, referring to dissidents such as Lekota and Mluleki George. Lekota, she said, was always "attention-seeking and very loud" and, in an apparent reference to the Greek myth of Daedulus and Icarus, had waited for him to "fly as high as he could" before they could any public statement about his actions.

The United Democratic Movement Women's Organization—UDEMWO for short—called on Motshekga to apologize. "She should be aware that what goes around comes around; she must not be surprised when in future her juniors refer to her as a 'dog' because they will be emulating her," said Udemwo. Secretary-General Kobela Raletjena said Motshekga ought not to refer to human beings as "dogs" which, she said, was "totally immoral and unethical". UDEMWO said this undermined the country's Constitution when individuals who exercised their rights were labelled with insults and were threatened.

"They could change it to POPE: Party of Pissed-Off Egos." Comment, *The Citizen*

The new party was finally launched under the name Congress of the People. The ANC objected on the grounds that Congress of the People was *their* name and nobody else had the right to use it, a contention that was unceremoniously chucked out of court.

In any event, Congress of the People was soon officially shortened, not to COTP or COP, as might have been expected, but COPE. Hayibo.com addressed the problem of the acronym, quoting constitutional expert Abacus Nyamende, who said that either COPE's leaders did not understand what an acronym was, they were keeping an extra word secret from voters, or they were "severely mentally handicapped".

According to the article, Nyamende also suggested that perhaps COPE's founders assumed that it was the voters who were mentally handicapped. The most likely explanation, however, was a secret word, such as 'enema', which would make it "Congress of the People's Enema".

Hayibo.com continued: "He said it was nothing to be worried about, as the ANC had been giving the country an enema for over a decade and that a change of personnel around the hose' might be what the country needed."

> "I don't want to hear songs about war and hatred." Mosioua Lekota, banning the singing of Umshini Wam' at COPE gatherings (hardly necessary, surely?)

Dead snakeskin jackets

After the launch of COPE, Zuma returned to the analogy of the snake, warning his supporters: "Remember, a snake will, from time to time, shed dead skin and leave it behind. The same snake comes out on the other end glowing and looking new. It is the dead skin that you see on TV trying to mislead you."

A few days later, he told his followers that the ANC no longer had to worry "looking for snakes under its jacket". During a public meeting in Bushbuckridge, Mpumalanga, he offered this intriguing piece of advice: "Stop following the snakes when they run into the bush. If you follow them you will end up cold because they will go into holes."

As Fred Khumalo pointed out, this was all rather confusing. First Mbeki was the snake, now the snake was the ANC, and the dead skin of the same snake was the breakaway movement. "*Hhawu*, this narrative is getting as unwieldy as an anaconda," he wrote.

Khumalo also felt that it was unfair to characterize the humble snake in this way.[3] "Who is speaking in forked tongues? How did the shed skin of the snake suddenly come back to life?"

Enter the donkey

Having apparently exhausted the potential of reptilian analogies, the ANC now turned to beasts of burden. Jacob Zuma likened COPE to a donkey when he addressed hundreds of Cosatu workers in Polokwane. He said there was a story in the Bible about how Jesus rode into Jerusalem on the back of a "lucky donkey. The people were waiting for the Son of Man who was on the donkey. The donkey did not understand it, and thought the songs of praise were for him," he said. Later, the donkey returned to Jerusalem on its own thinking it would experience the same adulation, but the people chased it away. COPE leaders were the same, said Zuma: without the ANC they were nothing.

> "Yes, I am the face of the ANC." Mosioua Lekota makes a Freudian slip on being asked whether he would be the face of COPE for the 2009 elections.

Foot-in-mouth disease

The leadership of the new party was not going to take all these insults lying down. "Vlakplaas is rising again," said Lekota after his bodyguard was kidnapped, robbed and threatened near Pretoria. "They told him, the party you and Lekota want to start, will happen in heaven. What they were really trying to say, was, 'If you don't do as we say, we will kill you'. That is exactly what P. W. Botha told me," said Lekota.

COPE's youth co-ordinator Anele Mda caused a furore when she told followers that if Jacob Zuma became president, rape would become legal. "We are going to have a government that is going to make raping official," she declared.

---

[3] Earlier in the year, he himself had written about the "snake of corruption". Reflecting on the experiences of the Nigerians, he wrote, "Look at them now, they can't sit on their asses in one place for any length of time. The snake bite of corruption and restlessness is pushing them to all corners of the world. They can't find peace because when the snake of corruption first reared its head in their country, they looked the other way instead of hitting it on the head right there and then."

"Does Anele have Tourette's or foot-and-mouth disease?" wondered Michael Trapido. "If I was the local veterinary surgeon I wouldn't be allowing her anywhere near our cattle anytime soon. The only time she seems to open her mouth is to change feet."

Fred Khumalo was disappointed by COPE's "lack of imagination" when it came to political insults. "Now, now, my dear, do you want to be another Malema?" he wondered. "The young man is way ahead of you; don't even try to catch up," he warned. Former head of COSATU Willy Madisha branded Zuma "SA's Stalin" and said that if Zuma went to the United Nations, people would say, "Here comes the rapist."

ANC spokesman Carl Niehaus said, "This is nothing else but hate speech of the worst kind. The outrageous rape statements fly in the face of the fact that President Zuma was found not guilty of rape."

"Where's my AK-47? I want to shoot Lekota!" ANC supporters chanting at a gathering in Port Elizabeth

Patricia de Lille condemned everyone. "This latest round of hate speech shows a level of political immaturity frowned upon by those of us who have not forgotten the ideals that we fought for.

"Those who gave their lives for the struggle against apartheid must be turning in their graves at the sound of this kind of hate speech coming from ANC number 1 and ANC number 2."

Well, as David Bullard once observed, "We've learnt the hard way over the centuries and discovered to our chagrin that the guy who looks good at election time often turns out to be a prize shit."

Hayibo reported on the new party's election slogan for 2009: "... new party organizers say they are confident that their new slogan—'Better The Corrupt And Arrogant Politicians You Know Than The Corrupt And Arrogant Politicians You Don't'—will make a difference at the polls next year."

"One Sinophile of Hogarth's acquaintance suggests that Top COP Lekota's foot soldiers are not terrorists, but 'terrorkota warriors'." Hogarth

The rise of the living dead

At a COPE convention in November, ex-ANC supporters from KwaZulu-Natal toyi-toyied outside the Sandton Convention Centre while holding up placards that continued the animal theme as well as the inevitable religious allusions: "Zuma you are a dead snake" and "Zuma: any relation to Lucifer?"

One man held a box to the ground symbolizing a gravestone; on it were written the words: "Zuma's funeral".

Hayibo reported on ANC protestors who attempted to disrupt a DA meeting: "According to security consultant Darrel Sundance-Kidd only a handful of ANC protesters arrived, the rest having been diverted by a rumour of a 25%-off sale at Markham. However, he said, those who did arrive outside the conference centre were "efficiently guided to an alternate venue" by trailing life-size cardboard cutouts of Mosiuoa Lekota and Mbhazima Shilowa on string behind a car."

Carl Niehaus was not the only ghoulish figure from the past to reanimate and emerge from richly deserved obscurity. Ex-Cape Town mayor and virtuoso sleazebag Peter Marais reappeared on the scene in order to join COPE. As Hayibo.com reported: "Veteran politician Peter Marais has vowed to serve the Congress of the People as faithfully as he served his last two parties, saying that his new comrades could count on him to remain absolutely loyal until he gets a better offer from somewhere else. "I give my blood, sweat and toil to the National Party," he said. "Ag, sies, sorry, I mean COPE.""

Jabulani Sikhakhane wondered why an entire comedy show had never been developed around why Peter Marais crossed the road while Hogarth could not help noticing the influx into COPE of "decrepit old has-beens who, like vampires, are signing up in the vain hope of reviving their dead careers".

"Marais has said COPE represents 'a second chance' for South Africa," Hogarth noted. "In his case, that's a third, fourth and fifth chance as well."

> "When I hear that people like Ebrahim Rasool, Avril Harding and co are joining COPE, it makes me worry that we are returning to the ANC in drag." Anton L., letter to *The Citizen*

Rats jumping ship

All these reports of people joining COPE had the ANC worried Deputy President Baleka Mbete—she of the fake driver's licence—as she pleaded with ANC MPs not to jump ship. "We are human, we make mistakes," Mbete apparently said to explain away ANC leadership mistakes. Zuma said, "We should tell [those who want to jump] there is no better home than the ANC. Therefore, we should continue to engage them as some are leaving the ANC on the basis of ignorance."

In December, Jacob Zuma told one audience, "Despite the splinter, nothing new has happened to the organization. The ANC is still intact." That's one way to cope with COPE, observed Hogarth.

Zwelanzima Vavi described the formation of COPE as a "right-wing backlash". It was "not a natural political phenomenon", he said, but rather the result of a "pro-capitalist agenda" and a failure to accept their defeat at Polokwane. Workers should support the ANC because if COPE gained ground, "it would blunt our weapons, and turn the trade union movement into a conveyor belt for the interests of big business".

"We are a family, and we stay in the house with those who are bravely suffering through all sorts of accusations and conspiracies," said Mathews Phosa, who told his audience that voters would "see right through the character assassination masked as matters of principle" of COPE. "COPE has not put a single matter of policy on the table that differs from the policies of the ANC. It leaves one with no other conclusion than to say that COPE is a house of people who are bitter about their democratic exclusion from the ANC."

"What do I think of COPE? My answer is simple. Yawn." Ndumiso Ngcobo

Besides, Lekota was a beneficiary of the very system he criticized, complained a writer to the *Daily Sun*. "Ironically, today he is pissing on the platform that paves his way to power forever."

"But Lekota must be applauded," added N. D. Ntshangase, "for having managed to fool white South Africans and the few who were present at COPE's inaugural conference into thinking that he cares for them. COPE is a black DA."

The Young Communist League called Lekota a baboon, prompting Cedric Mboyisa to criticize the use of a racially offensive word. "Our stable democracy does not need proponents of offensive insults to spoil it," he argued.

Fair enough, but insults do make it all so much more entertaining.

> "Let's face it; Dr Mvume has as much charisma and élan as a damp, clayey sod turned from the bottom part of your garden. He would battle to excite a crowd of long-term prisoners at a strip tease pole-dance." Comment on the new leader of COPE, Dr Mvume Dandala, *Mail & Guardian* Forum

The witches

If calling members of COPE snakes, dogs, donkeys or cockroaches wasn't deterring disgruntled ANC supporters from joining the new party, perhaps *Daily Sun*-style threats of the supernatural would have more effect. Speaking in Xhosa, Tokyo Sexwale told a crowd in Zwide township, "Our mothers are taken, house to house, they are also paraded on TV, these people are performing witchcraft with our mothers ... They are liars. You can't have respect for people who use older people in that fashion." It was not clear whether he was speaking metaphorically.

Sexwale said COPE was an organization that harboured racists. "Those who were defeated are trying to join this organization ... Once you are applauded by your former enemies, there's something wrong with you. Some of these disappointed racists are looking for blacks to lead them," he said. He stated that the ANC was not a violent organization, adding that COPE's inflammatory statements were violent. "If there is anything violent is the manner in which they have left the ANC, swearing at us that we are like P. W. Botha, but it is them who are behaving like Botha."

Charlotte Lobe of COPE responded by saying, "Our country has had many cases of violence visited upon elderly women on the basis of links to so-called witchcraft. I am sure you will agree that these comments are deeply irresponsible and undermine the dignity of women."

Sexwale defended his 'witches' comment by arguing semantics: "We speak rich African languages: mine, Sepedi, Sesotho, Sexhosa. And there will always be the danger ... to try to make political capital, to reduce very rich expressions said in African languages to a kind of kitchen English."

The elections, brought to you by Doom

Shortly before the elections, provincial ANC Youth League secretary in Mpumalanga, Isaac Mahlangu summed it all up nicely when he said that COPE in Mpumalanga would be "sprayed with Doom until it perishes". Addressing a press conference in Nelspruit, Mahlangu said the ANCYL would do everything in its power to make sure that COPE does not get any seats in the provincial legislature in the forthcoming general elections. "However, not one of those mad dogs who defected from the ANC and formed the Assembly of Polokwane Losers should get anything. We will spray these insects with Doom," said Mahlangu. He added, "Everyone knows that COPE was formed by insects that are hell-bent on holding onto power."

> "I will never vote a corrupt ANC into office. I am prepared to be called a snake, a dog and a baboon rather than endorsing a party and its leader Jacob Zuma whose moral values have declined worse than a Zimbabwean dollar." ANC head of policy in KwaZulu-Natal, Siyanda Mhlongo, who resigned and joined COPE a day before he was due to face an ANC disciplinary hearing for failing to execute his duties

An unknown animal

After the elections, references to snakes, dogs, donkeys or cockroaches seemed to go the way of the dodo. ANC Secretary-General Gwede Mantashe was reluctant to let go, though. Explaining why COPE was not given the opportunity to name the chairperson of any of Parliament's committees he said, "Because it is a new animal. We must develop a relationship with that animal. We don't know it yet. It is not about dishing out chairs, it is about work." What kind of animal COPE was now, he didn't say. A sheep, in wolf's clothing perhaps? A camel designed by a committee? An elephant in the room? Watch this space.

> "i argue everyone to be reasonable, no one before Lekota made this noise but now you like sheeps following one another crossing N2 without observing. as long as the first one is crossing, its fine. you people are just unbelievable … i rest my case on you if you cant open your eyes and use the powder inside your skulls." The appropriately named 'Brilliance' leaves a comment on news24.com

Chapter 4

Imbeciles in Expensive Suits:
Politicians

"Millions of not-so-gigantic turds find their way here, daily, and head for the open ocean. Or Koeberg Nuclear Power Station (which is a hop, skip and a jump away), creating not-so-gigantic radioactive turds that mutate and evolve and become politicians." Jeremy Nell

The previous chapter covered the dogs, snakes, donkeys and cockroaches of the political world. But what about all the other animals? Such as the pig, for instance?

"The tabloids have called me the 'Prince of Pigs'—while I'm the crown of God's creation," declared Truman Prince, newly re-elected mayor of Beaufort West. To underscore the merit of his claims, he explained, "I am a big man in a small town, with a big brain, a huge vision and above-average intelligence."

Not a man overburdened with modesty then. He also told the *Mail & Guardian*, "I do nothing half-heartedly. When I cause shit, I cause big shit. Sometimes, when there are no battles to fight, I would pick a fight because it activates my brain."

This is an insight that brings to mind the joke about the five surgeons who are discussing who are the easiest patients to operate on:

The first surgeon, from Durban, says: "I like to see accountants on my operating table because when you open them up, everything inside is numbered." The second surgeon, from Johannesburg, responds: "Yeah, but you should try electricians! Everything inside them is colour-coded." The third surgeon, from Bloemfontein, says: "No, I really think librarians are the best; everything inside them is in alphabetical order." The fourth surgeon, from Pretoria says: "You know, I like construction workers. Those guys always understand when you have a few parts left over." But the fifth surgeon, from Cape Town, shuts them all up when he observes: "You're all wrong. Politicians are the easiest to operate on. There's no guts, no heart, no brains and no spine, and the head and the arse are interchangeable."

"Just another poodle." Barney Mthombothi, editor of the Financial Mail, after President Kgalema Motlanthe fired Vusi Pikoli

"There's no progress. What has she done since she has been in office? What work can she account to? She's a disaster herself." SASCO on Education Minister Naledi Pandor

"She must use her fake accent to address our problems," Julius Malema on Naledi Pandor

"He now runs a one-man show. The UDM is an empty house and Holomisa is running up and down alone in that house ". Julius Malema on Bantu Holomisa

"They are a one-street party and their president is as good as a chairman of a street committee." Julius Malema on the IFP and its leader Mangosuthu Buthelezi

"Patricia de Lille calling for calm inside the ANC is like General Christiaan de Wet playing arbitrator between hostile camps in the British army during the Anglo-Boer War. Did the Nats teach them nothing? When there's discord, you sow more seeds of division." Ndumiso Ngcobo

"Dullish Blade Nzimande … is, by definition, quite a silly person, prone to superstitions about pink fairies and the workerist nobility that comes with undergraduate jargon and a fierce-looking beard and yet, by the same token, remarkably quiet about the dismal failures of Soviet and Maoist social engineering." Andrew Donaldson

"This man is dangerous and stupid. That he's in charge of our education system is particularly worrying." Duncan Mcleod on Blade Nzimande

MORE South African Insults

The continued popularity of circus metaphors in South African politics is perhaps apt. Julius Malema was widely dismissed as a clown (though, as political commentator Stanley Uys pointed out, no one was laughing). After the DA tried to lay charges over corruption at the ANCYL's investment arm, treasurer Pule Mabe said: "They have run out of things [to do] ... there are other serious issues of national importance. [The DA are] grand-standers, clowns, political jokers." DA treasurer Jack Bloom had accused the League of setting an "appalling example".

"To be drawn into a circus would not be something we are ready for," said Mabe, directly contradicting the assumptions of the South African public. "We are a very serious youth organization. We've got important things to do. We are introducing a new regime of corporate governance to make sure that there is accountability."

Perhaps this is what prompted Patricia de Lille to dress up "like a cross between a circus ringmaster and a Cape minstrel in her blue pantsuit and matching hat," as Lauren Cohen and Gabisile Ndlehele described de Lille's "eye-popping outfit for the 2009 opening of Parliament.

One blogger wondered whether de Lille was "auditioning for next year's coon carnival?" and continued, "Though no one is asking her to have herself injected with Botox, there is at least an expectation that a leader of a political party is properly groomed. Who on earth would trust this to run a coon carnival, much less a country???"

Others thought she looked like Charlie Chaplin or Johnny Walker. Given the popularity of the latter, perhaps it was an appropriate choice after all.

> "She was clearly taken with the opportunity, saying that she had dreamed of featuring in the country's longest-running soapie. Heads up Pat, politics IS the longest-running soapie in this country." Busi Bling on Patricia de Lille's guest appearance in *Egoli*

Beyond the three dominant figures of South African politics over the last two years—Jacob Zuma, Julius Malema and Helen Zille, who feature later in this volume—there are others worthy of special mention. Among them are Thabo Mbeki, his loyal cohort Manto, and those spiritual brothers in the Jacob Zuma camp, Carl Niehaus and Schabir Shaik. Though Niehaus and Shaik are not strictly politicians, they are both deeply embedded in our political fabric.

But first, let us reflect on the Shakespearian tragedy of our poetry-quoting former president, a man who was his own—and some said, the country's—worst enemy.

Thabo Mbeki: the colossus of odes

"What a tragedy, what an absolute waste, President Thabo Mbeki's tenure has been. And today it is unravelling like a badly woven quilt. It is incredible that such a colossal failure remains in office." Justice Malala

How quickly things change. After Thabo Mbeki fired Jacob Zuma in 2005, it seemed that his position was unassailable. Nothing was ever the same after Polokwane, though, and that does not only apply to the N1.

As *Times* editor Ray Hartley interpreted Mbeki's state of the nation address, "I've got Jacob Zuma and my mother watching, so have a little appreciation for the political minefield I'm about to walk through, okay? We're sorry we stuffed up the electricity thing but we are really, really, really trying to fix it by whatever means possible ... Things look pretty weird with the Police Commissioner on trial and the Scorpions boss suspended, but we are a resilient people that have been through a lot of weirdness before."

Sipho Seepe was not convinced by Thabo Mbeki's state of the nation address. "An assessment of Mbeki's presidency reveals a reign in the age of foolishness, the epoch of belief and of incredulity, and a season of darkness, both literally and figuratively," he wrote in *Business Day*. "We have become prisoners of hope. The sooner we disabuse ourselves of the notion that changes will occur miraculously, the better."

Hartley concluded, somewhat cynically: "All the other promises to fix things and speed up the government made in previous speeches still stand, only this time, I'm going to kick ass because I only have a year or so before Jacob takes over ... and you know what's going to happen then."

As it turned out, a year is a long time in politics.

"Whew! What a load of time shedding that parliamentary speech was, and to think that many people had been eagerly anticipating it!" Jon Qwelane's assessment of Thabo Mbeki's state of the nation address

Months before Mbeki was eventually forced to resign, there were strident calls for him to step down. "President Mbeki must go and he must go now. In a constitutional democracy such as ours, it is untenable for a president with his track record to remain in office," declared Helen Zille, agreeing—for once—with the SACP. She said he was a "lame duck" president: "He has failed to lead, failed to inspire and failed to offer hope. He has made it clear that his government will not accept responsibility for the very real crises facing our country."

Peruse, if you will, the following selection of opinions on the man formerly known as President Mbeki:

- Jon Qwelane, in the wake of Polokwane: "The self-conceited Mbeki cannot swallow his pride to accept that he is hated and was beaten fair and square in an openly democratic contest by someone for whom he clearly has no respect. He cannot believe that his borrowed English airs and graces from Exeter counted for sweet bugger-all at Polokwane, and his favourite Du Bois and Yeats as well as Shakespeare quotations impressed no one, except perhaps his sycophants who worship him like a god."
- Journalist Charlene Smith: "Thabo Mbeki must go. The president who has failed to see any crisis with the world's highest rates of Aids, worst crime statistics, exploding power stations, the stolen election of a neighbouring country and scenes of unmitigated barbarism against foreigners is destroying our nation."
- *Sowetan* columnist Lucky Mazibuko: "Our outgoing president, Thabo Mbeki, has set the lowest standards for our country and our people, and yet he is dismally failing to meet them. I think the less of a public role he plays in the few months left in office, the better for all of us. President Mbeki has become a menace to our society; he is like a fly in the pudding."
- *Business Day* columnist Sipho Seepe: "Mbeki's government rewards incompetence, celebrates mediocrity, and denigrates expertise and scholarship. It is uncaring and unresponsive. Accountability is a foreign concept."
- *Business Day* political editor Karima Brown: "Thabo Mbeki is really yesterday's man. He's done."
- Professor Ian Taylor of St Andrews University: "It's way too late for Mbeki to regain his reputation. He is yesterday's man. Mbeki has proven he can't produce the goods."
- Risk analyst Mark Schroeder: "Mbeki will revert to his lame-duck status."

- Justice Malala: "I am praying for the elections next year so that this incompetent can be bundled out of office. He is a disgrace to South Africa and to Africa."

"If you make bad decisions you need to correct them, but Thabo Mbeki's political style was autistic—you don't hear voices outside your own head." Tony Leon

In the midst of the xenophobic violence, Mafuta Baloyi complained that Mbeki and Shilowa were "two peas from the same pod" with their "frightening lack of leadership qualities".

"They are big on flowery speeches delivered from high in their plush offices, but the longer they are in office the more afraid they are to get dust on their Gucci shoes, walking in the communities and leading from the front.

"I am reminded of the famous words of Cromwell in the English parliament: 'You have sat too long for any good you have been doing. Depart, I say, and let us have done with you. In the name of God, go.'"

"The problem in this country is Thabo Mbeki and his people ... We don't want him." Julius Malema

After Mbeki was forced to resign, Hogarth wondered if the Thabo Mbeki Leadership Institute would offer courses in "effective denialism, silent diplomacy, intellectual tyranny and of course, peer enrichment". Perhaps Jean-Bertrand Aristide could be offered a chair in governance, Mad Bob would teach multiparty democracy "and the Trinidadian Shinehead could be appointed master of hagiography".

Several months after Mbeki had vanished into obscurity, Zackie Achmat of the Treatment Action Campaign argued, "He covered up his own deceit, his own lies and deep role in the arms deal." He also accused Mbeki of "double-speak", with veiled attacks on anyone who disagreed with him and criticized Mbeki's "race-based nativism", saying it had permitted black South Africans to use the race card to invalidate criticism of laziness and incompetence.

Just prior to Polokwane, Jon Qwelane had written: "The self-anointed patron saint of the African Union with all its unconvincing platitudes about good governance is actually an ungracious has-been, a yesterday's man who refuses to accept defeat."

Ultimately, though, Mbeki had little choice.

"Mbeki was poison by the end. Poison. I would have voted for de Lille and Rajbansi's love child at Polokwane had that been the alternative," Paul Berkowitz said on Facebook.

Manto overboard

In September 2008, Manto wept. Not over the suffering of ordinary South Africans in a barely functioning public health system. Not over the people effectively denied access to antiretroviral medication, the newborn babies killed by infections caught in hospital or the dashed hopes of the dying who believed in quack cures. No, what drove Manto to tears was the fact that people had been horrible to her friend Thabo Mbeki, and forced him to resign. "For all South Africans, this is quite unfair," she said, tears rolling down her face.

Fair or not, South Africans were astonished when one of Mbeki's most loyal cohorts failed to resign in solidarity with their leader—perhaps, some speculated, she was too busy at the pub to get the memo—and even more astonished when instead of being kicked out on her arse, a fate she richly deserved, she managed to score an alternative portfolio.

"As a disciplined and loyal member and deployee of the African National Congress, I remain committed in my duties as the country's Health Minister serving at the pleasure of my movement, the African National Congress," she said. Asked if she planned to resign, Manto replied that she remained, "obliged to perform all the public service duties associated with her office". Nope. There was just no getting rid of her.

> "But to pick up a picture of a politically elected person and throw it into a dustbin, I don't think that is correct; it smells of anarchy." Manto Tshabalala-Msimang comments on the suspension of KwaZulu-Natal doctor Mark Blaylock, who threw a portrait of Health MEC Peggy Nkonyeni into a dustbin after Nkonyeni suggested that doctors in rural areas cared only for profits, not for people

"The war is over," Aids activist Mark Heywood said when the government, with Barbara Hogan now at the helm of the Health ministry, agreed to roll out ARVs. Meanwhile, researchers at Harvard concluded that, compared to countries in a similar financial bracket, 330,000 South Africans should not have died.

Technically, this makes Thabo Mbeki and Manto Tshabalala-Msimang the most successful mass murderers in South African history. Daisy de Melcker and the Station Strangler have nothing on these two.

"We need to assess the impact our government programmes on women have had," she said. "There are general calls for the establishment of this ministry. We are hoping to have it phased into government. In our view, the ministry would consolidate our gender machinery," said Tshabalala-Msimang.

After Home Affairs called on South Africans to "confirm their alive status", it did seem possible that the explanation for Manto's extraordinary capacity for survival had been under our noses all along. She was undead, a creature that had crept through a portal from a parallel universe and was unleashed upon us to wreak havoc and sow death and destruction. Rather like those bits of ectoplasm that flew around in *Ghostbusters*.

The only happy aspect of this sorry tale is that she replaced the truly creepy Essop Pahad, who possesses more than a passing resemblance to Slimer.[1]

> "I just feel like crying." Health expert upon being informed that Manto had been appointed African Union goodwill ambassador for maternal, infant and child health

Besides the possibility that Manto was an evil spirit from another dimension, there were several feasible explanations for this woman's apparently impossible gifts of survival:

1. She was a vampire. The problem with this explanation, apart from its unacceptable Eurocentricity, was her well-known fondness for garlic.
2. She was a zombie and therefore undead.
3. She was a member of the Illuminati and was actually George Bush's long-lost half-sister. Though they may not look all that similar, they were both fond of the odd tipple. Her magical ability to escape anything resembling accountability was thanks to protection by powerful global interests.
4. She was one of those lizards that David Icke keeps going on about and, as in point 3, is George Bush's long lost half-sister.

---

[1] The little green ghost in *Ghostbusters*.

5. She was an alien, possibly related to the creatures featured in District 9 (the problem with this theory being that the prawns were addicted to cat food rather than booze).
6. She was preserved in alcohol and therefore impervious to decay.

In an especially cruel April Fool's joke, The Times reported that Manto was set to be reinstated as minister of health after Barbara Hogan angered the ANC with her comments about the Dalai Lama. "Controversial former health minister Manto Tshabalala-Msimang is poised to make a dramatic comeback," read the report. "Well-placed sources said Tshabalala-Msimang, who is renowned for her opposition to the use of antiretroviral drugs to fight HIV-Aids, will regain her position this week in a Cabinet reshuffle."

In a final sick twist, Manto was appointed African Union goodwill ambassador on maternal, infant and child health, prompting howls of outrage from healthcare activists across the land.

"She has done very badly in this country, and now she is going to destroy the whole continent," said Treatment Action Campaign General Secretary Vuyiseka Dubula.

Manto has largely faded from public view, replaced in the mind of the public by Julius Malema and others. Alas, her legacy will last long after she eventually shuffles off this mortal coil.

"We are confident that Comrade Tshabalala-Msimang, with her expertise would represent us well in the global community and deal with these challenges exceptionally." Spokesperson Asanda Fongqo of the Democratic Nursing Organization of SA

"I doubt if I'll vote again for a party providing such a fertile breeding ground for ANC apologists." *Sunday Times* reader Henry Kenney expresses his disappointment at former DA leader Tony Leon's about-turn on the ANC, after accepting a position as ambassador to Argentina

"I still bear the scars on my back of my grisly encounters with Marthinus van Schalkwyk and his merry gang of political mercenaries." Tony Leon on the DP's "marriage made in hell" with the NP

Maybe Myanmar for Bantu Holomisa?
Good suggest
He used to be
general.

Kenneth Meshoe could convert the heathens in Albania
And Terror Lekota would do well in Afghanistan.

And Helen Zille? Where could they send her?
I've heard the government is already in talks with PyongYang.

Carl Nohouse

"There's a post to be created at ANC headquarters for Director-General of Weasel-Worded Apologies. Carl Niehaus is the front-runner." Comment, thoughtleader. He was apologizing on behalf of the deputy minister of foreign affairs, only a week before he became mired in a scandal of his own

When the *Mail & Guardian* confronted ANC spokeperson and former ambassador to the Netherlands Carl Niehaus with the vast piles of dirt it had dug up, he burst into tears. "Most of what you've confronted me with is true," he wept. "I wish it wasn't. I've made massive mistakes and I've disappointed a lot of people terribly. I've no illusions that if you publish this article it will mean the end of my career."

And what a career it was. Revelations included the fact that he owed money to virtually everyone in the ANC. He had forged signatures while he was chief executive of the Gauteng Economic Development Agency. At one point he had asked to be introduced to Brett Kebble because he was desperate for money, and had been forced to leave his job at Deloitte and Touche. While he worked for Rhema, he bought a Porsche and a C-class Mercedes and the church had stood surety for R700,000 worth of debt.

The implosion riveted South Africa for at least a week, especially when Niehaus became no-house as the owner of the Tuscan Mcmansion he was renting in Midrand demanded R300,000 worth of unpaid rent. Hayibo reported that Niehaus had admitted to a "sick obsession" with pretentious, tasteless architecture. "Midrand just looked so beautiful that morning," they reported him saying, "with the sun glinting off hundreds of identical satellite dishes, the wind rustling through thousands of identical ornamental palm trees, the buzz of electric fences, the yapping of Maltese poodles, the bleep of car alarms."

Then out slipped the story that he had been arrested and spent a night in jail for failing to pay a R70,000 debt owed to the Lost City; he tried to use his former wife's Porsche as surety but the hotel refused. A Joburg advertising agency, Mortimer Harvey, told the media that they had never been paid for more than R1.5 million worth of work they'd done for the Children United Foundation South Africa; Niehaus was the chief executive of the foundation at the time.

As the story progressed, the lies piled up like back copies of *Garden & Home* in a dentist's waiting room. First it emerged that he had never obtained a doctorate or a master's in theology at the University of Utrecht in the Netherlands. Then Wits University confirmed that he had never obtained a BA from the institution, never mind summa cum laude.

> "Niehaus, you are a disgrace to the Afrikaners and I urge you to never speak a word in Afrikaans again." Letter to *The Citizen*

On his CV he claimed that he served on several boards, including those of the South African Netherlands Chamber of Commerce, Civirello Pty (Ltd), the Nederlandse Maatschappij der Letteren and the Afrikaanse Skrywersvereniging, as well as the President's Awards for Young Achievers and that he chairs the finance committee of the South African Council of Churches (SACC).

All of this turned out to be made up. In fact, there's no such thing as the President's Awards for Young Achievers. Or a company called Civirello Pty (Ltd). The Afrikaanse Skrywersvereniging is real, but it doesn't have a board.

Niehaus even scored a free holiday to Mauritius from a travel agent in East London by telling her that he needed to recover from chemotherapy for leukemia.

Hayibo noted, "The ANC has reportedly put pressure on Niehaus to provide full disclosure after the party became unsettled by claims he was making around the office that he had once wrestled a grizzly bear to death while making love to identical Swedish sextuplets."

Gauteng Premier Paul Mashatile, who was Finance MEC at the time that Niehaus was attempting to defraud the GEDA, said he warned the ANC about Niehaus who, he said, was a "liar who could not be trusted".

> "Brilliant one, Carl, blame apartheid and prison. The man is a scurrilous and pathological liar and a cheat. He is the epitome of the worst sort of conman hiding behind a fictitious religious degree." Letter to *The Citizen*

Then it emerged that Niehaus had failed to pay a R2 million mortgage on a house financed by Standard Bank and still owed R230,000 for unpaid rent to the management of Michelangelo Towers. In 2006, Tzaneen businessman Magula Makaana took Niehaus to court after he failed to repay a loan of R420,000. And while Niehaus was drowning in debt, he still managed to scrape together R35,000 in lobola—paid in two instalments—for his third wife, who was 18 years his junior. In the couple's prenuptial agreement, Niehaus listed his personal wealth at R12.5 million. "Someone described him as a habitual liar and I think that's a fairly accurate description," said Makaana. How Niehaus had survived to this point with his kneecaps intact was something of a mystery.

Predictably, Niehaus blamed apartheid for his addiction to Tuscan mansions and German cars. "Carl Niehaus has … sought professional assistance in the two areas vital to dealing conclusively with his personal situation and reconstructing his life," said his lawyer, Ian Small-Smith. "He is seeking psychological counselling to assist him in dealing with the long-term and deeply negative affects of his time spent in prison for his principled opposition to apartheid."

Small-Smith said he had taken on Niehaus as a pro bono client, which is probably just as well. "Carl feels terrible," he told the media. "He feels that he has failed the ANC and tarnished its image, but he will face the music."

The best Carl Niehaus story appeared in the *Cape Argus*. Apparently, Niehaus had told his then employer, law firm A. L. Mostert, that his sister had died and that he needed money to pay for a ticket to fly to London to arrange her funeral. This despite the fact that he was being paid more than R100,000 a month as a consultant.

"[Linda] Thango, who was then still his wife, was employed as Niehaus's personal assistant at his insistence." Niehaus was reportedly caught out on his return from London when he dropped Thango off at the front entrance to the law firm before parking his car. "Staff had arranged flowers for the couple. Thango reportedly asked what they were for. She was told it was a gesture from the staff as sympathy for the death of her sister-in-law. Her response was: 'When did that happen? We were with her yesterday.'"

In a rare acknowledgment of outstanding achievement in the area of nincompoopery, Niehaus was honoured by Hogarth as Mampara of the Week two weeks in a row and, in an intriguing postscript, after the elections, he was spotted driving a "very new-looking BMW". "Or," wondered Hogarth, "has some kind soul given him a job as a chauffeur?"

Schabir Shaik

"Shaik's doctors have confirmed that he is in the final stages of a terminal condition called 'life', and that the condition is irreversible. We can only pray he makes it through the next 30 years." Hayibo.com

In many ways, Carl Niehaus was a spiritual brother to Schabir Shaik, even if the former never got to spend time in jail. Not that Schabir spent all that much time in tjoekie: to absolutely nobody's surprise, he was released on medical parole after serving all of 28 months of his 15-year sentence.

Apparently the diabetes and high blood pressure he suffered from placed him in imminent danger of expiring. "As much as we wish Shaik the best of health, it is important—from the perspective of upholding the rule of law in South Africa—that our message of sympathy change soon to one of condolences, because the implication of Shaik's premature release on medical parole is that his death is imminent.

"Not your average get-well card, that," Hogarth observed.

Shaik's release, Andrew Donaldson was at pains to stress, had "absolutely nothing whatsoever to do with Shabby's fraudulent and corrupt relationship with Mr Love Pants, the singing groovy who, mere months after his investiture as our next president, may or may not find himself in the dock answering to the very charges that got Shabby into so much trouble in the first place ... absolutely nothing ... so don't even go there ... even if you are a convict suffering from asthma or tuberculosis and are wondering why you are still stuck behind bars".

COPE complained that Shaik's release represented "yet another clear case of abuse of power" by the ruling party. The ANC has once again proven unashamedly the length they will go to protect corrupt officials who have links to the ANC president."

Patricia de Lille said it was "completely disgusting that there is such scant regard for procedures and the law in our country when a criminal has connections to high-profile politicians".

Asked what he would buy Shaik as a welcome home gift, Max du Preez said it was a toss-up between a coffin and a home gym.

"Were he not at home right now, chained to a wall in his bedroom, the fraudster—or rather, his reanimated corpse—would probably be wandering the streets of Durban, mindlessly attacking people and devouring their brains." Andrew Donaldson surmises that Shaik is a zombie and South Africa is "dwelling in the realm of the undead"

JZ lashed out at South Africans for wanting Schabir Shaik dead, saying that he had been "deeply saddened" by the fact that many South Africans were convinced that Shaik was lying about being at death's door.

Tutu also questioned the medical parole that was granted to Shaik. "It's not a laughing matter—it's people saying 'go jump in a lake' if you have objections. Is this why people died, is this why people went into exile, is this why people were tortured?"

> "According to the Democratic Alliance MP who spotted and filmed the alleged outing, the sighting was 'manna from white whinger heaven, as if God himself had reached down from the clubhouse of the celestial golf estate' and revealed Shaik to him." Hayibo.com

After Shaik was spotted out and about in Durbs—buying balloons of all things—questions were asked about his apparent state of rude health. I saw him pulling over at a driveway in Essenwood Road—I could not believe what I was seeing. For a man said to be so gravely ill to be driving alone is unthinkable," said DA councillor Dean McPherson.

Correctional Services spokesman Thami Zondi responded to queries about this apparently miraculous recovery, saying: "As a department, we cannot force one to die. If one doesn't break the parole conditions then there is nothing we can do."

Zondi also questioned reports that Shaik had been seen driving a 7-series BMW. "It is a family car that could have been used by anyone," he said.

"Could it have been a ghost behind the wheel?" Andrew Donaldson wondered. "Could these mysterious appearances be the stuff of the paranormal? Are we talking Twilight Zone here?"

Correctional Services Minister Nosiviwe Mapisa-Nqakula said she was not sure that "terminal" meant a parolee must be confined to his home. "I know it means dying," she told Parliament. "But if you have you a terminal disease does it mean you cannot move around? You cannot go into your car?"

Patricia de Lille asked what would happen if Shaik had made a full recovery: "If some miracle happened and Mr Shaik is not dying and he's fit again—you have been drinking French wine and eating curry and then you recover—will he be sent back to jail because there is certainty that he did not die?"

The Minister said she didn't know.

A taste of paradise

"The ANC government is all about delivery. Delivery of pizzas and KFC buckets to ministerial residences; delivery of customized BMWs to ministerial garages; delivery of airline tickets to MPs; delivery of brown paper bags full of non-sequential unmarked US dollars to arms dealers." Hayibo quotes government tax advisor Caesar Augustus Dipoko

Imagine the news without politicians. Could you? That's exactly what a reader of *The Citizen* did, calling for news shedding or a blackout on all ANC activities for a week.

"Let's face it, every utterance by inept leaders and parliamentarians has been proved to be a load of twaddle … Just imagine, a week without the face of failure in all media! A time to get on with our lives without having the likes of the Zumas (both), Mantos, Erwins and their ilk, shoved in our faces. A taste of paradise?"

A news blackout would at least ensure a measure of freedom from what Andrew Donaldson described as the "proliferation of tired and pompous clichés continually thrown our way by a government which seems to have cornered the market when it comes to vapid posturing".

It's not just the ANC though. As one anonymous South African blogger sums it up: "Nearly all politicians … are notorious bullshitters (cue sarcastic act of surprise), endowed with the principles and ethics comparable to that of rabid dogs coupled with the money-extraction skills of a one-armed bandit at your local casino."

That's probably being too kind.

"Imbeciles in expensive suits—they come in all shapes and sizes. You find them in every field of life … these creatures feed on other people's sweat and blood. We have asked for leaders but God sent us criminals." Jabulani Mncube, Orange Farm, letter to the *Sunday Sun*

Chapter 5

Only in South Africa

"We really call upon citizens to confirm your alive status." Local Government minister Richard Baloyi, alerting South Africans to the fact that they might have been fraudulently declared dead

Ja, sometimes this is a strange place, hey. A land of zombies, where you have to check with Home Affairs to find out whether you're alive or dead,[1] People who were deemed deceased would have to report to their local Home Affairs office with an affidavit confirming that they were alive.

The department, noted the media report, "did not elaborate on why anyone would be fraudulently declared dead".

It's hard to imagine another country in the world where the Department of Transport would promote donkey carts and bicycles as innovative forms of getting around. Ben Trovato, writing about Transport Month, noted that the highlight for him would be the Promotion of Animal-Drawn Carts[2] at the Nokaneng community centre in Mpumalanga. "I hope the rest of the government is taking note," he wrote. "There is no reason why the housing department shouldn't promote Living in Caves. I would also like to see the department of science and technology promote the Wheel and the department of communications promote Grunting as a Means of Conversing."

---

[1] Dead people can still collect their pensions. In Witbank, three women strapped a dead man to a wheelchair to claim his pension money from the Post Office. "He didn't look so great," a witness told *Beeld*. After the women said that they didn't have money to bury the deceased, a supervisor made a print of the corpse's thumb on a receipt slip and handed the women R960.

[2] Occasionally, the animals end up inside cars, as was the case in Emanguzi in northern KwaZulu-Natal, where a Fiat Uno was stopped and found to contain a cow and two goats.

It's hard to imagine another place where a motorist could die after being "playfully" shot by one of the passengers in the car he was driving. (It seems that in January 2009, Sibusiso Mahlaba stopped at the side of Dambuza Road in Durban to talk to the occupants of another vehicle. According to KwaZulu-Natal Superintendent Henry Budhram, one of the passengers "playfully produced a firearm and while pointing it in the direction of Mahlaba, a shot went off". The passengers rushed Mahlaba to hospital, where he died.)

> "The distributor was chained to the engine and the brakes were non-existent. The driver was using his handbrake to slow the vehicle down a bit." KZN provincial traffic spokesman describes a vehicle impounded for not being roadworthy

Or a country where the main opposition party expresses outrage over the hiring of 25 sangomas by the National Intelligence Agency to cleanse its facilities in the national capital. According to the DA, the sangomas were paid R30,000 each to clear the NIA facilities in Pretoria of bad vibes. The NIA said this was ridiculous and that the ceremony had in fact involved representatives of several religions. It was understood that several cattle were slaughtered.

While on the subject of fresh beef, it was reported in November 2008 that a cow ran through an Mpumalanga shopping centre with a small dog attached to her muzzle. "Witnesses said the dog—possibly a mix between a terrier and a corgi, or even a sausage dog—had latched onto the cow's nose after finding her grazing in his owner's vegetable garden," reported Oris Mnisi and Tshwareloeseng Mogakane. "The beast kicked and mooed and ran, with the dog attached to her snout, through the Thulamahashe shopping complex."

Security guards locked themselves in their office to escape the cow. "When we first saw the dog we thought it was a plastic bag, but when the cow got closer we saw it was dog hanging tight while the cow was bleeding," said Vusi Shabangu.

The mongrel let go after it was called by a family member of the owner. Centre manager Nomsa Ngomane said damage amounted to over R2,000, but none of the tenants had laid charges of malicious damage to property. There was no word as to whether the dog was, as had been rumoured, a member of Congress of the People.

The political allegiances of the cow remained open to speculation.

"Other people say I may not be able to fight again while others say anything can happen. My choice, to be honest, is to go the cultural route because I believe this dislocation is caused by witchcraft." Boxer Tyson Sixhakuma, who was prevented from fighting by a problematic shoulder

If it wasn't cows and dogs, other domestic animals caused trouble. Earlier in 2008, the *Mopani News* reported that two chickens in Nyanyukani village outside Tzaneen were abandoned in the bush to be killed and eaten by wild animals after they started walking upright like penguins. Their owner, Nomsa Mlangeni, was convinced they were bewitched. She finally got rid of the birds after neighbours accused her of being a witch, and vowed never to keep chickens or eat chicken again.

In a similarly avian vein, Mervin Senna of Benoni was tormented by a strange black bird that appeared to his kitchen after the lights went out.

"Mervin Senna and wife are living in hell," the *Daily Sun* reported. "... they are being tormented by a strange black bird ... and the man needs help ... FAST!"

Senna explained that the bird, identified by sangomas as a tokoloshe, had started haunting him and his wife about four months before while they watched TV. Mervin heard and saw a black bird moving around the house in the dark. It would come out to eat their food and play in the kitchen.

"This bird is violent. It recently attacked my wife and wanted to sleep with me," he reported.

None of the church leaders, traditional healers or sangomas they had consulted with had been able to help. One sangoma said that somebody had put powerful muthi in the Senna's property.

"These fights leave me tired and my body sore. Recently my hair started to fall out of my head and I felt like I was dying. I have lost hope," he said, adding that he no longer had any cash to pay sangomas for more help."

Perhaps the parents who withdrew their children from two schools in the North West were afraid of a similar fate, after it emerged that five Venda-speaking sangomas had planted muthi in the grounds.

The reason for the presence of the sangomas was unclear, but it seemed that a local councillor had arranged for them. Parents demanded that cleansing ceremonies be performed at Makuka Secondary School and Sefikile Primary School before their children would be allowed to return.

> "There are people that suck bodily fluids out of a person at night when they are asleep. This is the work of witches. They must have put my bodily fluids there."
> 26-year-old Caswell Nkanunu's novel explanation for the compelling evidence of his involvement in the rape and murder of a 47-year-old Elliot woman

Prophets, witches and magicians are everywhere, though perhaps not all of them are as deft with a Bic disposable razor as Free State resident Ndoyisiwe Paulos Notito. Notito posed as a prophet and promised to heal the assorted ailments of the women who sought his help. Notito told them that they were bewitched and that the cure included the removal of the hair from their heads, pubic areas and armpits. After shaving them, he would then rape them and steal their belongings. Notito was eventually convicted on seven counts of rape, eight of theft and two of indecent assault. The judge indicated that he would have to serve 28 years before being considered for parole.

Also in the Free State—evidently a flattish brown version of Twin Peaks—48-year-old Nqadike Makoetla was tricked into falling asleep in a field by an evil ghost and awoke to find three men chopping at his legs with pangas. When they found that he only had R6 on him "they got furious and like hungry wolves fighting for a piece of meat, they attacked me with their weapons". Makoetla fought the men off and escaped with his life, but had to be pushed around in a wheelbarrow. Doctors told him that the cuts to his legs were so deep that he might never walk again.

None of this should surprise us. After all, as Deputy Police Minister Fikile Mbalula (ex ANCYL) informed the public in August 2009, criminals are "people who are possessed with evil spirits" and "animals" who should not be glorified, and the evidence in the *Daily Sun* would tend to bear him out:

> "The ingredients of the products are guarded under oath by its developers. The claim regarding swollen legs and the healing properties of the product are targeted at a market that knows and understands the cause of swollen legs and its remedy."
> Defense by the manufacturers of a herbal product called *Thoba o Thobe*

The Advertising Standards Authority ruled that the product could not be advertised by making such claims. A (white) reader had complained to the ASA after seeing an ad for the product in *The Citizen*.

Confidence tricksters continued to exploit the vast legions of the gullible. None of them as colourful, perhaps, as the woman—the colourfully named Nomatter Tagarira—who convinced the Zimbabwean government that pure diesel would pour from a rock she had struck with her staff, but each was creative in his or her own way.

Most snake oil salesmen promise help with matters such as erections and 'early sperming', but others claim to be able to bring more than one's rusty tackle back from the dead.

In January 2009, Canaan Mdletshe reported that the family of a man who died in 2007 were demanding R45,000 from a priest who said he could bring their relative back to life, if they dug him up. Jabulani Xulu was dug up in front of hundreds of onlookers at the Mbongolwane cemetery in Lanowe, then placed on a table in order to be raised from the dead. When nothing happened, the crowd became furious and police had to take the priest to safety.

Xulu's cousin, Timothy Shandu, said the priest had approached him and told him that he could resurrect Xulu. "The priest and my cousin were very close while he was still alive. He told me that God had told him raise my cousin from the dead because he had died prematurely," he recalled. "As shocked as I was, I asked him to put it in writing and he did."

Shandu explained that, while the priest did not want to charge for his services, Xulu's family agreed that if he did not succeed, they wanted R45,000. (Why not go for a nice round R50,000? This was never explained.)

"Our chief called him to a public meeting and he confirmed having written a letter to the effect that he had been instructed by God to resurrect my cousin. He was granted permission by the chief and we went to the grave site to exhume the body. Yesterday he prayed for hours over the remains but my cousin didn't rise from the dead. This angered the community," said Shandu. "I regret to have ever listened and believed him."

Two Ugandan men were arrested after they persuaded a Pietermaritzburg man to part with R60,000 after convincing him that they could turn his money into millions by "washing" it in a river. Edward Borgere and Unam Semakule told the victim they could turn his money into millions by washing it, praying on a mountain and sacrificing a goat. When, after two weeks—the time taken for the magic to work—the riches failed to materialize, the victim lured them into a police trap by offering them more money.

Then there was the bank employee who embezzled R1,472,587 after being manipulated by a "witch" who said she could help her fall pregnant. Fadia Poole consulted a neighbour who told her that an evil spirit was preventing her from falling pregnant. Once she had given birth—and thus been convinced that the woman's witchcraft was effective—she was convinced to steal more.

In Ntuwe in the Eastern Cape, a man was arrested in August 2009 for burning eleven people's feet in a bizarre healing ritual. "Police found eleven people who were badly burnt in their feet in a house in Ntuwe this morning [Wednesday]," said Superintendent Mzukisi Fatyela. "The man said once a person's feet were burnt with hot stones they would be healed from their disease," he said.

Fatyela explained that this had been going on since the beginning of the year. "Lots of people come here and pay to be healed; the man burns their feet and tells them they will be healed after," he reported. "All the people found by the police cannot walk … The situation is bad."

> "Opportunistic use of culture against one another lies at the heart of what is killing us in the region." Associate professor Pumla Dineo Gqola on the link between HIV/Aids and promiscuity

Oh, it's easy to laugh. But for those of us who consider ourselves too advanced to be taken in by such obvious superstition, it's worth remembering that none of those con artists managed to score a fraction of the cash that Barry Tannenbaum netted, and he was targeting the cleverest people in the country.

As you will see in the following chapter, white men also go to sangomas. They just call them investment advisers.

Chapter 6

The More Bulls, the More Bullshit: Business

Q: How do you make a small fortune on the JSE?
A: Start with a large one.

2008 and much of 2009 were dominated by news of the Global Financial Crisis and all-round perfect economic shit storm. Fred Khumalo tried to get his head around the collapse of several banks around the world. "See, I can understand if I give Mkhize nine of my best cattle, and four of them die because of some disease. Still, Mkhize has to show me the carcasses. Mkhize can't tell me that all my cattle have disappeared, and the next thing I see Mkhize at the local taxi rank driving a Toyota Cressida with flashy wheel caps and sheepskin-covered seats, eating a kota and chasing it down with a can of Sparletta Raspberry, and he cheekily tells me that my cattle—Awu, my favourite bull uVelevutha!—have just disappeared. There will be war."

Dedicated cynic and blogger Llewellyn Kriel was not impressed with the South African government's response to the world's worst economic crisis in seven decades, saying that Trevor Manuel and Kgalema Motlanthe had failed to show any "intestinal and testicular fortitude ... Where we need Chuck Norris full of skop, skiet and donner, we've got Woody Allen full of clichéd satire and black comedy."

"The toxic chickens of job losses have now come home to roost indeed," announced COSATU's Zwelanzima Vavi.

Nobody really understood how all these clever people could have stuffed up on such a gigantic scale. But there are clues here and there. For instance, when Barry Tannenbaum's R4-billion Ponzi scheme came to light, *noseweek*—reflecting on the extraordinary number of high-profile businessmen he had manage to con—wondered. "How do we face a recession with that level of business acumen?"

Indeed.

"The writing was always on the wall: this is one gigantic global fuck-up and everybody is getting hurt." Llewellyn Kriel

"This is economic terrorism. Those workers, their families, everybody is going to suffer." National Union of Metalworkers of SA provincial secretary Zanoxolo Wayile responds to Volkswagen's announcement that it would retrench 400 workers at its Eastern Cape plant as a result of the recession

Tannenbaum's spectacular fraud would only come to light later in the year. In the meantime, it was necessary to find explanations for how the financial kak had hit the global fan. After businessman Tokyo Sexwale's comments at an ANC rally about COPE's use of witchcraft in its campaigning, Hayibo reported that Sexwale had always been "strongly anti-witch" and understood that "bull markets are caused by friendly water sprites and that bear markets are the work of witches".

Sexwale spokesman Ponzi Qozo told Hayibo: "We've been adamant for some time: just look under the boiler or in the air ducts at Merrill Lynch or Lehman Brothers and you'll find a jackal's foot or a calabash full of dried frogs.

"Business is about making tough decisions. That's how we operate here. If a deal floats, then it's a witch. If it sinks, then it's a good investment and we buy in, with an exorcism clause."

In an issue of the *Sunday Times* that screamed "Jobs bloodbath" on the front page, Ben Trovato offered sage advice. "If you haven't already been laid off, get out now," he urged. "Set fire to your desk and run. Boardrooms are awash in treachery and fear stalks the corridors. Nobody can be trusted and everyone is afraid.

"Around the world, malevolent men in Persian-blue power shirts and lupine women with sharp breasts and pencil skirts are using the credit crunch to rid their offices of what they like to call the deadwood."

How ironic then that, in many cases, the deadwood was actually running things.[1]

---

[1] To survive in this environment, you would need to perfect the art of what Michael Waddacor describes as Amaschloep-schloepä. "Welcome to Amaschloep-schloepä where almost anyone can claw and grovel their way to the zenith of corporate power provided they master the arts of sycophancy, self-interest, quasi-brilliance, callousness and avarice."

"Listening to Citi's new boss for SA, Naveed Riaz, discussing how his bank is 'fundamentally strong' must be a lot like hearing a Roman commander reassuring the troops as the Ottoman Turks storm Constantinople during the last hours of the Roman empire." Rob Rose of the *Financial Mail* in January 2009

One of the worst performing shares on the JSE in 2008 was Super Group, which not only had to contend with the slowdown in the economy, but also a large amount of money that went astray in a deal with Angola. The company's management was lambasted by Imara SP Reid analyst Warwick Lucas, who advised investors to "sell and avoid" the stock. "Watching management bumble their way from one mess to the next," he wrote, "brings back boyhood memories of watching the class clown standing on top of a rickety ladder to change a light bulb."

Another consequence of the GFC was Absa's spot of bother with single stock futures. South Africa is the world's biggest market for SSFs, and several ABSA clients found themselves unable to make margin calls. "The fat lady has only just started warming up her voice," said Deutsche Bank analyst Voyt Krzychylkiewicz, who boasts lots of consonants in a name you hope you never have to pronounce out loud.

Absa said it would be a "strategic investor" in the companies whose shares it now owned. Moneyweb readers were not impressed. "As far as bankers are concerned the only difference between strategic and speculative is that a speculative investment gets sold in time whilst 'strategic' investments usually means someone has been fired," wrote one.

"You have to love Absa. They are like Herschelle Gibbs," snorted another. "They always give you a chance to be short. Accident prone must be the ultimate description when thinking about that bunch of plonkers."

Others blamed Absa's owner Barclays Bank, which saw its own market capitalization shrink from $91 billion to $11 billion. "Arrogant pommies walked into Absa thinking they knew everything; in the meantime, they just were surfing an artificial wave of non-existent surf," ranted one reader. "Their house of cards has come tumbling down after telling Absa how to do things. Luckily there wasn't enough time for them to change Absa and drag them down. The pommie losers should be shown the door, thrown out of Absa and out of SA."

"In the home loans business you get Ricoffy and biscuits. Times are lean."
Economist John Loos of FNB

Property was one of the hardest-hit sectors, as the bubble that had steadily inflated over the past few years popped like an overstretched film of Chappies. When Andrew Golding was asked to address the subject of what was happening in the residential property market at a conference, he said he had been tempted to tell the conference organizers that delegates needn't bother to come back from tea to listen to him. "Actually nothing is going on in the residential market—that's the quick answer to that one," he said. To illustrate his point, he showed a Powerpoint slide of a car balanced precariously on the edge of a cliff.

Economist and male chauvinist Erwin Rode was not brave enough to make any forecasts about the market. "Yes, it is a very brave man who makes forecasts. You have to have balls to do that, which immediately excludes all women from making forecasts," he said at a conference in Stellenbosch largely attended by white men, which was perhaps just as well. He also said that the retail sector depended on women for recovery. "They are very good shoppers and it is a question of time before they start shopping again."

"How did you get here; on a bicycle?" Shoprite's Whitey Basson to an analyst from Merrill Lynch, in February 2009

As for investing in Africa, it was not for the faint-hearted. Mike Flax, an executive director of JSE-listed Madison Property Fund Managers, told delegates at a conference on retail property: "Putting out the risks this morning, I kakked myself." Helpfully, he explained what he meant to the foreign delegates: "This is the kind of thing that happens in your underpants when you are very, very scared."

"This is too much information," said the conference moderator.

For his part, Whitey Basson was upbeat about Africa. Once people in Angola and Nigeria experienced air-conditioning and shopping malls, they would never go back, he said. The man behind Shoprite Checkers told analysts that he was disappointed not to have won the World Retailer of the Year Award—taken by Pick 'n Pay—but was trying for a doctorate from Nigeria.

"While Nick Badminton was swanning around New York, Whitey was selling groceries," one analyst remarked.

Later, asked about the performance of his hyper stores, Basson said that they were losing out because, unlike competitors, they did not stand for anything. "It's like going to the beach with ten girls and going for a swim with the fat one," he said, somewhat cryptically.

> "The accord is a nice idea, and manna for the PR folk who dutifully spammed the email inboxes of journalists across the country. But, apart from that, it is unlikely to achieve much more than the handshake between Robert Mugabe and Morgan Tsvangirai did in September 2008." Rob Rose on an accord between SARS and the banks

The paraffin mafia

Price fixing scandals rocked the bakery, milk and paraffin industries. Sasol's German subsidiary was named as the ringleader of a 'paraffin mafia' in Europe and fined €318.2 million.[2]

Sasol was also forced to admit there were Competition Act contraventions in its Sasol Nitro, Sasol Gas and Sasol Oil divisions. A Durban fertilizer company, Nutri-flo, had lodged a complaint to the competition authorities as far back as 2002. At the time, Sasol said there was little chance that they had fixed prices. But now it changed its tune, saying that new information which had been uncovered that indicated that a "finding of unlawful conduct under the Competition Act is more probable".

"When it comes to Sasol Oil, they've been very secretive," the CEO of the Public Investment Corporation, Brian Molefe, complained. Molefe was unhappy about the appointment of the euphonious named Hixonia Nyasulu as chairperson. "We asked Sasol for information about who was involved and what took place, but they refused to tell us. We believe the public should be told what took place," he said, and it's hard to disagree with him.

The SACP[3] called for Sasol to be re-nationalized. "The EU [European Union] fine once

---

[2] Specifically, a paraffin-wax mafia. It turns out that paraffin wax is used to make a wide variety of products, from the chewy bit in chewing gum, to candles, to the red coating on Gouda cheese. The raw material used to make paraffin wax is called 'slack wax'. You learn something new every day.

[3] If any organization knows about slack wax, it's the SACP.

more underlines the correctness of the SACP's call for the re-nationalization of this strategically critical corporation," they said.

> "In 2007 one 'Michael Thembinkosi Mahlaba'—in reality a tractor driver living and working near Howick, KwaZulu-Natal—was inserted as the director of Hellermanntyton, Renold Crofts and MacSteel Tube and Pipe." James Myburgh of politicsweb reports on fraud at CIPRO, the Companies and Intellectual property Registration Office

The cheese mafia

As if Sasol's status as the godfather of the European paraffin mafia wasn't sufficiently riveting, it turned out that South Africa has mafiosi specializing in everything from plastic pipes to bread and milk. In the wake of the bread scandal in which Tiger Brands was fined R99 million, Foodcorp was fined R45 million. Foodcorp's chief executive, Justin Williamson, said that the contravention of the Competition Act was "highly regrettable and extremely embarrassing", which at least was an attempt at honesty, not something one sees often in the business world.

Judge Dennis Davis was not impressed with Clover, which, together with several other dairy producers, was found guilty of price-fixing. "That a party enters into a leniency agreement, admits certain egregious uncompetitive behaviour and accepts the consequences thereof, but later seeks effectively to resile therefrom by way of a range of technical arguments, should not be countenanced, particularly having been advised by experienced lawyers in the first place," said Davis, which when translated from legalese apparently means that Clover said it was sorry and then tried to sweet-talk its way out of being punished.

Davis also said that price-fixing was morally wrong. "In a country such as South Africa, where food prices have risen at an alarming rate and where maldistribution of wealth continued to be a blight on this nation, such behaviour is unconscionable."

There was a more general problem in the legal system, he said, in that "all too many cases are run ... on the basis of all manner of conceivable technical arguments ... to ensure that matters are never brought to finality."

In business, it seems, it is possible to pay indefinitely to keep justice at bay.

"I'll eat flippin' bread and water if I can have my house. It's my son's and my home." Legal secretary Julia Lloyd, struggling to make ends meet after she resigned from her job and eventually took another for half the salary

How can we screw you?

"The old 'boere' must be choking on their 'boeretroos & beskuit' with all these commies churning through Absa's revolving door. Maybe Absa's corporate colours turn them on!" Comment on moneyweb, reflecting on involvement in Absa by Maria Ramos and Reserve Bank governor-elect Gill Marcus

Which naturally brings us to the businesses that everybody loves to hate. The banks, for instance.

"The less we know about their excessive fees the better, but we are constantly bombarded with feel-good promises that remind me of campaigning political parties' rhetoric," noted *Financial Mail* reader Tony Ball. "Not only do their actions belie their words but they have incredible arrogance to go with it."

Rod McKenzie was furious about the way "greedy guts" Absa charged R100 every time he sent money to his mother. "I can understand that bloated, self-serving porker, Absa, would still want to squeal for something, maybe R1 or R2, but not R100. For my mom I would imagine that is easily four or five decent meals. Or a contribution to her next hearing aid.

"Absolute Blessing to Screw Anyone ... Absolute Bonus to Steal from Anyone," he fumed.

One property owner who had lost his job wondered whether banks were just greedy. Why, for instance, did banks rush to repossess properties instead of finding another solution? "Are banks really devils' dens, I wonder?"

Mortgage originators were even worse, according to one moneyweb reader. "Banks are bastards, this everyone understands, but originators are worse and don't deserve any right to existence. Breeding ground of all those too useless to get real jobs, even as life insurance salesmen."

"An honest estate agent—that's an oxymoron." Andrew Golding, overheard at a property conference and quoted on propertyweb.co.za

In one comforting sign that the more things change, the more things stay the same, South Africans also loathed Telkom as much as ever. Llewellyn Kriel described them as a "national disgrace" and "the worst telecommunications outfit in the world" with "substandard technology" and "abysmal management". "There is absolutely nothing good to say about Telkom.

"Millions of hard-pressed landline users will testify that, aside from being polite (usually), Telkom's battalions of disconnected staff battling a crumbling infrastructure, unreliable technology, its own brain drain, antique governance paradigms and an apathetic, overpaid and woefully unqualified 'management' cause more damage than good. Lies, falsehoods, deliberate half-truths and concealment are easy within a labyrinthine and obstructionist maze."

One reader of Thought Leader described the typical message callers would hear when phoning to report a problem:

"Please hold, you're 10577453434 in the queue, Telkom appreciates your call and you will be attended to >>> Beep >>> Crap Music >>> Arb Message for useless Ad"

There were no alternatives. "Neotel is less than a fart in a hurricane," sighed another reader.

In terms of sheer incandescent hatred, the only serious rivals to Telkom and the banks must the bunch who lure unsuspecting victims to timeshare presentations with fake promises of prizes. David Bullard related the tale of how a woman phoned him up one day to tell him that he had won a Chevy Spark—and all he had to do was go along to a hotel to claim his prize. "Being a bit of a car snob I thought a Chevy Spark was a brand of gas braai," he recalled, "so I told the lady phoning that I already had a gas braai and probably wouldn't bother."

Blogger Donn Edwards discovered to his cost that even being rude about timeshare was not allowed, after he was sued by Quality Vacation Club to the amount of R461,500 for offering his opinion about them on his website. Despite overwhelming public sympathy, Edwards eventually settled the case, which required him to remove all references to QVC from his site, and suspending the case for five years provided he did not mention them again. Bullard suggested that the next time somebody from a timeshare operator phoned to tell you you've won a Chevy Spark, you should tell them you would like to donate the car to your previously disadvantaged domestic worker: "My guess is that the line will go dead."

> "BEE, M&A, BBBEE were the cesspool where greed knew no bounds. The instigators and advisers to these processes did not grow employment opportunities, they did not add to the export base of SA and they did not grow our intellectual property base. May the grim reaper remove them from our midst." Comment, moneyweb[4]

Lord Tito of the belt-tighteners

"Pretoria feels to me like living in exile ... there are very few restaurants, and very few friendly people," said Tito Mboweni. He also told the gathering that he hated the Reserve Bank building, explaining, "It's one of the worst examples of architecture for many years, and I'm on the 32nd floor. It's awful!"

At his farewell dinner, outgoing South African Reserve Bank governor Tito Mboweni related how his predecessor Chris Stals had told him: "Once a central bank governor becomes popular, he must retire immediately ... if you're doing your job you have to be unpopular."

Mboweni evidently took Stals's words to heart. At one press briefing, Mboweni waved a small ornamental knobkerrie about and jokingly warned journalists that they would be "clobbered" if they asked difficult questions. The Reserve Bank also banned photographers

---

[4] To add to which, one should also echo the words of Jo Maxwell: "It's not just our BEE heroes who were pillaging the country. There are also our WEE brothers, with more money than morals, lining their already fat pockets with even more dosh. It makes me positively sick reading of the lying, cheating, thieving greed of those who can manipulate the law, bribe the authorities and fool the uninformed public."

from snapping the governor in heated moments. "He was taking pictures when I was wiping off my sweat," Mboweni complained of a photographer after a news conference.

"If women glow, men perspire and horses sweat, what do central bankers do?" one publication asked.

When it came to getting others hot under the collar, Mboweni was a master. Here was a man who was in the habit of telling South Africans to tighten their belts while remaining demonstrably incapable of taking in his own. After the gov scored a 27.5% pay rise on top of his already huge salary, Police and Prisons Civil Rights Union spokesperson Benzi Ka-Soko fumed at the injustice of salary increases for public servants amidst a sea of poverty. "These big-bellied buffoons are currently earning millions of rands and live luxurious lives filled with opulence, abundance and unparallelled wealth." At the same time, ordinary workers were expected to do the "donkey work and earn slave salaries whilst the aristocracy continue to live Ivory Tower lifestyles".

"We are very, very angry that somebody whose policies have slowed down economic growth and job creation, and put existing jobs in jeopardy, will get such a high increase," said COSATU's Patrick Craven. "At the same time he has failed to keep down inflation, and now he accepts a salary increase that is more than double the rate of inflation."

"All I ever wanted was a Jaguar," said the gov.

> "Bizarre and quite shocking." ANCYL spokesperson Floyd Shivambu comments on Tito Mboweni's 27.5% salary increase

The Bank's policy of inflation targeting ensured that there was little love lost between Mboweni and the unions. In October 2008, he said that critics of the government's fiscal policies needed to be "prayed for".

"If you hear anybody saying the inflation targeting must be abandoned … If you hear anybody saying that we need a larger fiscal deficit, go to church," Mboweni told guests at a function. "If you hear anybody who says that they need a weaker exchange rate go to church, pray for them, because they don't know what they are doing."

The following year he used a different analogy, saying that the Reserve Bank should not be seen as a group of currency traders running a casino in Pretoria. After COSATU issued calls for Mboweni's contract not to be renewed, he told the press, "Disregard most of those statements ... they are irrelevant and of no consequence. Focus on the fact that there's work to be done."

After the governor refused to receive a petition from the National Union of Metalworkers of South Africa, NUMSA General Secretary Irvin Jim said the governor's actions were "arrogant and unacceptable".

"We wish to inform Mr Mboweni and all public and Constitutional office holders that the precedent set by Mr Mboweni must never, ever be employed," said Jim. "Anyone who rejects peaceful demonstrations and refuses to accept petitions from the South African working class, who are currently experiencing extreme economic and social difficulties not of their own making is inviting big trouble," said Jim. "You are warned."

Earlier, NUMSA workers protesting against high interest rates threatened to storm the Reserve Bank. One of the liberation songs they sang included the words, "Tito lento oyenzayo ayilunganga (Tito what you are doing is not right)."

The decision not to send a representative to collect the memorandum, observed *Finweek's* Greta Steyn, "was an act of utter contempt towards the left."

> "I would like to make a suggestion to the unions to leave monetary policy to the adults and the adults will leave behaving like toddlers to the unions." news24. com reader, responding to calls by COSATU for an interest rate cut of 200 basis points

Zwelanzima Vavi criticized Mboweni's conservative monetary policy, saying it was to blame for a slowdown in economic growth. "They dismissed our concerns and our calls for aggressive cutting of interest rates, but now today workers are paying the price for their short-sightedness."

"We won't be supporting Tito's contract renewal later this year. We need change there at the Reserve Bank," said COSATU President S'Dumo Dlamini. After it was announced that Gill Marcus would be taking Mboweni's place, COSATU said that it trusted that she would be "guided by the spirit of Polokwane".

"By the way," wondered Greta Steyn, "is it safe now to refer to Tito by his catchy first name since he will soon have less power to exercise against journalists for the alleged disrespect? Or will he emerge from early retirement on his unprofitable avocado farm in Limpopo in a new top job, from where he will resume being oversensitive to perceived slights from journalists?"

Reflecting on the governor's career, Mathatha Tsedu observed, "Being governor of the SA Reserve Bank is a huge task and an important appointment. You live in a world populated by bankers and you live a life of luxury. But that can never be an excuse for becoming the snob Tito changed into."

Asked for suggestions on what Mboweni's next career move should be, moneyweb readers suggested "photographic model" and "personal trainer".

"He requires a golden shower, not a golden handshake." Comment, *Mail & Guardian*, on similarly well-remunerated executive Dali Mpofu's R11-million payout by the SABC

Oh Christmas tree

"In the same way it shocked America to learn that Madoff operated a thriving Ponzi scheme, Tannenbaum's success in duping SA's wealthy will puncture holes in SA's corporate facade." *Financial Mail*

In June 2009, South Africa's business establishment was rocked to the core by the revelation that we had a Bernard Madoff of our own. Granted, R2 billion hardly compares to the $95 billion that Madoff siphoned off from his victims, but you had to give Barry Tannenbaum credit for conning some of South Africa's most prominent businessmen.

"Barry," explained *noseweek*, "is the famously pious son of Harold Tannenbaum, mega-rich son of one of the founders of Adcock Ingram, South Africa's second-largest pharmaceutical company."

His investors included former Pick 'n Pay CEO Sean Summers who invested R50 million, the former CEO of OK Bazaars Mervyn Serebro who invested R25 million, former JSE chairman Norman Lowenthal and former Bond Exchange CEO Tom Lawless among others. From Australia, Qatar, the UK, the US, Russia and South Africa, they all fell for the promise of extraordinary returns.

Later National Prosecuting Authority spokesman Mthunzi Mhaga would explain that

Ponzi schemes usually consisted of four characteristics: the bait, the hook, the line and the sinker. "The bait was promises of high returns and was used to lure investors; the hook was a complicated, but fictitious business model used to justify the promised returns; the line was the standing in society of the fraudster; and the sinker, which usually ended the scheme, was absence or paucity of commercial activity."

And so it was that the scheme started to sink when Tannenbaum was no longer able to pay interest to his investors, and one of them hired an investigator to do some digging. Christopher Leppan then filed an urgent application in the Johannesburg High Court to have Tannenbaum declared bankrupt. Hundreds of other investors emerged from the woodwork. The game was up.

Tannenbaum himself was far away from the fracas. Now resident in the South African enclave of St Ives on Sydney's north shore, he had left South Africa in 2007 because of South Africa's high crime rate, quite possibly his own. "Why do they all run to Australia? I thought convicts were no longer welcome!" wondered one *noseweek* reader. The editor explained: "That only applies to broke criminals ... those with loads of ill-gotten cash will always get a home wherever they so desire!"

"I live in Sydney, will pop over and hurl insults at him for a few AUS$," offered a moneyweb reader. Later the same man offered: "OK. Offering a new service. Barry lives just up the road from me, and for a few AUS$ will throw a pork chop at him every time he leaves his house. Special offer: four-letter insult words for $4.00."

> "Is it a coincidence that Tannenbaum means Christmas tree in German? The greed bags must have seen Barry as Santa Claus." Comment, *noseweek*

Nobody could believe that such a nice guy could rip off so many people. Wayne Gadden, one of Tannenbaum's investors and a personal friend, was stunned. "Barry's a great human being," he told the *Financial Mail*. "He lives in a modest home, and he's so trusting. I just can't fathom that he was involved in this."

"I started slowly and was sucked in," said one victim. "If one's due diligence is based on falsified documents, which match independent bank statements, one assumes things are okay. It is very easy after the fact to say investors were driven by greed."

Others found it difficult to believe they had been swindled by a man who came from a "highly, highly reputable family". Tannenbaum defended himself via email, saying that the allegations were "outrageous". He denied that comparisons to Madoff were apt. "Your attempt to compare me with Madoff isn't only odious, but is blatantly and patently incorrect, without any factual foundation and sensationalist," he fumed at the media.

Hendrik du Toit, the chief executive of Investec Asset Management, said that schemes like Tannenbaum's highlighted "the naivety of investors who were prepared to back, with vast amounts of their savings, an almost entirely unknown entity, in an investment offering ludicrously high returns, without any comprehension of how those returns were to be justified and without any form of operational due diligence."

> "I am an investor and have taken many investment decisions in my life, and this is one of the less fortunate ones." Sean Summers comments on his investment with Barry Tannenbaum's Ponzi scheme

A High Court order eventually froze R43 million linked to Tannenbaum's scheme, while Tannenbaum's attorney Darryl Leigh had assets seized—including two Lamborghinis (spraypainted to match) and three properties. Tannenbaum's main agent in Johannesburg, Dean Rees, had already organized himself a house in Switzerland, to which he conveniently decamped when interest in the scheme became a little too intense.

Barwa, a Qatari company that had lost money to the scheme, then obtained a worldwide freezing order on Rees's assets which was later overturned—somewhat reluctantly—by a UK judge. Tannenbaum confessed that "a number of documents including invoices, bills of lading and emails were altered or fabricated by me", and that he did this "with the active encouragement and full knowledge of Dean Rees". Rees argued that Tannenbaum was a "self-confessed fraudster and demonstrable liar" who is trying to "extricate himself from a massive fraud by seeking to lay blame [on me]".

Again, Tannenbaum complained that had been "tried and pilloried in the media", which, he said, was not the right forum "to debate all the complex issues".

Noseweek posed a couple of obvious questions relating to those complex issues. "The bottom line: how come all these smart businessmen somehow, with all their lawyers and accountants, never got around to using some plain common sense and asking themselves: if Barry Tannenbaum can afford to offer 20% for an eight or ten week investment—

secured by firm advance orders from South Africa's biggest generic drug manufacturer, Aspen—why wouldn't he take the same firm order contracts to his own bankers, RMB and Investec, and borrow the money there at an extravagant 4% for two months—and keep the remaining 16% for himself?

"Charitable feelings for his fellow millionaires?"

These are questions that, one hopes, will continue to be asked as the scandal runs its course over the next few years. For the moment, though, it appears that Australia's reputation as a destination for those of a criminal bent is safe.

> "Up until last week, my head was telling me it would never work, but my heart was saying please let it work … Now I feel stupid. It's our life savings and wasn't easy to accumulate." Johannesburg businessman who invested with Tannenbaum

The end of capitalism?

> "There is no counterweight in society if you have cowards in business. You have to have counterweights or you don't make progress." Trevor Manuel accuses South Africa's business community of cowardice in dealing with organized labour

Did Tannenbaum's con, dwarfed as it was by the huge international Ponzi scheme that was the consumer credit-fuelled global economy, signal a crisis for capitalism itself?

Julius Malema thought so. "At the moment, when the imperialist forces are accepting the failures of capitalism," he declared in the pages of the *Sunday Times*, "we should ask whether the time has not arrived for the government to make sure that the state owns the mines and other means of production, as called for in the Freedom Charter."

Certainly, some capitalists were suffering. "The meltdown of the global economy has reportedly halved the fortune of South African tycoon Patrice Motsepe, leaving him only filthy rich.

According to the Forbes List of those most likely to be put up against a wall when the revolution comes, Motsepe had been stinking rich last year but will now have to cut back on lunches of nightingales' tongues," reported Hayibo.

The same article noted that the Oppenheimer family had increased their net worth, and noted that they attributed their success to "lots of hard work, many wonderful friends, and a monopoly in a police state that supplied them with dirt cheap labour for 120 years."

"In for a Penny, in for a Pounding." De Beers intranet, as reported by moneyweb

Which is perhaps why capitalism has been blamed for so many things in South Africa. The xenophobic violence of May 2008? Blame capitalism, according to a gathering of socialist organizations. Incidentally, even those Tito-baiters COSATU were considered too capitalist by one group, which dismissed them as "pro-capitalist misleaders" and the ANC as "bourgeois". "It is the ANC, SACP, COSATU Tripartite Alliance government that oversees neo-apartheid capitalism under which the overwhelming majority are locked in grinding poverty and black people remain at the bottom," declared the organization known as 'Spartacist' in a pamphlet.

Poverty and inequality? Blame capitalism. (Well, the communists would, wouldn't they?) "The liberation will not be worth anything if the persisting economic dominance of white- and imperialist-owned capitalist monopolies remains unchanged," the SACP said in speech celebrating Freedom Day. "The narrow and compradorial black economic empowerment and the increasing super-exploitation of the black working class through outsourcing, casualization and slave-like conditions under which most black farm workers continue to be subjected to, must change."

Robert Raine had a different view. "Capitalism's new competitor is not collectivism, but pragmatism," he argued. "Capitalism, in fact, is all about taking responsibility."

As they say: yeah, right.

"Admiring advertising for its creativity is a bit like admiring Nazism for its cool uniforms." Chris McEvoy

Perhaps it would help if capitalists were nice people. But it seems that, for the most part— like socialists—they are not. But then, as Jeremy Gordin argued, if one thought that any of South Africa's businessmen, "from Cecil John Rhodes onwards, or downwards, was a sweetie-pie, or that any top capitalists are plum puddings or even peppermint ice creams, well then, as I said, one needs to get out more."

Gordin was commenting on the outcry over comments by the arthritic 84-year-old former deputy chairman of Anglo American, Graham Boustred. Interviewed at his Sandhurst home by three journalists from *Business Day*, Boustred's politically incorrect views of the current Anglo CEO Cynthia Carroll reverberated around the business world. "This woman's hopeless," he declared. "There's no morale. Do you know why it's difficult to find a female CEO? It's because most women are sexually frustrated. Men are not, because they can fall back on call girls, go to erectile dysfunction clinics. If you have a CEO who's sexually frustrated she can't act properly."

At one point in the interview, Boustred said to one of the journalists: "I thought you were from *Business Day*. I thought you knew about business."

"I don't know," said one journalist.

"Then fuck off," said Boustred.

Which pretty much sums it up, really.

"If there are a lot of bulls in the market, there has to be a lot of bullshit." Estienne de Klerk, chief financial officer of Growthpoint Properties, at a property investment conference

Chapter 7

Freedom of Speech:
The Media

"The levels of attack expose the immaturity of media coverage of politics in South Africa, which subjectively and repulsively define leaders of the ANC outside organizational mandate and process." ANCYL spokesperson Floyd Shivambu in response to reports on President Kgalema Motlanthe's extramarital involvements

"Living in South Africa is exhausting. We are always one small step away from mass hysteria," Jarred Cinman argued in the wake of reports that Trevor Manuel had resigned. "Or that, at least, is the impression you'd get if you based your knowledge entirely on the news media."

The media, he argued, was a messenger "of the most dangerous kind", whose only interest was in provoking a reaction. "To say it clearly: the reporting of the entire saga around Zuma and Mbeki over the past months, and especially the last week, has, on the whole, been appalling, irresponsible, alarmist and destructive. You, the media, should be ashamed of yourselves."

Julius Malema and Zwelanzima Vavi would certainly agree with him. After Julius was taken to task for his "kill for Zuma" statement, for example, Zwelanzima Vavi attacked the Human Rights Commission, calling it "liberal" and "yesterday's guardian of human rights". Blade Nzimande—who isn't necessarily the sharpest tool in the shed—dismissed the HRC as a "kangaroo court". Referring to the decision to demand that Julius retract his statement, Nzimande said, "Such actions unjustifiably unleash the always 'battle-ready' media lynch mob, without observance of any due process as contained in our constitution, thus severely prejudicing the individuals concerned."

The irony—that Vavi and Nzimande were simultaneously questioning the right of the media to freedom of expression while defending the right of one of their own to abuse it as he chose—was apparently lost on them.

The kill-for-Zuma debacle was not the only issue around which the freedom of speech debate raged. There was Kgalema Motlanthe and reports of a relationship with a woman many years his junior, Deon Maas and his column about Satanism, David Bullard who was fired, and Jon Qwelane who was not, and finally, Steve Hofmeyr and *Huisgenoot* and Joost van der Westhuizen and *Heat*.

But no issue brought debate over the limits of the right of the media to freedom of speech than the Zapiro cartoon that depicted Jacob Zuma and his supporters about to rape Justice.

Zapiro, political assassin

"While rude, risqué or extremely hard-hitting cartoons are bound to offend some readers, this is a risk worth taking." Jonathan Shapiro, aka Zapiro

For a week in September, Zapiro dominated the headlines with a cartoon that showed Jacob Zuma unzipping his fly, preparing to rape the metaphorical figure of Justice, while Julius Malema, ANC Secretary-General Gwede Mantashe, SACP boss Blade Nzimande and Cosatu General Secretary Zwelinzima Vavi held her down.

The ANC, the ANCYL and the SACP said the *Sunday Times* had disguised abuse as press freedom in publishing the cartoon. "The cartoon rubbishes the collective integrity of the alliance and constitutes yet another continued violation of the rights and dignity of the ANC president," and added that the paper's editor Mondli Makhanya was a "ranting dictator who finds joy in manipulating the truth".

The statement issued by the three organizations also declared that the "hard-earned, good public perceptions" of the ANC and alliance could not be swayed by any amount of "half-truths" the *Sunday Times* published.

Cosatu said that, while it had appreciated Zapiro's skill in the past, it wanted an apology from the *Sunday Times*. "While we accept that cartoonists have the licence to express controversial views," they argued, "yesterday's cartoon is in extremely bad taste and goes way beyond limits of acceptability."

MORE South African Insults

ANC spokesperson Jessie Duarte denounced the cartoon as "vile, crude and disgusting". She said that Makhanya "screams press freedom when he is attacked but misuses that freedom every week. He tries to show that the new leadership of the ANC will loot the country in the future".

SACP General Secretary Blade Nzimande said Zuma's rights had been raped. "Zapiro, don't try and make fun of rape. Our sisters, our mothers are victims of rape on a daily basis. Don't play with rape. It's you, along with the other media people who are rapists."

> "Zapiro is misinterpreting press freedom to mean free character assassination."
> Comment, *The Citizen*

Zapiro defended himself, retorting: "I get the feeling that South Africa tends to exceptionalize our politicians ... We seem to think our politicians are more sacrosanct than other politicians around the world. If politicians like Jacob Zuma were to live in another part of the world he would be the subject of harsh criticism."

Political commentator Ebrahim Harvey disagreed, arguing that cartoonists were not royal game. "We can never allow satire and satirists to occupy some holy ground and not be subject to critical scrutiny," he argued. "We must not defer to sacrosanct and unaccountable cartoonist power. Cartoonists who have licence to do as they wish with callous disregard and impunity and editors who condone this do both the Constitution and freedom of expression a great disservice."

Jody Kollapen of the Human Rights Commission thought that Zapiro might have gone too far. "The view of the Commission is that while the cartoon captures a significant political and social issue within society today—on the role of the judiciary and its place in society—the cartoon may well have gone a bit too far in terms of how that particularly relevant social, political, legal issue was captured. I'm not saying that the cartoon necessarily breaches any laws and clearly that is something that would need to be looked at."

> "Satire is not a very familiar alphabet in Africa. In the last 15 years of democracy, I've been celebrating my freedom; we tend to forget how free we are and how far we've come. But if Zuma tries to curtail freedom of speech, he's going to be busy, because we'll bite him whenever we can." Pieter-Dirk Uys

Meanwhile, *Business Day* cartoonist Brandan joined the fray with a sketch depicting the same characters—Julius Malema, Gwede Mantashe, Blade Nzimande and Zwelanzima Vavi—pushing the head of 'Lady Liberty' into a toilet bowl with their feet on her back. *Star* cartoonist Yalo drew her running away from a car with the licence plate 'Public Interest' speeding up behind her.

The following week, after Judge Nicholson's judgment regarding Zuma's corruption case was released, Zapiro reproduced exactly the same cartoon—upended with the note "Still valid"—except this time it was flanked by two new panels. In the third, the would-be rapist was now Thabo Mbeki, and Justice was held down by former justice minister Penuell Maduna, Bulelani Ngcuka, Justice Minister Brigitte Mabandla and acting NPA boss Mokotedi Mpshe.

"I wanted to hit back at the Mbeki side without letting the Zuma side go," Zapiro explained.

Zuma later demanded R7 million from Zapiro for the attack upon his dignity. In December, Zapiro and Zuma clashed live on 702. "He [Zapiro] is quite vulgar in what he does," said Zuma, arguing that Zapiro had continued to find him guilty even though a court of law had acquitted him of rape.

Zapiro, unrepentant, called in and challenged Zuma on the concept of media freedom.

"A responsible press is one that holds politicians to account," he argued.

To which Zuma replied: "My brother, I think you have said something very important which you ought to understand. You put a white lady, Zuma opening his trousers, that can't be right. You are invading my own dignity."

Zapiro went on to accuse Zuma of merely paying "lip-service" to the freedom of the press, arguing that Zuma should not be depicting himself as the victim when he was the one with all the power. "I don't think the media has been fair," Zuma complained in response. "They have gone beyond the border."

"Inspired by the historic firing of the Large Hadron Collider in Switzerland, the ANC Youth League says it intends building a similar device to explore, at a subatomic level, the bias of the media and the judiciary against Jacob Zuma. According to a spokesman, this would be done by colliding newspaper editors and judges at close to the speed of light 'to see what happens'." Hayibo.com

MORE South African Insults

The Zapiro lawsuit was only one of several. Even respected soft-left UK broadsheet *The Guardian* was targeted for printing an article in which Simon Jenkins described the soon-to-be president as a "polygamous, leopard-skin-draped Zulu boss" and an "unschooled former terrorist, communist sympathizer and rabble-rouser".

In the article, under the heading "Get used to a corrupt and chaotic South Africa. But don't write it off", published on 6 March, more than a month before the corruption charges against Zuma were withdrawn by the National Prosecuting Authority, Jenkins said that Zuma's hopes were pinned on being president so "he can protect himself".

Jenkins quoted "a friend" as saying God was "about to give us a criminal and a rapist as president". The columnist argued that sceptics viewed Zuma as the "harbinger of Armageddon", with the ANCYL "disrupting meetings of COPE with blood-curdling slogans worthy of Robert Mugabe's thugs".

Jenkins added that Zuma was "just another African crony politician for whom power is not about government, but personal enrichment" and that "Zuma's style of government is morally contaminated, administratively chaotic and corrupt".

Zuma's lawyers said: "Mr Zuma believes that the published column contains grossly defamatory, false and indefensible allegations, the most serious of which is the false claim that he is a rapist." Zuma himself added that the world needed a media it could rely on "even in the United Kingdom", not one that printed lies and distortions.

A settlement was finally reached at the end of July in the British High Court of Justice, Queen's Bench division. "The president firmly believes in the freedom of the press as he has fought hard for freedom of expression and other basic rights during the struggle against apartheid," the presidency said in an official statement. "In this matter, the *Guardian* newspaper disregarded the basic principles of journalism and media ethics."

> "Look, you guys, there is no soap that will wash a *Times* journalist in my eyes. It's not unfortunate, it's reality. I think that if you are a South African who wants to see transformation then you've got to join in the fight for it, not become part of the third force. But you all sound exactly the same so there's no point." Jessie Duarte to *Times* journalist Philani Nombembe

The Bullard brouhaha

"It's not only about the money, although that is a large part of it. It's about the lack of vision, the pettiness and the creeping mediocrity." David Bullard on the *Sunday Times*, writing before the offending column appeared

Another subject of a Zuma lawsuit was David Bullard, who was targeted for writing that Zuma was "stupid". The column that got him fired, however, was not about Zuma at all and—ultimately—would lead to one of South Africa's unlikeliest reconciliations.

"Imagine for a moment what life would be like in South Africa if the evil white man hadn't come to disturb the rustic idyll of the early black settlers," began the Out to Lunch column of 6 April 2008. "The vast mineral wealth lying undisturbed below the Highveld soil as simple tribesmen graze their cattle blissfully unaware that beneath them lies one of the richest gold seams in the world. But what would they want with gold?

"Every so often a child goes missing from the village, eaten either by a hungry lion or a crocodile. The family mourn for a week or so and then have another child."

All is peace and quiet until men arrive from a place called China. "Suddenly the indigenous population realize what they have been missing all along: someone to blame. At last their prayers have been answered."

The response was predictable. Some readers thought that Bullard had a very good point. Others were incensed.

Xolela Mangcu, for example, accused Bullard of hate speech on the grounds that he recreated African societies "that exist only in his racist imagination ... Not only does the *Sunday Times* have the responsibility to let Bullard go, but it may well be that the authorities need to investigate whether he has broken the laws of the land. But the greater challenge is for white colleagues to make sure the racists among them are consigned to a sectarian existence."

"He is the type of person South Africa does not need within its borders," declared Pallo Jordan, speaking in Parliament. He likened Bullard's insults aimed at South Africans to "coming into someone's living room and defecating on their carpet".

Sunday Times editor Mondli Makhanya fired Bullard three days later. "He wrote a racist column on Sunday. I had a conversation with him on Tuesday; I told him that what he wrote was unacceptable," he explained to *Business Day*. Speaking on Talk Radio 702, Makhanya said the column was "extremely, extremely, extremely offensive" and "totally against the values of the *Sunday Times* and the country".

Vincent Maher speculated that the column was a way to fire Bullard "without having to go through the tedious process of firing him according to labour regulations". "Racism is a trump card;" he observed, "you can't beat it even if you're innocent, and no one will listen to you defend yourself."

One moneyweb reader was at a loss. "Jon Qwelane still has a job and Bullard doesn't. Hell, Jon's writing makes David's look like that of a choirboy in comparison."

> "I have never in my life met a man so consumed by hatred ... on this occasion hatred for me, hatred for Zuma and a liberal dash of well-justified self-loathing."
> David Bullard on Jonathan Shapiro, aka Zapiro, who accused him of "licking Jacob Zuma's Guccis"

Later Bullard apologized for the column and then, in a move that surprised many, apologized to Zuma who subsequently dropped his lawsuit. Bullard even appeared on stage at the Sandton Convention Centre to endorse the ANC for the 2009 elections and, in line with the spirit of the times, also sued his former employers for unfair dismissal.

Writing for moneyweb, Bullard argued that Zapiro, Max du Preez and others were hypocrites, demanding freedom of speech only for those with whose opinions they happened to agree. "Once you start tinkering with people's constitutional rights you are on a slippery slope and I certainly wouldn't want to live in a world ruled by media fascists like Zapiro and du Preez."

"People ask if Julius Malema should be gagged? Of course not. He is always original and every so often he unwittingly says something quite intelligent. The South African political landscape would be quite barren without the Malemas and Quntas."

Bullard argued that editors should take responsibility for "shoddy journalism" and proposed a special court to protect the right of citizens who felt they had been wronged by the media. "After all, doctors, lawyers, accountants and dentists can all be sued for malpractice so what puts journalists in a special category, particularly considering the reputational damage they are capable of doing?"

Earlier, he had accused the *Sunday Times* of deliberately targeting and victimizing public figures at will. "Mondli Makhanya, the Jorrocks of the newsroom, would sound the hunting horn and we would all go off to write some poisonous invective about that week's chosen quarry, comfortable in the knowledge that, even if we were sued, the case would take ages to come to court and the shareholders would pay anyway," he wrote. "That's why the term 'journalistic integrity' is an oxymoron."

Many of his fans found all of these events quite perplexing. "The real David Bullard has been taken over by a virus from alien beings—this communist-supporting girlie-man that has taken over his body is not him," commented one moneyweb reader after Bullard endorsed the ANC. "Whatever you do, don't look him in the eye as it is very contagious."

"If evidence were ever really needed to show that 'the personal is political', then Pallo Jordan's attempt to wave his flaccid intellect in the *Mail & Guardian* editor's face provided that evidence in spades. The patronizing tone, the intellectual dishonesty, the preoccupation with elite egos rather than ordinary lives: all are emblematic of much of the ANC leadership." Sam Sole responds to Jordan's criticism of the media's coverage of Kgalema Motlanthe's private life

The Qwelane kerfuffle

The Bullard brouhaha was followed by the Qwelane kerfuffle.

In an April 2008 column for the *Sunday Sun*, Jon Qwelane told readers that he hated the concept of gay marriage. In fact, he was offended by men "kissing other men in public, walking holding hands and shamefully flaunting what are misleadingly termed their 'lifestyle' and 'sexual preferences'.

"Homosexuals and their backers will call me names, printable and not, for stating as I have always done my serious reservations about their 'lifestyle and sexual preferences', but quite frankly I don't give a damn: wrong is wrong! I do pray that some day a bunch of politicians with their heads affixed firmly to their necks will muster the balls to rewrite the constitution of this country, to excise those sections which give licence to men 'marrying' other men, and ditto women."

Not surprisingly, South Africa's gay and lesbian community was somewhat offended. In the 21st-century equivalent of toyi-toying, they started a Facebook group and campaigned to have Qwelane fired.

"This is hateful stuff. Ignorant stuff. The kind of thing written by a man who is not very secure about his own sexuality," charged law professor Pierre de Vos.

Alex Matthews was hardly surprised: "The *Sunday Sun* is gutter press and Qwelane's equally contemptible opinions are part and parcel of a paper that believes that stoking xenophobia and perpetuating intolerance is a prerequisite in speaking to the 'blue-collar man'."The editor of the *Sunday Sun* ignored calls to fire Qwelane, something that David Bullard applauded, incidentally. As Chris Roper noted, many felt that the slap on Qwelane's "aggressively non-limp wrist" suggested that there were double standards afoot. "They say that the fact that Jon Qwelane doesn't get fired from the *Sunday Sun* for implying that gays are like animals but David Bullard gets the boot from the *Sunday Times* for implying that black people are like animals, shows that it's okay to be a black homophobe, but it's not okay to be a white racist." What this showed, he said, was that the editor of the *Sunday Sun* had guts. Public pressure should not decide your editorial policy, he argued, adding that he thought that firing David Bullard "for writing unspeakable crap" was a "cowardly" thing to do, "although not as stupid as hiring him in the first place".

Press ombudsman Joe Thloloe found Qwelane not guilty of hate speech on the grounds that he did not advocate violence against gays and lesbians but did breach Press Council codes by "implying that homosexuals are a lower breed than heterosexuals", and that the *Sunday Sun* was guilty of "publishing denigratory references to people's sexual orientation".

"… the hypocritical and lickspittle mainstream press …" Jon Qwelane weighs in on the debate over whether reports of then President Kgalema Mothlanthe's extramarital dalliances were in the public interest or not

"Pahad's lonely, but relentless assault on the media, which is doing everything in its power to destroy South Africa, will be much missed. In his absence stories may appear which do not properly toe the party line on politics and we all know how dire that will be for this delicate land." Ray Hartley on Essop Pahad's resignation from Parliament

What Snuki said

"SABC warned to be unbiased in adulation for ANC." Hayibo.com headline

The SABC, an organization that for much of its history has been more comfortable with supporting the ruling party than representing the interests of the public, continued to slide ever more deeply into the mire. In an interesting case of reverse evolution where, having reached the reptilian phase, it then slipped back into the swamp, grew gills, lost them, and finally became one with the primordial slime: to the tune of some R2 billion.

Michael Trapido commented: "The crisis at the SABC seems to literally deepen by the hour as it haemorrhages money like a crazed gambler at the slot machines, drives out its most talented performers and continues to bolster its reputation as a crude propaganda organ of the ruling party."

Ray Hartley, editor of *The Times*, observed that the public broadcaster had "transformed itself from apartheid propagandist to distributor of flaccid political blancmange in 15 short years".

Marianne Thamm noted that SABC News under the benign guidance of Dr Snuki Zikalala, spent R5 million setting up a Washington bureau, and R600,000 a month running its Nigerian office. "With that kind of investment of taxpayers' money you would at least come to expect a shit-hot nightly news bulletin with reports from these far-flung corners of the earth," she observed. "Instead, the SABC main bulletin is more parochial than a local knock and drop and its coverage of political events so appalling that it is, in the main, unwatchable. Even its propaganda is the bargain-bin sort.

"Nature hates a vacuum," she concluded, "and the SABC is a big heaving, pulsating, sucking void that is going to implode and fall in on itself like an old drop lavatory ... Watch this space."

"I think there's confusion at the SABC and a power struggle. There are a number of top people who suck up to the notion of what the government would want them to do." Zapiro

Earlier, there had been reports that the ANC had complained that the SABC was making President Kgalema Motlanthe look, well, too presidential. Apparently he looked too like a statesman compared to Jacob Zuma, who looked more like a pop star. Dancing and singing can have that effect on audiences.

"We were asked in October to reduce our coverage of Motlanthe and focus on putting out a better image of Zuma. We have tried to resist this, but there is only so much we can do," said one SABC source.

ANC Secretary-General Gwede Mantashe said this was nonsense. "They do not cover us objectively, so we don't have the luxury of saying 'increase this or reduce that'."

"Meanwhile," reflected John Scott, "get used to the idea of the ANC president trying to appear more presidential on TV than the president of the country. It won't come naturally, even with the SABC's help."

"It was a protest, and as you know protests can be messy." Azapo leader Pandelani Nefholovhodwe explains why a group of Azapo members invaded an SABC TV studio. They were protesting against media bias

COPE accused the SABC of sabotage and "blatant bias" following the public broadcaster's failure to broadcast the party's final election rally in Polokwane. It wasn't deliberate, said the SABC; it was a technical problem. COPE's communications chief Phillip Dexter said this was unconvincing, especially when the ANC's final rally at Coca-Cola Park in Johannesburg received extensive coverage. "The SABC's repeated failure to be an objective and even-handed purveyor of the news to the people of South Africa continues as it again knuckles under to the ruling party to the detriment of fair-handedness and democracy in our country." After the SABC failed, again, to broadcast a documentary on political satire, Zapiro responded ruefully. "What more can one say?" he said. "The SABC has been a constant disappointment and I naively imagined the show was going to air."

"The ANCYL says good riddance to Snuki Zikalala and wishes him the best on whatever career path he pursues, hoping it will not be in the media." ANC Youth League statement after the SABC did not renew news chief Snuki Zikalala's contract at the end of April 2009

The departure of Snuki Zikalala at the end of April 2009 was mourned by nobody. The Youth Communist League was especially pleased. "We welcome Zikalala's long-overdue departure within the context of eliminating abuse of the SABC news division for narrow and factional battles," YCL spokesperson Castro Ngobese said.

The DA's Dene Smuts said, " ... any high would be coming off a very low base."

"Goood riddance. What goes around comes around. We still know what he did last summer," added one reader of Thought Leader.

Widely blamed for the parlous financial situation at the public broadcaster, Zikalala had previously been involved in blacklisting commentators that were critical of Thabo Mbeki. (Zikalala himself said that the word 'blacklisting' was perhaps too strong. "There wasn't a blacklisting, but perhaps a greylisting," he explained. "What I found was that the same people were being used day in and day out on radio and on television as if they were the only people of intelligence in our country. All I was saying was that other analysts should be sourced.")

Asked how he felt about the state in which he was leaving the SABC, Zikalala said, "It's not easy to leave the SABC on a good note, but I did." He added that he was proud of having transformed the SABC and said any criticism he faced was because certain people in the South African National Editors' Forum (SANEF) did not believe that a black man could run such a large organization. "They feel that a black man cannot run such a huge organization," he told Tim Modise. "A black man cannot have the good and courageous ideas that I have. They have something against me, but I don't care. I am focused on what I am doing, and I make sure it does happen and it works."

Some noted the irony that Zikalala had obtained his PhD from Bulgaria in 1986 for a thesis entitled: 'SABC as the Racist Propaganda'.

Perhaps, one could say, Snuki learned from the best.

"The truth of the matter is that most black editors are fence-sitters who are afraid to rock the boat." Sandile Memela is annoyed that no black editor endorsed the ANC prior to the 2009 elections

Steve Hofmeyr is going to moer you now

Steve Hofmeyr has a history of encounters with the media.

In 2002, he attacked Jan-Jan Joubert, the editor of the Klein Karoo Nasionale Kunstefees newspaper *Krit* after an article referred to his "kak" shoes. Hofmeyr apparently screamed obscenities and told Joubert, "Take off your glasses because I'm going to moer you now!" Hofmeyr then removed the journalist's glasses and slapped him, hit him with a rolled-up newspaper, and told him he was a "little poes".

Earlier in 2008, Hofmeyr grabbed a *Rapport* journalist by the throat at the Deuriemikke music festival at Loftus Versfeld; he was apparently unhappy with the paper's "one-sided reporting" after news of a ten-year affair with his mistress, Janine van der Vyver, became the scandal of the year in trefferland.

It was as a result of a series of reports on VanderVyvergate that Hofmeyr chucked a cup of tea at *Huisgenoot* editor Esmare Weideman at a breakfast held at Sun City to celebrate the Miss South Africa pageant. (The temperature of the beverage in question remains a mystery.) One witness to the tea-throwing said, "Steve said to me recently that he holds three journalists responsible for the fact that he will be without a tree and his two sons this Christmas.[1] One of them is Esmare."

Weideman said she was considering criminal and civil action against Hofmeyr and would donate any proceeds to a cause for abused woman. "We report on the comings and goings of celebs," she said. "If he has been in the news for the wrong reasons, he can't blame us for that. He's known for bashing the media when it suits him."

"Press freedom is me breaking your jaw." Steve Hofmeyr to journalist Jan-Jan Joubert at the Klein Karoo Nasionale Kunstefees, in 2002

Cliff Saunders, once the face of Nat-era TV reporting, now haunts the letters pages of *The Citizen*.

Weighing in on the Hofmeyr/*Huisgenoot* imbroglio, he said that if Thabo Mbeki could

---

[1] This comment raises a couple of questions. Firstly, why wasn't Hofmeyr sad that he won't have his *wife* and his sons with him this Christmas? And surely a man—even if he is newly single—can still put up a Christmas tree of his own?

get away with knocking Winnie's hat off in public, "why crucify Steve Hofmeyr for pouring a cup of tea over ... Esmare Weideman's cranium?"

Hayibo.com reported that white South Africans were traumatized by the feud, which had caused "millions of white South Africans to run to their room, lock the door, and beg Mammie and Pappie to stop fighting." They quoted counsellor Cadenza Mbete who said, "Steve Hofmeyr and *Huisgenoot* are the Alpha and Omega for millions of white people in this country. In many ways they are parent figures."

She said that "Father Steve" and "Mother *Huisgenoot*" had taught white South Africa most of what it knew. "He taught us that the sky is the limit as long as you leak your personal life to the media at strategic moments and do a middling Neil Diamond impression. "And *Huisgenoot* taught us that most of the country's problems are caused by Satanists and feminists, and that the two greatest moments in any woman's life are when she produces her first son and self-publishes her first book of inspiration poems."

Pearlie Joubert was irritated. "Helloooo! You can't cry victim and ask for a special brand of protection and sympathy with a corporate title and a printing press under your arm," she argued.

"As an editor, Weideman is fair game. Tits and all."

Childish wankers

Just what was in the public interest anyway? The editor of *Heat* magazine, not otherwise known for its commitment to the moral upliftment of South Africa's youth, explained the importance of publishing still images of a video purporting to show Joost van der Westhuizen snorting drugs and cavorting with a stripper (*see also* chapter 9). Joost, said Melinda Shaw, "had a responsibility as a public figure and role model for tens of thousands of young people ... When we saw the video for the first time, we were just as shocked as you are now," she assured the public. "We cringed on behalf of Joost and immediately thought of Amor. We debated whether we should destroy the tape and maintain the illusion [of Joost] or whether we should reveal who he really is."

Last time he checked, observed Chris Roper, "*Heat* magazine wasn't exactly a magazine that had 'pushing Christianity' and 'building better families' as two of its editorial pillars."

Roper wondered why readers wanted to read stories exposing the failings of celebrities. "The only possible answer must be—because we're childish wankers, voyeuristic vampires whose lives are empty and meaningless without the constant fort-da of erecting tinpot gods and then tearing them down, erecting them and tearing them down."

Joost had considered suing *Heat* and *Rapport*, but changed his mind after realizing how much it would cost. He and Amor were forced to make the ultimate sacrifice: retreating from the limelight until the furore died down.

> "South Africa's sportsmen and women are our pride and joy. Yes, they do get into trouble and are rightfully exposed but what about cases where an individual of the highest integrity is juxtaposed to bilge because nobody bothered to check the facts?" Michael Trapido comments on another Joost's problems with the media, this time involving reports on the travails of a group of companies with which he was involved

Tough speech

Whither freedom of speech in South Africa, both for the media and for the country's citizens?

In the lead-up to the 2009 elections, Jody Kollapen warned that South Africans should expect to be shocked by what politicians would have to say as the election race got heated. "The difficult issue one often has to deal with in society is whether speech that is tough, that is disturbing, that may be shocking should be circumscribed," he said.

Kollapen did not think that "tough speech" should be restricted. "I think we should ensure that we are able to encourage that kind of open dialogue, debate, and in each case determine where the line should be drawn appropriately.

"I'm inclined to say people should be allowed to express their view as long as it does not constitute incitement to cause harm."

Someone who knows all about incitement is Julius Malema. At a speech to commemorate Youth Day, he criticized the media for being "hostile" and "unpatriotic". Complaining that the media propagated respect for the judiciary but not "respect for politicians", he said that the press enjoyed freedom and the judiciary was independent "because of politicians".

Never mind that politicians only got to be politicians because the public, the schmucks we are, voted them in, and the media, for all their sensationalism, still offer us one of the few means to keep them on their toes. Though, granted, of course that's when their feet are not firmly wedged in their mouths.

"I'm being sued by the president and it's disturbing—it doesn't give a good signal to the world. It could happen that he would have to come to court and testify against me. But I'm not worried about either court case because I'm sure that freedom of expression would trump any argument." Zapiro

Chapter 8

BMWs and Blue-Light Gangs: Road Rage

"At least a penis enlargement pump can be safely tucked away under your bed without bothering anybody else." BMWs, according to a comment on Thought Leader

The greatest divide in South Africa is not between the haves and the have-nots or Jacob Zuma supporters and people punting for Helen Zille: it is between BMW drivers—and wannabe BMW drivers—and everybody else.

Just ask Blade Nzimade, who said he needed a 750i because it had a big boot to transport papers. Others have suggested that a big boot would also come in useful should he ever find himself having to transport R500,000 in cash. Just ask Willie Madisha what a schlep *that* is. Julius Malema, a Merc driver himself, rejected criticism of the purchases, saying: "If you want to talk morality, your morality is not my morality."

BMW drivers are just ... different. Not even physical disabilities can cramp their style. In May, *The Star* reported that a 40-year-old woman on crutches was caught travelling at 187kph in her silver BMW near the Olifantsfontein offramp. She was also charged for removing her licence plates.

Tony Jackman has a theory that may provide us with some answers. BMW drivers, he reasons, are aliens. This would explain their inability to indicate, for example, and their desire to drive up the backside of motorists on the road in front of them. Not that he is prejudiced or anything: "I am only prejudiced against BMW drivers," he explains, "insofar as they are a bunch of arrogant, headlight-flashing, rear-bumper-caressing road-hoggers who believe they own the road and that all other cars should stand aside to make way for them at any time of day or night. Other than this, I have nothing at all against them."

BMW drivers themselves acknowledge that they are a different species entirely. As one respondent to Jackman explained: "For those who are still looking like a deer in truck headlights while I roar up behind your sorry excuse for transportation, those flashing lights that blind you (even on a good day) are actually structured Morse code signals, embedded into all our ancestors' DNA by the BMW Illuminati centuries ago."

BMW owners also get beautiful blondes as standard on all six-cylinder engines and higher. As he put it, M3 and M5 owners "get more ass than a public toilet seat".

Because speed limits did not exist in the distant eons when BMW drivers were evolving, they do not recognize them today. "So," advises Jackman's source, "next time you're pulling into the middle lane as fast as your little lawnmower engine can handle and you're thinking how much you hate me—just remember your woman is probably wondering how she could be my 'optional extra' and I'm probably deciding whether to use my sixth gear or not."

> "There is nothing stylish about a BMW. It's for people who are new money and don't know any better, who are overcompensating for small bits or who can't afford a real luxury car like a Bentley. Even a Mercedes reeks of class where a BMW reeks of Brylcreem and bling." Comment on Thought Leader

For three months over late 2007 and early 2008, Vodacom advertised a competition in which it would give away 100 BMW 320i's in 100 days. Well, 'give away' is perhaps not the correct term: in order to enter, subscribers had to send an SMS costing R10. The more SMSes sent, the more chances you stood to win. Easy.

First there were the phone calls to talk-radio stations. Then came the reports of subscribers racking up enormous bills in order to enter the competition. Hendrikus Wessels spent R48,000 on SMSes. Marelize spent R27,000. One Johannesburg man managed to send R150,000 worth of SMS entries before his cell-phone service was suspended. How he managed not to notice and why it did not occur to him that, having set up a system in which his computer sent SMS entries automatically on his behalf, this eventuality might manifest itself, is a mystery.

The competition was eventually investigated on the grounds that it could be an illegal lottery. While Vodacom remained adamant that the competition was legal, they closed it early anyway and allocated the remaining cars, leaving many hopeful entrants disappointed.

Nearly two years later, the competition was in the news again after it emerged that Tsheko Maloma, a security guard who worked for the Greater Sekhukhune District Municipality in Groblersdal, won one of the cars after he ran up an SMS bill of R277,484 on a 3G data card stolen from the municipality. Maloma attempted to sell the car, but it was impounded. Eighteen months after Maloma won the car, it was finally confiscated by the municipality.

Since a used BMW 320i was now worth substantially less than the money that Maloma had spent on text messages, the municipality decided to keep it as a second car.

> "They gave me a PT Cruiser convertible as a loan car, which in itself is a calculated insult. When they brought my Jeep back last week, they told me, again, that they couldn't find the problem. So now I have an untrustworthy Jeep that I'm not inclined to take into the bush, which means I might as well have a BMW X5 or some other piece of crap disguised as an off-road vehicle." Chris Roper

Nobody should be surprised at the level of hysteria. Vodacom merely took advantage of the innate desire of a frightening number of South Africans to possess a BMW. Even the wildlife wants to be in a BMW, judging by the experience of a resident of Lonehill in northern Johannesburg who was perturbed to discover that her 3-series had somehow become home to several dassies. Displaying the compassion and consideration with which all non-BMW drivers are familiar, she attempted to get rid of them by driving at high speed on the freeway. When this failed to dislodge the animals, staff at the Johannesburg Zoo were called in to remove them. Eventually, six dassies were extricated from the vehicle and sent to Free-Me; sadly, one died of trauma.

> "I am always muttering darkly behind the wheel: 'Christ, another fucking BMW', then desperately trying to shift into the left lane in time while my wife checks her seatbelt and takes a swig of voddy." Tony Jackman

The passion that BMWs excite in South Africans is perhaps best illustrated by an incident that took place on the N1 near the Botha offramp in Centurion. A 3-series BMW tried to persuade a 7-series to move over. When the 7-series remained in the fast lane, the driver of the 3-series felt affronted. Rather unwisely—one would have thought—the two cars then pulled over for a BMW-driver-on-BMW-driver confrontation. The driver of the 3-series fetched a sword from his boot (non-BMW drivers may not be aware that luxury German vehicles come equipped with the iconic weapon of medieval knights, which are stored alongside the emergency triangle and the first aid kit) and started hitting the roof of the 7-series with it.

Wanting to get a bit of a run in before launching the next assault, he took a step back and was promptly taken out by a passing Honda.

What can one say? The Almighty clearly moves in mysterious ways, some of them involving reliable Japanese sedans.

"Quite a Wagnerian lot, BMW drivers. It's all valkyries and the smell of napalm in the morning ... All arriviste bling. That is the soul of the BMW driver. Those that grow up graduate to Audis or Mercs." Comment on Thought Leader

Lord of the Rings

"Lord of the Rings." Slang for Audi (from the logo), Sowetan slang blog

In light of the generally well-deserved reputation of BMW owners driving like poephols, it's surprising that the biggest speedster of all achieved this feat in an Audi TT rather than a BMW. In December, DJ S'bu was trapped doing 257kph at night, south of Johannesburg. The car was a vehicle sponsored by Audi South Africa. He explained on his Facebook page that the car was so comfortable that he didn't realize he was speeding.

"You can tell me what you like," blogger Michael Trapido commented in the wake of this revelation, "but anyone who is driving at 257kph and doesn't know it has to have found the mother lode. I don't care what it takes—I'm leaving no rock unturned in the quest to find out what it was this genius was smoking."

"Giving a powerful car to this fool was about as reckless and dangerous as handing out razor blades to babies," said Andrew Donaldson, who was deeply unimpressed with DJ S'bu. "So, this German cowboy walks up to his car and says: 'Audi'," he wrote in his *Sunday Times* column. "Except that it wasn't a German cowboy; it was some wanker called DJ S'bu. A man of many talents, S'bu (real name Sibusiso Leope) is an award-winning record producer and hosts various popular radio shows. He is also (it says here) a 'television personality', which—despite the apparent contradiction in terms—means, in media-speak, that he is just another spoilt, bling-soaked suckhead who passes as a celebrity."

Audi took the car back. As it turned out, DJ S'bu was not the only celebrity to lose a new TT. In June, celebrity choreographer Somizi Mhlongo was distressed when his brand-new vehicle was taken without his permission by a friend who managed to kill himself when writing it off outside Diepsloot.

Expressing a sentiment with which South African car lovers everywhere could sympathize, he said, "I am not sure which is the worst nightmare—losing a friend to a horrific crash after he had betrayed my trust or losing a new car."

> "I think that my Zulu ass would look great on the leather seats of a Mercedes-Benz C-class. Fuck the kids' educations. I went to a Catholic mission school in the middle of nowhere in northern KwaZulu-Natal and I turned out alright. Plus, this year is my 20th high-school reunion. I can't possibly arrive there in a ten-year-old Opel." Ndumiso Ngcobo

Sadly, not everyone can drive a BMW or an Audi. Some of us are required to drive cars like the Toyota Auris which, according to Robert McKay, "looks like a Yaris suffering from serious water retention or the consumption of too many Big Macs."

Or you might, horror of horrors, have been tempted to buy a Chrysler Sebring. The Americans describe this car as "the spawn of Satan" (and no, Deon Maas had nothing to do with it), but overtones of evil would be an improvement on Alex Parker's assessment: "As a driving experience it is about as inspiring as lettuce ... It's right up there with cucumber sandwiches and Randburg. It's whatever on wheels."

The only thing he liked about the Sebring was the release catch on the inside of the boot. "That means if you get kidnapped, you can hop out at a traffic light," he noted. "Or, if you're like me, travelling in the boot is the best way of not being seen in this completely dreadful car."

> "Honey, if you find Toyota exciting, you'll find Riaan Cruywagen exciting." SMS to 702's Leigh Bennie, who told listeners to the Word on Cars show that she found Toyotas, well, exciting

Motorists gullible enough to part with the bank's money for a Sebring might well end up hoping for a close encounter with some of the wildlife for which South Africa is famous, and that does not include drunk divorcees in Fourways. A rhino in the Addo Elephant Park attacked a hired Yaris driven by two Dutch tourists, causing considerable damage. Whether or not the notoriously short-sighted animal mistook the vehicle for an Auris was not confirmed.

"The rhino stomped on the bonnet and gored the windscreen a few centimetres from the woman," reported a park official. Similarly, in June, one of the last remaining Knysna elephants left little doubt about his presence when he took exception to a brand-new tractor, completely trashing it. In what may have been a commentary on the rocketing oil price, the large bull was said to hate the smell of diesel.

SanParks official Hylton Heard was philosophical: "Look," he shrugged, "an elephant is a big animal and ultimately if something's in his path and he doesn't like it there, he can make a plan."

In contrast, a large bull elephant in Hluhluwe took a shine to a Citi Golf, and who can blame him? Even if it's a piece of tinny rubbish, it's a firm favourite with local motorists. The elephant in question was photographed lovingly caressing the vehicle with his trunk, his distended penis clearly visible, all in the story that appeared on the website of the UK's *Daily Mail*.

> "This is about as glamorous as genital warts, but if it's glamour you want, buy a copy of *Heat* magazine." Alex Parker on the 2.4-litre diesel engine fitted into the Land Rover Defender

Beware of the mielie

Presumably the men who attacked Citi Golf driver Zander van Biljon in Pretoria did not feel quite the same way as that elephant. Van Biljon was driving in the fast lane on the N14 when a white Jetta flashed its lights at him. He could not move over because a truck was in the lane next to him, so the Jetta then squeezed into the gap between his car and the truck, before the Jetta driver spat at Zander and threw a mielie at him.

Seriously. You couldn't make this up.

After being forced off the road, Van Biljon was punched by the Jetta driver, while one Jetta passenger whacked him with a cane. During the assault, Van Biljon managed to flag down a passing police car, but the officers were not interested in helping him. "The police told me they couldn't help me," he reported. "They also told my attackers it was a road-rage incident; they had to just get into their car and go."

The mielie was an unusual touch, though, according to Synovate's annual road-rage study, this sort of thing was most likely to happen in Gauteng. The survey revealed, among other findings, that sports cars and small vehicles were most likely to be the target of road rage. Drivers of SUVs and bakkies were least likely to be the targets of road rage (which is surprising because they are usually the worst on the road; perhaps they are the ones picking on the drivers of small cars). Drivers in Gauteng were most likely to be on the receiving end of road rage, and also most likely to get out of their vehicles to confront another motorist.

To nobody's surprise, Capetonians were the most relaxed.

> "In Bloemfontein, I am always more at ease at traffic lights. I'm astounded that it happened in Bloemfontein and that it was a woman." Barbara Möller, who was sprayed with pepper spray by a fellow motorist during a road rage incident

Laurette Ndzanga was unlucky enough to live in Gauteng and therefore, inevitably, the victim of road rage. She was slapped by a Putco bus driver, apparently for driving in the right-hand lane. "I kept on driving and stopped at a red robot. He got out of the bus and came to my car and started insulting me. He then slapped me on my face after I had rolled down my window to hear what he was trying to say." Ndzanga opened an assault case with the Kliptown police.

Similarly, in Pretoria, Comfort and Zanele Mkhonto were attacked by the driver of a double cab—a Nissan Navara. Mr Mkhonto felt that the double cab was driving too slowly, so flashed his lights to get the driver to move over. The latter then made rude gestures, liberal use of the K-word and shot at them with a pepper-spray pistol. Mrs Mkhonto ended up in ICU after an allergic reaction to the spray.

Durban drivers would do well to take note of the fact that so many of them are prepared to climb out of their vehicles in order to take things further. One of the victims of the province's short tempers was an off-duty taxi driver who asked a driver from a rival taxi organization for an apology after a minor prang. He was shot dead for his trouble.

Just a short way up the highway, Pietermaritzburg resident Simanga Wiseman Mthembu—a male nurse—was sentenced to 18 years in jail after he shot dead a taxi driver. After the taxi failed to stop at a stop street, Mthembu told the driver: "Get a proper licence because that is not the way to drive." Each man went his separate way, but six hours later fate brought them together again. During the second confrontation, Mthembu shot the taxi driver several times. Judge Chris Nicholson (yes, the same judge who effectively forced Thabo Mbeki to resign) said that even if people were irritated by taxi drivers, they could not take the law into their own hands.

"TYPE: Motor Vehicle
COLOUR: Cream
MAKE: Isuzu
SPOTTED IN: Monument, Johannesburg
DRIVER: Tall white male
OFFENCE: Rude driver showing his ID with his hands and dangerous driver swerving in front of everybody. An insult even for a pig."
As reported to roadhog.co.za

The principle of Laerskool Jan van Riebeeck in Springs had his kombi rammed by a disgruntled teacher in her Getz. "I could hardly believe my eyes when I got there and the Getz was wedged under the kombi, with the teacher still behind the wheel," he told a reporter. "She looked dazed. I didn't say a word, I turned around and walked away to get myself under control first. Some of the staff got her out of the car and she was taken to hospital by ambulance.

"I'm not cross with her, I'm actually sorry for her," he said of Jackie Swanepoel, who was angry because her contract had not been renewed. "It's upsetting that it had to happen on the eve of the school holidays. It's been a big blow to my holiday plans. I don't know if she acted intentionally, because you can see that she slammed on brakes; the marks are there on the rugby field."

"I don't have words to describe the incompetence and unprofessional actions of the State." Magistrate Sigqibo Mpela, acquitting 2010 executive Linda Mti on charges of drunk driving

Licensed to cause havoc

"We will leave no stone unturned in our investigation. Some people who have licences can't even start a car … Let's all arrive alive with a lawful driver's licence." Captain Leonard Hlathi (what is it with the police and turning stones?) comments on the arrest of an Ermelo traffic official who issued more than 100 bogus driver's licences

No local could ever hope to match the achievement of the Korean grandmother who failed her driving test 771 times; any self-respecting South African motorist would long since have paid a bribe in order to pass. Indeed, hiding in a toilet for 20 minutes while you pretend to do your test is considered adequate qualification for a driver's licence, at least in White River. The motorist in question and the driving-test examiner later both appeared in court.

Who can blame motorists for trying to find a way around the system, when a visit to the local traffic department is like an expedition to one of the inner circles of Dante's inferno. "If outside looked like a refugee camp, inside looked like Catholic limbo," reported Ben Trovato. "Sad, hollow-eyed people drifted from counter to counter, lips moving in silent prayer. I joined the other lost souls in the queue of the damned that led to Persephone's cubicle. The earth revolved, reptiles evolved, another ice age came and went."

"If you badly want to die, rather take a rope and go to the nearest tree [to hang yourself]." KwaZulu-Natal Transport MEC Bheki Cele, launching the province's holiday motoring safety campaign

Things were different in the old days. Charles Mogale reminisced about his own driving test during the apartheid years, where the testing officer told him, "Jy weet fokol van parking nie." Asked what the 'golden rule' of the road was, Mogale suggested, "You have to be courteous to other drivers and road users, be alert and do not endanger other people ..." The officer corrected him, saying: "Keep left, jou bliksem!"

Though, whether 'keep left' would have helped the East London learner driver who lost control of the vehicle and ended up on top of one of the greens of the Cambridge Bowling Club, causing damage estimated at R5,000, is doubtful. "It turned out to be a driving lesson that turned out bad ... I later found out that the driving instructor had fled after the learner driver had lost control of the car and it landed on the green—an embankment about three or four metres down," reported resident Neville Harris, who had wondered how the Citi Golf had ended up where it had.

As if that wasn't enough, when the owner of the driving school showed up at the scene, police smelled alcohol on his breath, found him to be three times over the limit and arrested him for drunken driving.

"It is difficult to say how much he had to drink as it depends on a lot of factors such as his weight, what he had to eat and what he was drinking, but we can safely say he had a lot to drink." KwaZulu-Natal department of transport spokesperson Zinhle Mngomezulu commenting on the arrest of a truck driver who was found to be 16 times over the limit. According to police, the man was driving on the wrong side of the road before crashing into another oncoming truck.

Water buffalos in uniforms

"Given the unenviable Metro police record around South Africa, most people wouldn't spit on a metro officer if he/she was on fire." Ian Catton of Boksburg, letter to *The Citizen*

"Just back from a trip which normally would take 45 minutes," complained one Moneyweb reader. "It took me two hours. Traffic lights down all over the place and what are the dumb, stupid phuqueing lazy blue-bellied Katzenjammer Kops doing? Hiding behind trees, standing in driveways and harassing the citizens when they should be attempting to keep the traffic flowing. What a bunch of moronic fools; their bosses must take the cake for ineptness, venality, stupidity and just pure laziness."

"The fact is that the metro police are rapidly becoming another lawless force in this country, like the taxi drivers," opined David Bullard. "The only solution is to disband them and start again and the first thing to do is to disarm them. Giving people who can't do joined-up writing guns, is never a good idea as many parts of Africa have found out to their cost.

"Nobody respects them because it's very hard to respect people who only made it into uniform as part of some ANC job-creation programme. They are unprofessional, their attitude is all wrong (they forget they are public servants), they have a well-deserved reputation for being corrupt and, last but not least, many of them are hideously fat."[1]

In Cape Town, protesting taxi drivers spontaneously changed the slogan "Kill the farmer, kill the boer" to "Kill the traffic police, kill the city police" (somehow it's not quite as catchy). About 2,000 members of the taxi industry caused major disruptions when they marched to the city's civic centre, where they set a rubbish bin and a road sign alight to indicate their unhappiness with the city's new transport plans. Mitchell's Plain taxi owners said they could not guarantee the safety of commuters and advised them to use buses instead. This was a nice gesture, but not especially helpful as buses were either being stoned or not allowed to enter the townships at all.

"I don't mind traffic cops lacking a sense of humour if I'm caught speeding but I don't want to be asked for a bribe by a water buffalo bulging out of his uniform."
David Bullard

The light at the end of the tunnel is the oncoming train burning because angry commuters set it on fire

---

[1] Given that so many traffic cops are overweight, it's somewhat ironic that an obese women won R50,000 in damages from the Thulamela Municipality after a traffic officer ordered her out of the taxi she was travelling in. "I felt like my weight was a disability. I was really humiliated," she said. This was not the first time an officer's rudeness cost the taxpayer money: earlier, the department of Safety and Security was ordered to pay Professor Ignatius Maithufi after police called him "hardegat", pointed their guns at him and accused him of being drunk.

"Killing machine … a coffin on wheels." KwaZulu-Natal Transport MEC Bheki Cele describes bus operator SA Roadlink. The previous month, a Roadlink bus was involved in an accident in which eleven people were killed

If you don't possess a car of your own, you're forced to use public transport, which in South Africa, amounts to taking your life in your hands and handing it over to someone who hasn't quite yet mastered the art of using opposable thumbs.

Passengers on a Putco bus from Sandton to Soweto were treated to a re-enactment of the movie *Speed*, only without Sandra Bullock. "We got on the bus in Sandton and the driver reeked of alcohol," one traumatized passenger reported. "He did not take the normal route and once he got onto the M1 South highway, towards Soweto, he began driving recklessly. Cars were swerving and hooting at him. We asked him to pull over but he said: 'Don't ask fucking questions'," she said.

Another passenger reported: "The man in front of me fell back on top of me which the bus tilted. I asked the driver to stop, but he swore at me and said: 'You can report me but nothing will happen to me—I am Putco's number one driver'."

The driver was eventually forced off the road by metro police near the Kliptown police station.

"In December, [another] driver and his friends had a braai on the bus. They stopped at a bottle store in Sandton and bought alcohol. They had a skottel on the bus and braaied chicken." A Putco passenger reports on the joys of public transport

If public transport proves unreliable, South African commuters have a novel way of solving the problem. They burn things down. At the beginning of 2008, Pretoria commuters set seven trains on fire after power cuts delayed them for two hours. "The trains were not moving and commuters got angry and started setting trains alight," said a police spokesman. As a result of the violence, Metrorail suspended services along the Mabopane and Ga-Rankuwa lines.

In Daveyton, commuters torched a Metrorail ticket office and threw stones at police attempting to restore order. "The commuters are complaining that there are constant delays from Northmead to Daveyton station; they are also demanding that we release the arrested people," said Inspector Nakedi Rapholo. She added that trains could not move through Daveyton station as there was a risk that the commuters would set them alight. Presumably, as a result, the delays were even longer.

In Brits, about 300 angry commuters burnt two buses and damaged another ten because they had run out of diesel. "The commuters became angry and started throwing stones at the buses," said Superintendent Koos Degenaar. "Ten other buses were damaged with broken windows and so on. The damage is estimated to be around R250,000."

"How long will it take commuters to destroy the Gautrain as they have destroyed others? Maybe they won't be allowed to use it. I fear this train will also go up in flames. Only a few will benefit, the rest of us taxpayers will have to use our poor road system." Letter to *The Citizen*

Thick-skulled barbaric illiterates

"Shut up and don't act like the so-called 'free women' who make noise and talk too much." Taxi driver to Hillbrow woman who complained about getting change for a R100 note in coins

Of course, if your bus or train is reduced to ashes, you could always just catch a taxi. Taxi drivers are perennially hated by the South African public and the past year was no different. At last count, there were at least eight Facebook groups dedicated to the hatred of minibus taxis. But if motorists hate taxi drivers, so do many of their passengers.

"Commuters are generally inhumanely treated everyday at taxi ranks," said Popcru spokesman Benzi Ka-Soko. "It is so painful to see old women being subjected to such degrading treatment by taxi drivers. More shocking is the deafening silence from men during these dastardly acts." Male commuters, he said, kept quiet and displayed "sheepinshness" while women were abused by taxi drivers. "Body-shrinking insults fly in our taxi ranks as if it is normal social conduct. Have these human beings lost the human touch of being human, humble and respectful?"

In February 2008, taxi drivers at the Noord Street taxi rank attacked a young woman because she was dressed in a miniskirt. Twenty-five-year-old Nwabisa Ngcukana was humiliated when her clothes were torn off in front of a cheering crowd. A taxi driver named Phineas interviewed by the *Mail & Guardian* said women abused men by being "half naked". "Before 1994, women wore clothes neatly and properly; now they say they have rights," he complained.

David Kau suggested that taxi drivers be forced to recite a pledge every morning: "I will treat my passengers and fellow motorists like human beings." On the other hand, schoolchildren should be pledging not to turn out to be a taxi driver. "If this pledge does not make them want to stay in school and get good marks, in ten years' time these high-school dropouts will kick your ass when they catch you wearing a miniskirt not only at the taxi rank, but also in your driveway."

> "No illiterate will tell me what to wear." A female *Sowetan* reader in response to reports of attacks by taxi drivers on women wearing miniskirts

Readers of *The Sowetan* had plenty to say about taxi drivers in the wake of reports of the attacks. Words like 'stupidity' and 'barbarity' came up many times:

> "I think the law should show those barbaric taxi drivers who is in charge and they must make sure that they get the message in their thick skulls by giving them their deserved punishment. Taxi drivers are very rude and DISRESPECTFUL of everyone: women, old citizens and men and think that they own this country and everything in it."

> "I could not believe it when I read the story; it is such barbaric behaviour that confirms stereotypes about black people and, I bet my bottom rand that if asked, the perpetrators would hide behind and abuse the words culture and decency as an excuse for their actions. What hypocrisy from so-called advocates of cultural morality."

> "These beasts have been allowed to do as they please for too long. They force people to get into filthy unsafe taxis; if you raise your concerns or object, you are in trouble."

and

> "Taxi drivers are idiots; they have developed the lunatic perception that they rule our country. To me taxi drivers' skulls are empty. They don't think; they just do anything anytime … Anyway, what do you expect from someone who spends 365 days without taking a proper shower?"

Even when women do succeed in getting their own back, taxi drivers have their ways and means of exacting revenge. Miriam Malebatja was 'banned' from the Marabastad taxi rank as punishment for reporting a driver to the police. "He started touching me between the thighs and I jumped because I was offended and did not expect that," she explained. "But he was not even embarrassed. He just kept laughing and making fun of me in front of everybody. I was really embarrassed and offended by what happened so I opened a case against him."

The taxi driver was fined R2,000 or six months' imprisonment. But now other drivers refused to transport her. "They were angry that I reported the case to the police because, according to them, it was a small issue that most women did not report," Malebtaja said. "It seems that they are used to doing this to other women who do not report such cases."

> "As is set out in Section 1 of the How To Survive South Africa Act (1 of 1652): Notwithstanding any laws elsewhere contained never ever ever fuck with the Minibus Taxi-Drivers." Michael Trapido

After a taxi strike brought Johannesburg to a grinding halt, Mondli Makhanya reflected on how the industry had become an "uncontrollable monster". Absolutely everybody hated the taximen. "You see, what needs to happen is that Mugabe must come down here and rule South Africa for a while," said one of two workmen, in a conversation Makhanya happened to overview, "Then he can wallop these taximen and set them straight. Thereafter, he can return to Zimbabwe, and Zuma and Lekota can fight it out for the presidency."

Makhanya was struck by the anger of Joburgers and the "universal sense of disgust and helplessness" over the strike. The arrogance of the taxi industry was breathtaking. "We are mobilizing. If they don't address this, we will bring the entire country to a halt for a week or two," Joe Mophuting, a spokesman for the United Taxi Association Forum threatened. "The government's limp-wristed ways have bred an industry that operates almost as a parallel state," Makhanya charged. "A rogue parallel state at that."

The Sowetan agreed: "Enough is enough. It's time for the government to assert its authority and stamp out the taximen's banditry."

The chances of that seemed slim when the ego of the industry knew no bounds. It's hard to imagine anyone but the taxi industry claiming ownership of transport routes, as the National Taxi Alliance (NTA) did when it said it wanted "full ownership" of the Bus Rapid Transport system because it had developed the routes the BRT system was targeting.

"The taxi industry is therefore justified in claiming intellectual property or goodwill on the taxi routes and taxi ranks," NTA secretary-general Alpheus Mlalazi said.

Some observed that claiming intellectual property did tend to imply that the taxi industry possessed an intellect in the first place. Intellectual property specialist Herman Blignaut pointed out: "'Transport routes do not constitute subject matter which can be termed intellectual property."

"What shocked the sisterhood was the outing of taxi nudists. Several strikers stripped to show contempt for the government and Minister Jeff Radebe. I understand that the shocking scenes put the minister off his ProNutro." *Sowetan* columnist Nthabi Moreosele

Blue-light gangs

"All of a sudden there is a hullabaloo about blue lights. I suggest it is because some people are aware that in the blue-light car today, there is a darkie inside there." KwaZulu-Natal transport MEC Bheki Cele, interviewed by Carte Blanche for a story on a motorist who was killed in a collision with a 'blue light' convoy

If there is any rival to taxis for the title of the most hated users of South Africa's roads, it's the VIP protection unit and their so-called 'blue light gangs', those convoys of expensive black motor vehicles that ferry politicians at warp speed between from one meeting in which they do nothing to another meeting to which they contribute bugger all.

In KwaZulu-Natal, eight people were injured after one of the bodyguards in a convoy shot out the tyre of a Mazda that failed to get out of the way fast enough. The convoy of vehicles was late picking up the KwaZulu-Natal MEC for social development, Meshack Radebe, who was to be transported to inspect storm damage.

Radebe said, "If blue-light drivers behave badly, we must also question the behaviour of road users. Motorists must give way when they see blue lights flashing. It means we have an emergency, we need to get to a place in a hurry and people's lives depend on it."

Presumably the downtrodden masses faced the imminent threat of their sad lives being further denuded of meaning if he were to fail to show up on time to offer them empty promises after their homes were damaged by stormwater.

"Our drivers are trained to protect us. We are heading to elections and they need to ensure our safety. If a motorist behaves in an unpredictable manner, how do our drivers know we are not being ambushed? Their reaction is to push aside and shoot," Radebe said. The Mazda in question was transporting three teenagers and a young couple to a subversive and possibly terrorist activity, in this case a dance recital.

Hlanganani Nxumalo, the bodyguard, was arrested on eight counts of attempted murder. Magistrate Thys Taljaard refused bail and said, "There's a history of VIP members terrorizing road users and having no regard for the law. Can one really blame the press for referring to them as the blue-light gang of KwaZulu-Natal?"

"Motorists are put under intense pressure when these blue-light thugs suddenly appear from out of nowhere, flashing their lights and tailgating drivers who cannot immediately move on to the slow lane. How can he justify making such a ridiculously insane comment?" complained motorist Ronnie Davids In a letter to *The Citizen*, Victor Mashishi defended Nxumalo, arguing that he had done the right thing under the circumstances. "For a long time motorists have refused to give way for convoys transported by the unit. Drivers even slow down to get a reaction from VIP officers. They disrespectfully call them 'the Blue Light Gang'. These people who were shot at showed no respect."

"He's not the only one," responded one *Citizen* reader to news that Radebe had gone on sick leave, saying that the incident had made him ill.

Mashishi was in the minority, however. Max du Preez waves his arms and swears in three languages if his child is not in the car with him. He also suggests that motorists put on their hazard lights and hoot until the convoy was out of earshot. "It is time every politician, whether he/she be the president, a minister, a premier, a provincial MEC or a mayor, took notice of how we citizens feel about their ridiculous sense of self-importance and their disregard of our rights."

The head of the VIP Protection Unit couldn't understand why nobody liked them. "The South African public doesn't respect the vehicles of the VIP Protection Unit," complained Commissioner Mzondeki 'Sean' Tshabalala. "They simply refuse to move out of the way. There is a general apathy towards us."

Peter van der Merwe was unmoved. "Sniff. Snob. Let's all cry him a river," he wrote, wondering, "Why is the government closing down the Scorpions, who actually fight crime, but keep the VIP Protection Unit, who merely commit crime?"

> "They were swearing at him and all he said was he was using a company car." Witness to a road-rage incident in which two bikers beat up a man who caused an accident near Pietermaritzburg. The driver was apparently a provincial MEC's bodyguard

> "I accept we are also an arrogant lot and think that we are above others, so using the blue light just boosts our ego." Anonymous VIP Unit driver, interviewed by the *Sunday Tribune*

Daddy's gonna steal you a Golf

> "Oh, and while I'm at it, can somebody please shoot those persistent car guards who refuse to accept that I have no money in my wallet and who somehow believe that gesturing me into a parking bay the size of Madagascar requires remuneration—notwithstanding the little card in my possession commonly known by many as a 'driver's licence'." Jeremy Nell

Finally, since we are on the subject of crime, here is a car-theft story guaranteed to gladden the heart of any of the owners of the 90,000 cars stolen annually.

In October 2008, Hemman Mathebe of Mamelodi East went on trial for an incident that took place almost a year before, when he was locked in a VW Golf 5 for two hours while the owner partied in a Hatfield club. Natasha Labotski unwittingly locked the man in the vehicle after she pressed the remote without looking back to make sure it was locked. After a couple of hours someone came looking for her to tell her that a man was locked in her car. Police Inspector Stephanus Dreyer recalled how he was patrolling the area when a security guard alerted him to the man locked in the Golf. "The person inside panicked," he said. "We tried to open the door, but couldn't. I told and gestured to him to open it from the inside, but he gestured back that he couldn't."

After Labotski was finally located, she let the man out of her car. "All he said was 'Sorry, sorry'," Dreyer said. Mathebe denied a charge of attempted vehicle theft and said that Labotski had asked him to sit in the vehicle while she was away, and had asked if he would mind being locked in.

Not entirely unexpectedly, Labotski denied this.

Hush my *laaitie* don't you cry
Daddy's gonna steal you a GTi
And if that GTi don't Torque
Another GTi I will stalk
And if the stalking don't go to well
Daddy's gonna steal you a Caravelle
And if that Caravelle makes some tricks
Daddy's gonna jack you a VR6
And if that VR6 won't fly
Daddy's gonna knock a BM from a Sandton guy
And if that BM's sound is kwaai
Da Lenz cherries will go with you to elke braai
And if the cops ask why
Daddy will buy the docket from a police spy
And if all these things still make you cry
Then you're not my *laaitie* ... your mom told me a lie!
From SAjokes.blogspot.com

Chapter 9

Schnaai the Beloved Country:
Crime

"Government says crime stats are wake-up call, presses snooze button." Hayibo. com headline

"Our law enforcement agencies are working tirelessly to ensure that crime is drastically reduced. Our criminal justice system is being bolstered to ensure that perpetrators of crime are dealt with speedily and effectively." Kgalema Motlanthe, report to the African Peer Review Mechanism

When former Capetonian Brandon Huntley applied to the Canadians for refugee status, he told them it was because he had been mugged seven times. African South Africans, he said, had targeted him, calling him a "settler" and a "white dog" and he could not possibly live in safety in South Africa.

The Canadians presiding over his case agreed. Huntley, said the board's panel chair, William Davis, "would stand out like a 'sore thumb' due to his colour in any part of the country." (Obviously, as Hayibo observed, the board had never looked at YouTube footage of a Patricia Lewis concert or a rugby match at Loftus.)

The South African government was incensed by what it said was—you'll never guess—a racist decision. "Canada's reasoning for granting Huntley a refugee status can only serve to perpetuate racism," said the ANC, and they probably had a point, though not necessarily for the reasons they imagined.

Jeremy Gordin observed that the reason everyone "from Sue van der Merwe, the deputy minister for international relations and potjiekos, to Ronnie 'Mampara' Mamoepa, the spokesman for that department, is so upset is that it is of course true—the government is both unwilling and incapable of protecting most its citizens".

"This is not a secret, after all."

Chris McEvoy suggested we should all get a little perspective. "Let's be honest: we haven't exactly lost a cure for Aids here," he argued, pointing out that Huntley was an unemployed irrigation sprinkler salesman who worked as a carnival attendant until his visa ran out, then stayed on illegally. "With his departure, South Africa is one redneck lighter."

The *Mail & Guardian* thought that Huntley was the "Mark Shuttleworth of con men", responsible for exporting "quintessential Capetonian attitude we call dofness". As for those who doubted that Huntley had been attacked seven times: "You only have to look at a picture of him to know: that is a face demanding to be slapped."

The southern African representative of the UN High Commission for Refugees maintained that crime could not be grounds for seeking refugee status. "Crime is not committed by the state," argued Sanda Kimbimbi. "To say that the state is not able to protect you is far-fetched. Anyone can be a victim of crime. If that was the case, then anyone in South Africa would be able to claim it."

Which, one supposes, is the point. Besides those politicians who enjoy the services of entire teams of blue light-flashing, BMW-driving bodyguards, nobody is safe from the attentions of South Africa's thriving criminal classes.

"We don't care for God. Let's stab these dogs". Robber to the Tanzanian High Commissioner, who was beaten unconscious during a robbery at his residence in December. The ambassador had been holding a farewell party

The least frightening place on earth

"South Africa has become a problem area." Ian Melas, manager of Johannesburg's popular Lion Park, makes what is quite possibly the understatement of the year while commenting on a robbery at the park's restaurant, during which a restaurant patron was shot dead

Another South African who fled for the northern hemisphere chose a slightly different strategy. Wanted sex offender and former Pretoria advocate Dirk Prinsloo was finally caught after a failed bank robbery in Belarus of all places. Police spokesperson Sally de Beer said, "We were informed by Interpol that Prinsloo was arrested at 5.30pm on Friday following an attempted bank robbery in Belarus. Prinsloo and two other men allegedly attempted to rob a bank on Wednesday, armed with a pistol and a knife. The staff at the bank co-operated but managed to overpower two of the suspects and he ran. He was tracked down and arrested two days later."

Is jail in Belarus—notorious as one of Europe's most corrupt countries—better than jail in South Africa? Perhaps Prinsloo could offer a comparison for our edification when he is finally extradited after serving his sentence there.

> "The Homecoming Revolution is a fallacy! The Effingoff Resolution is reality!"
> Comment, *Mail & Guardian* Forum, during a discussion on crime

British motoring journalist and professional stirrer Jeremy Clarkson would have been mystified by Huntley's case. Clarkson, after all, was disappointed by his failure to experience crime in Joburg, writing that the city's "fearsome global reputation for being utterly terrifying, a lawless Wild West frontier town paralyzed by corruption and disease," is nonsense.

"Johannesburg is Milton Keynes with thunderstorms," he wrote, disgusted. "You go out. You have a lovely ostrich. You drink some delicious wine and you walk back to your hotel, all warm and comfy. It's the least frightening place on earth."

"So why does every single person there wrap themselves up in razor wire and fit their cars with flame-throwers and speak of how many times they've been killed that day? What are they trying to prove?"

He was "baffled" that South Africans would try to dissuade visitors to the 2010 World Cup. "Why ruin the reputation of your city and risk the success of the footballing World Cup to fuel a story that plainly isn't true?"

Jacob Zuma and former ANCYL president Fikile Mbalula would have been cheered by Clarkson's PR punt. As JZ told Al Jazeera, crime in South Africa could be gone within a year. "The only difference in South Africa is that our media is more open and report crime more than it is reported in other countries," he said. And crime is so yesterday's news: "Certainly, by 2010, you will tell me that violence will be the talk; that it has gone down."

"Perhaps it will be close to zero by that time."

Sure.

"We used to bliksem the truth out of them. But these days, you are supposed to say to them: 'Please state, tell the truth. I beg you.' No crook is going to take you seriously." Police officer bemoans South Africa's human rights laws, in conversation with *Sowetan* columnist Charles Mogale

Kiss the criminal

"There he is, then—our sheriff, Wyatt Twerp." Andrew Donaldson on police commissioner Bheki Cele

But there was no need to despair. For those who had given up hope that South Africa's criminals would ever be bliksemed by the forces of justice, a charismatic new figure appeared on the scene. Teetotaller, gym fanatic, owner of 48 Panama hats and dater of 20 year-olds, Bheki Cele was never going to be your run-of-the-mill copper. He dressed like a drug dealer—Huggy Bear of *Starsky and Hutch*, or Bra Georgie of *Isidingo* come to mind—and spoke like Dirty Harry. Shoot or be shot, he told police.

"You can't be soft and you can't be moving around kissing crime. You need to be tough because you're dealing with tough guys," he told the media after he was appointed as Jackie Selebi's replacement. Asked about his reputation as a 'cowboy', he said, "Well, cowboys don't cry. We will just fight crime."

Cele wanted the law to be changed to allow police to "shoot to kill" criminals without worrying about "what happens after that". He told the *Weekend Argus* that the police needed to match the firepower of criminals and use "deadly force" to create a country "where people aren't told they're safe, but actually feel safe". Cele disliked the laws governing the level of force police were allowed to use with criminals, saying that officers responding to an attack had to "arrest their minds, thinking is this right or is it wrong?"

"Police must think about what is in front of them and do the job," he said, "or else they get killed."

Cele, Andrew Donaldson observed, appeared to be "enforcing the law south of the Limpopo with an approach usually associated with the affairs to the west of the Pecos River about 150 years ago".

> "Police force members have said that if every police officer was dismissed for swearing in front of a superior, there would be no police officers left." Story on a Free State policeman who was fired for using the F-word in front of a superior officer

Cele was determined that the police should not be a refuge for people who were too useless to be employed elsewhere. "The problem we are facing is that the police force is seen as a failure organization. Whoever fails somewhere else will be asked: 'Why don't you join the police?'"

A fine example of the kind of individual Cele might have had in mind was the commander of East Ratanga station who set up residence there, washing himself every morning in front of his colleagues in the station's kitchen and holding meetings while dressed in his pyjamas. Johan Beeter, chairperson of the Heidelberg Community Forum, said the station commander had been taking sick leave in his office and that workers could not use the copier or fax machine. His car, which was broken down, was also being stored at the station.

Provincial police spokesperson, Superintendent Eugene Opperman, said that the case was an internal matter.

> "To spare my future grandchild the embarrassment of having a donkey pull up outside her house with a mannequin in a blue uniform tied to its back—because by then that's what the police force will have been reduced to—I went to the traffic department on Friday." Ben Trovato deals with a traffic fine

Cele was not the first to make colourful threats against South Africa's criminal community. In 2008, Deputy Minister of Safety and Security Susan Shabangu famously channelled the spirit of Steve Tshwete at an anti-crime imbizo in Pretoria West. "You must kill the bastards if they threaten you or the community," she told the crowd. "You must not worry about the regulations. That is my responsibility. Your responsibility is to serve and protect."

In March 2009, Jacob Zuma said, "I'm not saying that the laws are too user-friendly for criminals, but rather that they need a bit more bite," while in August, he told police, "Criminals have a lot of rights. One of them is the right to remain silent. So when they come to the station, don't ask too many questions, just put them in jail."

"Shoot him in the flesh," said Gauteng community safety MEC Khabisi Mosunkutu when asked how police officers should respond to a situation in which they were threatened by an armed suspect.

Deputy Police Minister Fikile Mbalula told a community police forum meeting in Guguletu that criminals were "not born of a man and woman". "These are people who are possessed with evil spirit," he informed the gathering. "We keep on glorifying these animals as if they are real human beings. The days for criminals to see their own coffins and graves have arrived."

> "Show your faces, you dogs. You will also die." A relative of slain reggae star Lucky Dube at the trial of his alleged killers in the Johannesburg High Court

In an apparent bid to make good on that threat and rival Martin's Funerals, Mbalula announced "Operation Wanya Tsotsi" in August 2009. The operation's name, he explained to Parliament, was a "radical African expression and display of strength and zealousness against one's enemy".

"It is a weapon to instil fear and respect to one's strategic opponent. It is an expression of readiness of one's forces of war. It is a strength exhibition! It is a war cry!"

A language specialist consulted on the precise meaning of the new initiative explained that an exact translation of the term was: "You will shit, criminal!", though at the same time conceding that a less literal, more polite interpretation might be: "You are in deep trouble, criminal!"

One *Mail & Guardian* reader was less than impressed with the name. "Sis, I smell shit with new operation," sniffed Mfusi Tshingilane. "I also hope it will create jobs not amavolunteers."

> "He told me that he was so angry, not because he lost a couple of hundred rands, but because he wished that the robbers were from the big city, and not some moegoes from a small town. Talk of the arrogance of the big city guys." Edward Tsumele reports on the case of a friend robbed in a small town in Limpopo

A rotten policeman

"Nothing is more dangerous to all of us than being protected by a rotten policeman."
Tokyo Sexwale

It was hard to imagine that Cele would not enjoy the support of the public. South Africans were so relieved that Jackie Selebi had finally shuffled off into the sunset that they would have welcomed a one-eyed Albanian midget with postnasal drip in his place. As Judge Nico Coetzee said of the then police commissioner's reputation: "So tarnished that nothing that happens can tarnish it more."

Pierre de Vos reflected that Selebi might never be proven to be corrupt "but he sure seems like a slimy and morally corrupt person to me, asking for money from Agliotti and others to pay for his lavish lifestyle. I, for one, would not want to be his friend—*finish and klaar.*"

Selebi survived for so long in part because he was able to convince others of the merits of his case. When Glen Agliotti and Clinton Nassif, both allegedly involved in the murder of Brett Kebble, claimed that Selebi had received payments from them, Selebi said he was being framed.

Embattled National Director of Public Prosecutions Vusi Pikoli believed him. Testifying at the Ginwala commission into his fitness to hold office, Pikoli told of an emotional meeting with Selebi. The police commissioner had denied receiving payments from Kebble-murder accused Glenn Agliotti.

"At the time I believed him," Pikoli recalled. "I cried in that meeting. He cried in that meeting. For me it was a cry of relief because I never believed that he could be facing accusations of that nature. We cried on each other's shoulders in that meeting and I told him that I believed him when he said he never received the money."

When Selebi was finally forced to make way for Cele, he said he had no feelings on the matter. "Ja, it was okay, it was okay," he said of his impression of Cele. "I'm not in a position to make comments about any individual that has been placed there. Those who made the choice must have thought about it carefully."

We hope so.

"Selebi will be remembered for his shockingly realistic portrayal of South African police chief Jackie Selebi in the highly acclaimed drama, *Schnaai the Beloved Country*." Ben Trovato

Squashing the Scorpions

It was at Polokwane, at the end of 2007, that the ANC resolved to squash the Scorpions, who had the inconvenient habit of targeting their own, including Jacob Zuma. "Hollywood-style tactics", they called it. Though the announcement was hardly surprising, there was widespread fury in the wake of Safety and Security Minister Charles Nqakula's revelation that the Scorpions were to be disbanded and merged with the SAPS.

"The arrogance of the minister to undermine Parliament is absolutely disgusting," said Patricia de Lille, while Bantu Holomisa said that dissolving the Scorpions would be "sheer foolishness". "The people who drove this campaign were themselves wanted by the law."

To jeers from some MPs, Nqakula said, "We are a dynamic organization that has always seized the moment to rise to higher levels and that is why we continue to occupy the moral high ground."

Director at the Institute for Security Studies Peter Gastrow commented: "The only ones cheering were the organized-crime bosses."

A valiant last-ditch attempt to save the Scorpions ultimately failed. Maggie Sotyu, head of Parliament's Safety and Security committee, ruled that tens of thousands of signatures collected in a 'Save the Scorpions' petition were irrelevant "because people in her own constituency did not know what the Scorpions were. "They think it is some fruit somewhere," she said with a straight face.

"I am not sure what is the opposite of 'don't give up the day job'—'don't give up the night job'?—but whatever it is, Maggie Sotyu should take it to heart," Richard Calland observed.

So it was that the Scorpions were replaced by the Directorate for Priority Crime Investigation, also known as the Hawks—so named, said Mthwethwa, for the bird's ability to see from afar. "My advice to you is you have to be thick-skinned as you weather the storms—there will be turbulence out there," said advocate Thanda Mngwenge, former deputy head of the Scorpions, as he handed 288 case files over to Anwa Dramat during a public ceremony.

"We expect the unit to zoom in on the activities of criminals and destroy their evil networks, at home and globally," said Police Minister Nathi Mthethwa

Observers seemed least certain. Zapiro depicted DPCI—pronounced 'Dipsy'—as one of the Teletubbies.

"The mafia … a liar." Former metro police officer Patrick Johnston describes his former boss Robert McBride, who was eventually fired from his position as head of the Metro police in Ekhuruleni

"If we are to believe the expression 'your body speaks your mind' we now have a better understanding of the flabby, drooping intellectual capacity of a certain Metropolitan police force. Messrs Johnnie Walker and Jack Daniels must be very proud of their elite progeny." Robert McBride, according a letter to *The Citizen*

Stranger the pulp fiction

"Please telephone the man that gave us a lift and we are sorry for stealing the car from him but we never made it threw to Soweto. So he is lucky but we got something and he has a nice fone. Thabo." Note left in a car stolen in Sandton and parked in front of the Langlaagte police station

Doubtless even the Hawks would have been baffled by one of South Africa's stranger homicide cases. An Mpumalanga woman died in January 2008 after being hit by a shoe during at argument with another woman at the Fetakgomo municipality offices in Sekhukhune.

Police spokesperson Superintendent Mohale Ramatseba said that Lydia Selebalo and Dipolelo Nkhomi had been involved in a fight in which Nkhomi's clothes were "torn apart". Nkhomi had then thrown a shoe at Selebalo, who then died. An eyewitness said that the shoe had not killed Selebalo. "The deceased was a longtime sufferer of epilepsy. It is unfortunate that she collapsed while she was engaged in a fight with another person—to the extent that an innocent person might be seen as a murderer," the eyewitness said. He further alleged that the deceased had instigated the incident by hurling insults at the accused.

The police spokesperson said: "At the moment we are just clutching at straws, not knowing whether to charge the culprit with murder, culpable homicide or whatever charge."

> "Shoot those faggots. Besides, nobody gives a shit about firearm-wielding retards who steal health pills from harmless old people." Jeremy Nell comments on a case in which four armed robbers held an elderly KwaNobuhle couple at gunpoint for over an hour before escaping with nothing more than blood pressure pills

In another intriguing case, Mcebisi Noji, accused of raping five women between the ages of 54 and 65, came up with a novel alibi: he told the court that he had not had an erection since the year 2000 (obviously a memorable year for him). "I am not capable of rape," he explained. "I did not commit these crimes and I cannot do it physically. Secondly, that is not the way I was brought up, and I do not find old women sexually attractive."

A doctor examined Noji and concluded that there is nothing wrong with him. Senior state advocate Nickie Turner then asked Noji the obvious question: "You mean someone dressed in the same clothes as you and left your blood and semen at the crime scenes. Is that what you want this court to believe?"

Noji said, "I am confused about that."

While we are on the subject, it's worth noting that perhaps one of South Africa's best examples of nominative determinism or, more correctly, aptronym, was the instance of the lawyer who was tasked with defending South Africa's worst-ever rapist. He went by the name of Harold Knobb. Mr Knobb lived up to his name by suggesting that Mongezi Jingxela should receive the minimum sentence because he had not given his victims HIV and they were in any case not virgins. The judge did not see Knobb's point of view, and sentenced Jingxela to over 1,000 years in jail.

> "Detroit, LA, Jo'burg? No, Melbourne." Headline in the Melbourne daily, *The Age*. A lone gunman had brazenly robbed a hotel in the middle of the night before getting away with tens of thousands of dollars in loot

In February 2008, a 21-year-old drug dealer, one Goodman Golide, was run over by his client, a 37-year-old Witbank man who was angry about being given Panado instead of cocaine. After the man discovered that the drugs did not give him the high he was expecting, he confronted Golide, who then tried to run away. The disappointed drug user then ran over Golide with his car.

In Willowvale in the Eastern Cape, a drunken good Samaritan attempted to help another man, also drunk. Thinking he was being attacked, the second man stabbed the first, killing him.

Meanwhile in Welkom, a seven-year-old child was busted driving a vehicle for a gang of criminals involved in counterfeit money. "One of the suspects was a seven-year-old and he was the driver of a vehicle when they were busted by the police in Welkom," the police explained.

"Fucking criminal." Lettering on cap worn by celebrity choreographer Somizi Mhlongo to his court hearing in Randburg on charges of indecent assault

A robber in Durban was caught with an AK-47 rifle, a pistol and a single box he had from Johannesburg in his suitcase, as well as R6,000 in cash, by the appropriately named Captain Anthony Lockem of the Durban Organized Crime Unit. (Captain Lockemup is probably too much to hope for.)

Before being caught, the man had purchased a pair of Italian woman's plastic sandals for R2,499, a pair of man's trousers for R895, a long-sleeved golf shirt for R900 and gun oil for R40, within hours of committing the crime. Presumably the golf shirt, trousers and shoes were not necessarily purchased as an ensemble.

Popular singer Patricia Majalisa was forced to sing one of her hit songs after being hijacked in Yeoville. "I pleaded that I could not sing because I was traumatized and crying," she reported after being dumped in an informal settlement near Vereeniging. "They insisted that I could sing and that I should not act funny. Afraid and even vomiting, I was forced to sing as they drove."

Freedom Front MP Willie Spies inadvertently rescued a cell phone repairman who jumped onto the bonnet of his Mercedes while Spies was driving from the airport in an effort to escape thieves who had attacked him. "I accelerated and stopped about 500 metres further down the road," he explained. "When I stopped, he rearranged how he was sitting on the bonnet and then I drove at about 40 or 50km/h into town." Spies called an ambulance and the man, whose face was bleeding profusely, was admitted to hospital.

"The killer is in prison, but it is like he is on holiday. I bet he has all the rights of an innocent human being. I personally think that is unfair." Ayanda Mlandu, best friend of Ivy Flietoor, who was murdered in Olievenhoutbosch north of Johannesburg. A taxi driver later confessed to the killing

"He missed. I didn't."

Sometimes, the least expected victims got their own back. A 78-year-old Greek granny fought off two youths who attempted to rob her store, while a 17-year-old Port Elizabeth ballerina got into an impromptu wrestling match with a hijacker—and lived to tell the tale. "I yanked the man from behind the steering wheel," she explained to the media. "When he was out of the car, he threw me to the ground. I jumped up and grabbed him again—I just didn't want him to get into that car again."

Another grandmother who fought back was a friend of veteran *Cape Times* columnist John Scott. He related what she did when one of the muggers tried to take her wedding ring while she was out walking with her grandson. "I told him that if he did I'd kill him," she told Scott. "So he stopped. He also kept saying 'fuck you, fuck you'. I can't stand it when people say that to me. So I shouted at him to stop that, too, which he did. He didn't say much after that. I think I halved his vocabulary."

"Give me baboons any day to some of the people you meet on the mountains," wrote Scott.

"Give us the phone or my friend is going to fucking shoot you in the head." Mugger to American student Matt Radler as he stood at a bus stop outside Campus Square in Melville

Twenty-two-year-old Equestria resident Shireen van der Walt bliksemed a burglar caught breaking into her home, "He was climbing out of the window of the spare room," she explained. "I started hitting him on the head. I wanted to hit him hard enough to injure him, so that my partner could get hold of him. I can't say if it was five blows or fifty. I just lashed out and kept yelling. Unfortunately, I couldn't get a hold on him. I didn't think of being afraid. All I thought was, what the heck's he doing in my house. It makes me so angry. I don't steal from anyone else. Why should he come and steal from me?" Despite her best efforts, the man still escaped with a laptop, a camera, DVDs, CDs (is there a market for stolen treffers?), jewellery and other personal items. She told the media: "I wish he'd come back. Then we can have it out, man to woman!"

Then there was the Bloemfontein hijacking victim who was rescued by taxi commuters. She had initially assumed her unexpected allies were in cahoots with the hijackers, but watched in wonder as they hauled the hijackers out of the car and beat up them up before handing back the woman's handbag and cell phone. Afterwards she told a journalist, "It's wonderful to think that people, who are perceived to be lawless, rushed to help me, especially in the present situation with regard to crime in our country." She added that she had no plans to report the incident to the police. "I'd just become another number in Bloemfontein's hijacking statistics," she explained.

> "He claimed that his bank card had been swallowed and that he wanted to remove it. We charged him with malicious damage to property." Police comment on the arrest of a man who attacked a Kempton Park ATM (where else?) with a wheel spanner in an attempt to retrieve his bank card

In a similar tale, Claudene Walsh, the owner of a construction business, was helped by fifteen casual workers who saw her chase two men who tried to hijack her beloved bakkie 'Pumbaa'. "I just became so angry. I just felt that I was sick of this kind of thing, tired of these kinds of things in our country," she explained when asked what had made her do something apparently insane. "So, when they touched me ..." Walsh was full of praise for the workers, who helped apprehend one of the hijackers. Later the man sat crying in the back of the police van. "In the end, the good and the bad were thrown together, all on one day," said Walsh.

"Well, he missed. I didn't," police reservist captain Marc Ishlove told 702 after an incident in which he shot dead two hijackers at a shopping centre in Randburg. Ishlove was widely hailed as a hero. Suggestions that Ishlove was a racist brought forth a sharp rebuke from *Times* reader Litheko Modisane, who argued that this view was "naïve in the extreme".

"This is because there is no cause to believe that he was acting in the service of a particular race. These criminals are not on some political mission to save the black race and annihilate the whites as some pseudo-commentators are inclined to think. They are out to get what they want at any cost and from whomever they identify as their target."

"I'm so angry that I just want to kill. I gave the police everything and they did absolutely diddly squat." Hijacking victim Claire Jones, who said that police bungled her case

In January the Safety and Security Minister and four police officers were ordered to pay R150,000 in damages to a frail, elderly couple and their daughter, after they were insulted, assaulted and unlawfully arrested and detained during a police raid on their home. Judas and Annah Mabena were hit and kicked when the police searched for their son at their KwaMhlanga home in Mpumalanga on August 3, 2003. The couple was arrested by one of the police officers who assaulted them when they tried to lay a charge. Their daughter Ivy Mabena (30) was awarded R20,000 in damages after the police told her that she "smelled bad" and should take a bath.

In July, Fanie Kriel was viciously assaulted by police after they mistook him for a burglar. After exchanging angry words with a neighbour who had called the police, Fourie was repeatedly hit with a baton, sprayed with teargas and kicked. "They kicked me in the stomach and the woman jumped on my legs and knees ... They yanked me by my hair and sprayed more teargas into my mouth and eyes." The police captain was unapologetic: "He said they had made a mistake, that I should calm down and 'leave it'."

"These cops should be arrested, charged and dismissed. Their motto is: 'When bored, get into a car, drive around, catch three or four foreigners and you have a cool R1,000 for lunch and girlfriends'. Ag sies, SAPS!" Letter to the *Daily Sun*

Suspending operasies

"There were makeshift beds under branches and blankets. Clothes hung on wire. A tub of moisturizer lay on the ground and a face cloth had been left on a branch to dry." *The Star* describes the "lair" of a pair of thieves in the veld in fascinating detail. The hideaway was discovered after a Randpark Ridge resident took matters into his own hands and tracked down stolen property in the servants' quarters of a nearby house

The economic downturn was blamed for all sorts of things. Even the spate of mall robberies that had South Africa's neokugels wondering whether they were prepared to die for manicures and skinny jeans was attributed to the recession. Fikile Mbalula explained the crime wave thus: "According to the experts it should be expected because of the economic conditions we find ourselves in today. The recession just hit us recently."

"There has been crime since before the recession," he added helpfully.

But others had suspended their operations until interest rates went down, as *Sowetan* columnist Nthabi Moreosele reported. "Mboweni forgets that it is the mothers who pay tjotjo to get their sons out of jail. Now the Magrizza's savings will only pay for minor crimes like assaulting a cheeky neighbour."

Relaying the comments of a young 'klevel' from Dundela in vernacular us, Moreosele wrote that mothers would not pay for "roof [robbery], dronk bestuur [drunk driving] or shoplifting. A R300 shake will have to go up to R1,000 to soften an official's heart so that the son can be released on free bail".

"He said mothers love their children very much and could not bear to think of their sons shivering in jail. He also said clevers like him had suspended their operasies until the rand and the interest rates went down."

"Judy Bassingthwaighte, director of *Gun Free SA*, firmly believes that the best defence against an armed murderer is to give him a back rub and read him romantic poetry." Blogger and cartoonist Jeremy Nell targets Gun Free SA

For others, crime was big business. Fred Khumalo noticed that in the suburbs the traditional Zulu watchmen, or *omantshingelane*, were no longer called security guards. "They were now called security executives, or security consultants. Many of them are now white! They've got huge companies such as ADT and Coin. And if you don't pay these buggers they'll do a David Bullard on you. If you don't pay these glorified *mantshingelanes* they'll turn a blind eye when you've pressed the panic button while you're under attack by the kwerekwere who's been doing your lawn."

A traditional Zulu specialty had been colonized by whites: "But the long and short of it is white big business has stolen from us, the Zulus, what we've always considered our terrain: looking after people's properties, especially if such a job held the prospect of beating someone up. Siyekeleni bo, sishaye izigebengu! (Leave us alone to beat up these criminals)."

"And, in any case, many of the Vusis I know are characters of shady reputation. Sun City prison is their preferred domicilium. So, I'd rather stay with what my detractors call a slave identity, or a Eurocentric identity, than be confused with some Vusi Khumalo who has been involved in some cash-in-transit heist." Fred Khumalo

What Australians need is a taste of the sjambok

"My name is Jeremy, and I am a South African. I am likely to steal you dry, so please keep all belongings close to you." Jeremy Nell, speaking at a wedding in Sydney

Australian criminals are no match for their South African equivalents, even if the Aussies are becoming more accomplished in fields such as car hijacking and ATM bombings. In August 2008, South African immigrant Dion Driman—and possible spiritual heir of the *mantshilinganes*—became a local celebrity after he sjambokked a group of gatecrashers who attacked him at his house in Wahroonga, which is a nice middle-class suburb in Sydney.

"It's a traditional African herdsman's whip," he explained of his weapon of choice. "It's something that won't maim or kill you but it will bloody well hurt."

Australians were impressed, "Dion Driman is the greatest Australian super hero, even though he's South African, and he has no actual super powers," wrote one blogger. "Just a big stick."

Others were a tad more cynical, "When Gen Y yoofs and Seth Effricans start fighting, it's not like there is any REAL downside is there?" wrote one Aussie. "I mean LET THEM FIGHT TO THE DEATH, I say."

As for the local police, another commented. "I'd like to think the NSW fuzzy muff are just trotting out the time-honoured 'don't try this at home' bilge for the meeja, and half-arsedly investigating any supposed use of excessive force."

"Nah, it's rare any of us give big ups to the Yaapies, and fair enough because they're not the most likeable of peeps (that whole apartheid thing seemed a bit, I don't know, racist?)," he reflected. But he did allow that "this was exceptionally cool".

Perhaps Bheki Cele, Brandon Huntley and Dion Driman should get together for a bosberaad. Between, they should be able to come up with something.

> "I'll say this much and you can quote me: This country's fucked until the government can start to do something about the crime." Lolly Jackson speaks out after one of his strippers was robbed. The police took so long to arrive that Jackson eventually flagged down a passing patrol car

Chapter 10

Men, Women and the Bits in Between:
Pomp and Ceremony

"The worst thing about drinking, apart from waking up to find a wedding ring on your finger, is the hangover." Ben Trovato

In South Africa, penis size is a matter of life and death.

We know this because in September 2008, three men died of gunshot wounds after an argument over the dimensions of their dingeses. The argument took place between two groups of white and Indian men at the Merseyside Restaurant and Bar at the Queensmead Mall in Umbilo in Durban.

As a police officer later explained, "The white man went to the toilet and an Indian guy followed him. While in the urinal, the Indian man told the white man that his penis was bigger than his [that of the white man]. The white man left the urinal and told his friends about what had happened and this is when the argument started."

Five Indian men—two of whom were police inspectors—then left to fetch their guns and returned a short while later, opening fire on their opponents and killing three of them. Two others were rushed to hospital in a critical condition, but survived. The killers claimed that they were victims of a racist attack and had shot their victims in self-defence.

"She said that I must go to a doctor to get my penis enlarged. She said she was tired of me and had another man." Ockie van den Berg, on trial for allegedly beating his wife to death with a spanner. His wife had also told him that he was not the father of one of their sons

Some would say that the Umbilo shooting suggests that some South African men have an inferiority complex when it comes to measurements of their genitalia. But if research is to be believed, South African men generally have a remarkably high opinion of themselves.

What women had always suspected was confirmed in a global survey by Synovate, which found that 78% of South African respondents believed that they were sexy.

By way of comparison, 78% of Malaysian and 66% of French men believed they were not sexy. Only Greek and Russian men outranked South African men when it came to shameless narcissism.[1]

Given the obsession of South African men with themselves in general and their dangly bits in particular, one can perhaps sympathize with the HIV-positive Standerton man who developed breasts as a result of ARV therapy. "I am forced to remain indoors because whenever I take a stroll on the streets, people stare at me and some even laugh uncontrollably when they see my big boobs," he said.

> "I am now in my 90s, married twice and the father of two sons, both 'intact'. I swim every day, wearing nothing and don't mind at all if friends and neighbours see me. In fact I recommend it!" Reverend John Oliver sharing a little too much in a letter to *The Citizen*, on the subject of circumcision

Not all South African women necessarily agree with this positive assessment. "What is it with men today?" wondered one *You* reader. "They don't know how to treat a woman. I always get the wrong type and I'd like to find a down-to-earth Christian man who would like to get married. Where do I find him? Nowhere, because there are no real men out there. They're spineless takers and should be shipped off to Mars to give us women a break."

One woman famous for a similarly low opinion of men is Kuli Roberts, who writes the Bitch's Brew column for *Sunday World*.

"I don't need a man," she declared. "Hell, I don't even need sex. I've been without it for a couple of months now and I feel fine. No itch or sudden rash; just getting on with life." There are plenty of advantages to "not having a man," she said, "including not having to be nice to toothless relatives with body odour," or being paranoid "when he sneaks into the bathroom to answer calls like the whore he is" and not having to listen to lies "about him

---

[1] South African men also favoured the clean-shaven look (90%) while 68% used lip balm. In a finding that deserves to be featured in the next South African Tourism campaign, 88% of South African men said they used deodorant, compared to a global average of 72%. South Africa: alive with the probability of encountering less B.O.

being out with the boys when he is with his slut who relies on R5 airtime."

One man who seemed to demonstrate Ms Roberts' low opinion of men was the husband of Maria Kubong. He beat her up for calling out her neighbour's name while she was dreaming. She was having nightmares after their house was robbed, she explained. "My husband began beating me, saying I was making love in a dream and calling out our neighbour's name."

The husband refused to give his side of the story, saying it was a family matter which did not include the *Daily Sun*.

> "Men's biggest problem is their pride. They should forget about their pride and become the head of the household again the way God intended them to be." Farmer, preacher and Hansie's boet's china, Angus Buchan of *Faith Like Potatoes* fame

Yolandi van Rooyen started a site called donotdatehim.co.za, saying she wanted to help women who had "struggles with men". "The aim is not for the website to be about mudslinging," she explained. "It is a serious matter."

Warnings about men on the site include comments such as: "Girls, watch out for this mommy's boy. He still lives with her in Roodekrans. He has no spine and has to sleep around (with the help of Viagra) to make himself feel better" and "This man targets women with property because he does not have a place to stay. Before you know it, he has moved in with you. Stay away!!"

By January, the site had over 14,000 registered users. An article in *You* prompted one woman to write to the magazine, saying she was married to a "self-serving psychopath" for seven years. "He didn't tell me he had cancer, lied to me, got me to pay for everything we needed, fraudulently, bankrupted my medical aid, and then died leaving me with nothing. I hope his soul rots in hell."

One woman came up with a novel way to deal with her cheating husband's mistress. First her husband moved out of their home into a double cab bakkie parked outside. Then, a couple of months later, the wife discovered that he was keeping a mistress inside the vehicle. She promptly caught the woman, tied her up with cable and wire, and called the *Daily Sun* to record the incident.

Another woman beat up her ex-fiancé with an umbrella in front of his new girlfriend and tried to set him alight after pouring petrol over him. "Fortunately, I managed to overpower her and took the matches away," said *Sowetan* Mpumalanga bureau chief Riot Hlatshwayo—what were his parents thinking? "She is a dangerous woman," he said." I am telling you. She even instructs her new boyfriend to intimidate and verbally assault me over the phone."

"I don't understand it. The man has pop-out eyes like [the old SABC TV character] Knersus. He's the meanest man on earth. He stole my wife when I lost my leg about two years ago. And then, a week after divorcing me, she realized her things had been stolen." Henk Schoeman, whose wife Ria left him for Oudtshoorn Casanova and con man Johann Garbers

The saga of rival lovers Bianca Ferrante and Donne Botha continued to take up column inches. In 2000, Botha allegedly attacked Ferrante with a champagne bottle while the latter shared the bed of insurance billionaire Douw Steyn. The state declined to prosecute, so Ferrante launched a civil suit. *Noseweek* reported that Steyn first threatened to kill Ferrante, then showed up apparently drunk at the Wynburg magistrate's court. Steyn emptied a bottle of Evian over his head, and then borrowed a knife from one of his bodyguards, which he used to cut off his shirt at the elbow and his trousers at the knees.

"I'm scared of women," wrote a *You* reader, and after reading these stories it's not hard to agree. "I know they'll move mountains when it appears God is taking too long, sweating and shovelling until they get what they want.

"Why did her husband's ex want him back, especially after he told her that he didn't want any contact with her?" she wondered. "I've been where you are lady and, believe me, you're wasting your time. Use your time to find your own man and move on."

"Do you know how difficult it is to find a decent-looking straight man? Most of the time I feel as if I'm in a zoo with all these creatures walking on two legs." Kuli Roberts

Former athlete Heidi McIntosh confessed to the murder of her husband after a decade of silence. "It was a very traumatic ten years," she told the judge. "I was never happy. Whenever something bad happened I thought it was happening to punish me." McIntosh said that she had wanted a divorce, but that her husband had threatened to commit suicide if she left him. She also said that one of the contributing factors was her late husband's racism. "I went to the gun safe and got the shotgun. I loaded it. I then went to my husband and shot him. I went to my neighbour and told him my husband had committed suicide."

McIntosh was sentenced to five years' imprisonment.

> "Makhwapheni/Roll-on—Origin: makhwapheni is a plural for armpits hence the referral to roll-on. When you are cheating you would like to keep the affair under wraps; refers to someone you are cheating with." *Sowetan* slang blog

Hendrika Coetzee was luckier; she got away with a five-year postponed sentence for killing her boyfriend—who was wheelchair-bound—over a fried egg. Prosecutor Sol Sefike had argued that she should face a jail term. "She asked a paraplegic to prepare her food, while she is normal and healthy. The defence witnesses paint her as an angel and the deceased as the devil, but a person lost his life and is now six feet under in a cold grave." Magistrate Kallie Bosch found that the abuse to which she had been subjected by her boyfriend, Gavin James, triggered the attack.

It was perhaps inevitable that one of the more bizarre love stories of the past year or so should emerge from Delmas, famous for dog murderers, keeping-it-in-the-family sex and various nasty diseases. Zelda Fourie, a 34-year-old deaf-mute abattoir worker married to a deaf-mute man, claimed that she was kidnapped, held captive and raped by a group of men from the local squatter camp.

Police, members of a commando, the community and her relatives, had searched for her for five hours before finding her late on a Saturday evening in a squatter hut in Botleng with four men and three women, all of whom were naked or semi-naked.

The following Monday, the cracks in the story started to appear. By Wednesday, Fourie's story had changed. She dropped the charges and admitted that she loved one of the men she had accused. The media did not follow up with any reports on the state of Zelda's marriage. One can only assume there were a lot of awkward silences in the Fourie household.

> "Ag shame. We women are tired of pretty boys who think they're God's gift. Give us real men like Daniel Craig." Letter to *You* magazine, in response to an article about Top Billing handyman Janez Vermeiren

Celebrity divorces included Mark Fish, Uyanda Mbuli, Herschelle Gibbs, Tumi Masha and Steve Hofmeyr.

Herschelle Gibbs's wife Tenielle filed for divorce two days before their first wedding anniversary. "I've got record of every payment you made whilst I have been away Tenielle, nice one! I am taking my credit card tonight thanks!" he SMSed her after hearing the news. Tenielle demanded close to R100,000 a month to maintain the standard of living to which she had become accustomed. She also said that Gibbs would think nothing of spending more than R50,000 on art and furniture in an afternoon of shopping. (What kind of art? Does Herschelle have good taste?)

Gibbs's mother Barbara never did approve of the marriage. "I was so unhappy about their marriage. He works so hard for his money and deserves a wonderful wife—not this woman, who's always been bossy and just wanted her own way."

According to Barbara, Tenielle was "aggressive", "manipulative" and "a barrier between my son and me". As far as she was concerned, Tenielle should get nothing. "Tenielle entered the marriage with no money, without a blue bean. And now she must leave it with no money. Her demands are bloody nuts! That woman never worked. All she did, all day, was sit in the sun smoking her long cigarettes, like a bloody madam. And now she's sucking him dry. What nerve."

Mark Fish also filed for divorce, saying that he and his wife Loui were no longer able to communicate. In court papers he described her as "moody, quarrelsome, belittling and bombastic" and said he had lost his love, affection and trust for her.

> "Inexplicably, women consider television watching, beer drinking and important scrotal-arranging activities to be the same as doing nothing." Ben Trovato

In May, *Huisgenoot* reported that Steve Hofmeyr and his wife were planning a ceremony to renew their wedding vows after he had recovered from being hospitalized for a perforated colon. This proved to be somewhat premature; by October, they had announced that they were going to divorce. In the mean time, Hofmeyr's long-time mistress, Janine van der Vyver, sued for damages. She claimed that Hofmeyr had promised to leave his wife and to fund a business venture.

Things got worse for Hofmeyr when Nelmari Kruger revealed that she had had a four-month affair with Hofmeyr three years before and still had burn marks on her calf from his motorbike's exhaust pipe from the first time they had sex—in the veld, on the day of his seventh wedding anniversary. Kruger said she would like to apologize to Steve's wife. "I'm sorry I did it," she told *Huisgenoot*. "I shouldn't have. I really don't understand how she can stay with him after everything that has happened."

You readers were not impressed. "Nelmari, why air your dirty laundry? You've got involved with an MBA (Married But Available) knowing what you were getting yourself into. Leave Steve alone. He's still my hero with the voice of an angel."

"You silly girl. What did you expect—a pat on the back? You've humiliated yourself in front of the whole country and you should be ashamed of yourself. Why didn't you just keep your big mouth shut!"

"I don't care how popular Steve is—he's nothing but a skirt-chasing dog. How could Nelmari even think of having sex with him in the house he shares with his wife and sons? She might as well have been paid for her services."

As for the news of van der Vyver's lawsuit, one *You* reader wrote, "Get real, ladies. If you get involved with a married man who already has a reputation as a womanizer you're nothing short of stupid or publicity-seeking gold-diggers. Steve, you should zip it up."

'Pathetic' of Strand said she had no sympathy for women who have adulterous affairs and then "bleat about being hard done by", but Steve Hofmeyr boggled her mind. "He's so full of his own importance yet he's so mediocre, even as a singer. The silly women he has used for 'popstar diversions' (asseblief!) have obviously bought into his illusion that he's someone special."

'Leave him' defended Steve on the grounds that he was human and everyone makes mistakes. "I'm disappointed in the women he's been involved with: he was good enough then, now they want to drag his name through the mud. I don't believe in affairs but I like Steve and enjoy his music."

> "Ask [the people with me] if there was any time to go even to the church on that trip—there wasn't even time for that, much less this nonsense." Springbok coach Peter 'Div' de Villiers, aka Twakkie, on rumours of the existence of a tape of him engaged in sexual activities with a woman who was not his wife

Joost van der Westhuizen was accused of being the mysterious figure in a video of a woman performing fellatio on a man. A man had phoned him up, he said, and told him,

"Jou kak begin nou." He swore his innocence, saying that the socks and underpants worn by the man in the video were unlike any he owned.

"First, I don't own a pair of Polo socks in any shade. Amor buys my clothes and she's never bought me Polo socks," he explained.

"Secondly, I don't have a pair of underpants, in any shade, with 'holes' in. If they mean holes as in the underpants need mending, it's nonsense. Our domestic worker has been instructed to summarily throw out any worn-out garments. If they mean those underpants that old men wear that's made from mesh fabric, I also don't own any of those. I wear ordinary Jockeys."

"It is common knowledge," noted the article in *Beeld*, "that Van der Westhuzen has a tattoo on his buttocks."

As for the footage of the man snorting drugs, "I snort nothing," said Joost.

Amor said, "In this crisis Joost and I find strength from Above, and from our many friends who support us and pray for us." Later, after she and Joost decided not to sue the media for releasing the video, special investigator Mike Bolhuis said, "Joost and Amor still love each other very much and are happily married. The longer this drags on, the more pressure it puts on them."

Never one to let a good advertising opportunity go by, Nando's put out an ad reading, "Joost, if you're not eating at home, eat at Nando's." At the broadcast of a Bulls game against the Blues, Darren Scott of Supersport said to Kobus Wiese, "The guy you're standing with sounds a lot like Joost, but doesn't look like him" while at the match itself, a banner in the stands read: "Joost soek Amor en More en More ..."

Joost told Jacaranda 94.2: "They can take my name and my body, but they cannot take my soul."

> "I have always felt that people can't go around grabbing my crotch willy-nilly without invitation. I have perfected the art of doing just that by myself since I was 13, thankyouverymuch." Ndumiso Ngcobo reflects on the latest Somizi Mhlongo scandal. Mhlongo was accused by a fan of indecent assault after he allegedly fondled the man's crotch when he asked for an autograph

Speaking of souls, one has to doubt whether either Stuart Ireland or his estranged wife Sylvia were in possession of such a thing, since it's likely that they would have mortgaged it off long ago to pay for all the bling. The most entertaining divorce case of the year first came to the attention of the public in the November 2008 edition of *Noseweek*. The article reported that proprietors of expensive boutiques across Cape Town were devastated when Mrs Ireland's money supply was finally cut off. Callaghan in Cavendish Square was owed R1.5 million and the Jimmy Choo shop on the Waterfront R664,000. Lulu Tan Tan, also on the Waterfront, got off relatively lightly with an unpaid bill of R342,000. That was for just three months' worth of purchases. (Mrs Ireland's long platinum blond tresses were comparatively cheap: only R20,000 to R30,000 a month.)

Noseweek was enthralled: here was a tale for the times. "For a start, the obsessive, heartless pursuit of profit, followed by equally obsessive and pointless consumption/shopping: the complete absence of sense and sensibility.

"Here it comes with obsessive, loveless, essentially masturbatory sex to match." For here was the clincher: "Wasn't it inevitable—even if we are a little shocked—that, in the midst of the money maelstrom, we would find a supposedly respectable someone fucking someone that he definitely ought not to have been?"

> "He showed me *Debbie Does Dallas* and told me that is how you have to do it. I was 24 years' old and still a virgin. I had no idea what a blowjob was." Cezanne Visser, also known as 'Advocate Barbie', tries to account for her transformation "from a prudish virgin to into a cheap woman", during her trial at the Pretoria High Court

For it turned out that Sylvia had been having a torrid affair with none other than the expensive psychiatrist who was charging her husband R2,000 a week to sort out her fragile mental state. It seemed that the time billed as "individual therapy" and "extended therapy" involved little more than bonking sessions, even at the Ireland home when Stuart was out walking the dogs.

Stuart was so oblivious to what was going on that he appointed the psychiatrist as a director of his company—no concerns about a conflict of interest there—and took him on luxurious business trips. Meanwhile, the psychiatrist started sending Sylvia what he imagined to be erotic SMSes at regular intervals during the day, every day, for months. (Those quoted by *Noseweek* mostly involved fantasies of being tied up, though one rather morosely acknowledged, "Sadly, I am nowhere near driving a Bentley.")

Sylvia, who said that the psychiatrist abused his power over her and that what they had was "slavery, not a relationship", finally ended the relationship in February. He resigned as a director of the company and she lodged a complaint with the Health Professionals Council of South Africa.

> "Some women, when they go to a party, get more emotional support from the expensive new handbag they're clutching than they get from their husbands." Former *Cosmopolitan* editor Jane Raphaely

Things finally came to a head in August, when Stuart had a divorce summons served on Sylvia. In an affidavit in which he accused Sylvia of "frittering away exorbitant amounts of money" and having "blatantly terrorist objectives", he stated, "She became emotionally manipulative and subjected me to endless threats to sabotage my business, damage my reputation and to do me physical harm if I did not acquiesce to her outrageous demands to transfer to her bank account large amounts of money she demanded on an almost daily basis." He accused Sylvia of shouting at his employees and insulting his business associates, including an SMS in which she told one of his business partners that his "bride looks like Frankenstein" and advising him to get a "personality transplant". He also claimed that she had attacked him with a meat cleaver, smashed his SL500 with a hammer, slashed its tyres and shredded 30 of his silk ties.

She in turn said he "threatened and bullied" her, and used visits to their dog, Jack, to gain access to their home in order to show it to estate agents. "My dear Stuart, I would like a divorce," she had written earlier in the year. "I have come to not only dislike you, but to also despise you … Anyway, on a lighter note, even my dogs have stopped scratching themselves since you were removed from the premises."

> "Google me, baby. You'll find that I'm well connected." Sandton pick-up line, as recorded by Nikiwe Bikitsha

Stuart hit back in an SMS. "Typical, you think only of yourself, you don't give a damn about Jack otherwise you wouldn't punish him, knowing full well how fond he is of me," it read. "The house has to be sold … Anyway, I wouldn't have thought that it holds many pleasant memories for you … As for me, since you told me that he [the psychiatrist] fucked you in almost every room you can perhaps understand why I have no feelings about the house being sold."

Stuart offered to pay Sylvia maintenance of R20,000 a month, but she said this would barely cover the monthly costs of the dog walker (R2,000), florist (R3,000) and security guards (R10,000). She also wanted him to pay for Botox, hair appointments, a new Mercedes C180 every three years and four first-class international air tickets every year.

To indicate the desperation of her circumstances, she said she had been forced to sell jewellery worth R30,000 to make ends meet after her husband turned off the money tap. She said this was unfair as he was paying R65,000 a month for his R3million Bentley while "pleading poverty".

> "Wow. I am happy for my ex-husband and his future wife. May they get what they deserve." Kuli Roberts

The credit crunch prompted the wives of rich men to start divorce proceedings on the grounds that the money no longer justified their husbands' affairs. Celebrity divorce lawyer Billy Gundelfinger said that his practice could not cope with all the new business. "A lot of marriages among wealthy people have been on the rocks for years, and wives have been prepared to overlook [their husbands' infidelities] because of the lifestyle—but no more," he explained. "The guys with big money are not just less wealthy; a lot of them have been badly, very badly, burned."

Less financially flush couples decided it was cheaper to stay together. A Sandton-based marriage counsellor called Debbie Bright told the *Sunday Times*: "My intake of couples in the last three months has doubled; the credit crunch is definitely bringing people into therapy." Perhaps they would be wise to keep in mind the case of Ixopo resident Bonisile Eunice Mveve, who murdered her estranged husband with a pickaxe one night in February 2009. The couple, who were in the process of getting divorced, shared the same house. Police said they had no idea what had prompted her to attack her sleeping husband.

> "Robbing lobolo of its dignity is like a Jew urinating inside the synagogue, or a Seventh Day Adventist drinking alcohol on the Sabbath, or a Muslim eating pork inside the mosque. Peace, baf'ethu!" Fred Khumalo

One man who clearly enjoys the married life—despite one divorce and one suicide—is Jacob Zuma. Reports emerged that Jacob Zuma, not satisfied with the four wives and one fiancée he already had in his harem, was already making plans to take a sixth. Michael Zuma said his brother was not bothered by criticism. "There are a lot of men all over the country—politicians included—who have more than one partner, but they do not have the courage to come out in the open. They choose to hide things. By coming out, my brother is showing his mettle. And he is strengthening our paternal home."

Just what the country needs: more Zumas.

"So what is the collective noun for first ladies?" Hogarth wondered. "A bevy, a chorus, a choir? Or could we borrow from the movies and call it the 'the first wives' club'? Hogarth prefers 'an embarrassment of first ladies'." Hogarth also suggested that Zuma take a look at Book Four of the *Kama Sutra* for advice: "As translated in the Oxford version of the ancient Sanskrit handbook, its sections include: 'The Senior Wife; the Junior Wife; the Second-hand Woman; the Wife Unlucky in Love; Women of the Harem' and, perhaps most important, 'A Man's Management of Many Women'. Hogarth is confident he would have no use for Book Five: 'Other Men's Wives'."

> "My darling, I'm already married. And I'm in the NG Kerk. There we believe you only marry one person. That's the end, but that's that. How would Pastor Zuma manage to be president in any case if it takes him all day to kiss all his wives goodbye?" Evita Bezuidenhout explains why she declined Jacob Zuma's invitation to be his next wife

Asked about which of his wives would be first lady, Zuma said, "There is no first lady ... I think it's an old debate between those who have been colonized and those who were colonizing," he explained. "It's a wrong debate which people write long columns about. There's no magic about the 'first lady'. If you've got wives, what is important is that you are able to deal with them. If there is an occasion, one day we will have the wife we are with, another day we will have another one, it's not an issue."

So first the position of first lady is a rotating one.

"It's not the first wife, or the second wife, or the third wife that's involved," Zuma said, "it's the president. Is the president able to lead a country?"

Which was the question everybody has been asking.

"The only number one is satisfying me." ACDP leader Reverend Kenneth Meshoe, referring to his wife Lydia

In contrast to Zuma, Kgalema Motlanthe was known as the Monk of Mahlamba Ndlofu. The acting president seemed to have no prurient private life to speak of, so when the *Sunday Independent* reported that he was separated from his wife and was in intimate relationships with more than one other woman including a 24-year-old, allegedly pregnant with his child, there were sighs of relief all round. "Motlanthe to wed his 16-V!" crowed the *Sunday World*.

As Pumla Dineo Gqoka observed rather glumly, "Sex with multiple partners is so entrenched in southern Africa that it is a religion, a basic moral philosophy for most people here."

Now that South Africans knew that Motlanthe wasn't some kind of ghastly asexual freak, they felt much more comfortable with him at the helm, and when the ANC condemned the media for intruding into Motlanthe's private life, everybody knew that things were back to normal.

A woman claiming to be Motlanthe's lover then phoned Kaya FM with a request to have her favourite songs played. These included 'Heaven Sent', 'Let's Get Married', 'When I Say I Do', 'Incomplete', 'Because of You', 'Never Love Again', 'Fallen Again', 'Don't Matter' and' Colour of Love'. "No prizes for guessing what she was trying to tell him," observed Hogarth.

The woman was later shown to have lied, but in the meantime, the *Mail & Guardian* canvassed ordinary South Africans for their opinion on Motlanthe's pecadilloes. It was perfectly understandable, opined Mike Mogale of Limpopo. "It is known in our societies that younger women are more exciting than older women ... they are soft and sexy. Married women tend to be very boring, that's why we men try to score the young ones. Personally, I think that Motlanthe behaved like a real man ... Real African men always have lots of women."

So there you have it.

In the end, those South African men who do wish to accumulate lots of women would do well to bear in mind the advice of Nikiwe Bikitsha, and stop assuming that women are only interested in how much money they have. "So, brothers, a little heads-up," she explains, "it's not what is in your pockets we're after but that little beating drum behind your breast pocket. Your hearts ... Maybe then we'll see about what's in your pants."

"If you never wear high heels, rather stand on a telephone book or two—you don't want to make an impromptu bollemakiesie by accident." *Women24*'s sex columnist offers advice to those attempting the "somewhat silly, very vigorous and proudly South African" Bouncing Bontebok, in an article on sex positions

Chapter 11

Talking Kak about Playing Kak:
Sport

"News just out: South Africa took three gold medals this morning. Security caught them at the gate." Joke that did the rounds online after South Africa's disastrous performance at the Beijing Olympics

"South Africans talk an amazing amount of kak about sport," reflects Carlos Amato. "If we could bottle and export our output of half-baked opinions about local soccer, rugby and cricket, we'd soon have a trade surplus to rival China's.

"After a team loses, we all get onto on our high donkeys, screaming that the coach blundered criminally by not picking the sublime player X. Had player X featured in the defeat, we would have lambasted the coach for picking that well-known palooka, name of player X.

"Hindsight is like dagga: it gives delusions of profound insight."

That said, the biggest load of kak served up in relation to any kind of sport was offered, not by South Africa's sports fans, but courtesy of Foreign Minister Nkosazana Dlamini-Zuma when she said, apropos of the government's decision to deny a visa to the Dalai Lama, "If there is a sporting event it must remain a sporting event. We have seen how messy it can be if you begin to pull all sorts of issues into the sporting event."

"You're grouped as incompetent ... disorganized ... irrational ... zero people skills! A bright future awaits you as national sports administrators!" A guidance counsellor in a Zapiro cartoon addresses three schoolboys

"Butana Khompela—piss off you racist pig and leave our Springbok alone. So much for reconciliation—Ha!" 'Butana Khompela hater', comment, Democratic Capitalist

Turning the bokkie into biltong

Chairman of the parliamentary sports committee, Butana Khompela, would surely not agree with her. "People say sport should not be political," he said during his campaign to turn the Springbok emblem into biltong. "Sport has always been political in South Africa; it has been used as a guillotine for black people."

(Komphela also charged that SASCOC (the SA Sports Confederation and Olympic Committee) was "full of whites and Indians who don't understand transformation and lack vision". His comments were slanderous and racist, said SASCOC president Moss Mashishi.)

"I will never buy a Bok item, attend a match or watch any Bok broadcast ever until the team coach and players are selected on merit again and the emblem is protected. That is my prerogative as it is the ANC's prerogative to destroy the game and the proud history of the Boks," a distraught rugby fan vented in the page s of *The Citizen*. Let's see how long this latest exercise by the ANC in political engineering lasts when the Boks begin losing games and money, and stadiums are empty. The Boks, like Bafana Bafana, and the country are ruined forever."

Khompela and his comrade-in-arms, Cedric Frolick, caused much angst for the rugby ous when they not only launched a vicious attack on the Springbok, but threatened to "take stadiums away from rugby". Frolick denied this, saying, "There are people who engage in criminal activity of a racist nature when they leave the stadium. But I never labelled all people who watch rugby as criminals." He said that new stadiums being built for 2010 should be "points of integration" without historical "baggage".

> "Yes, there is animosity between us, I told him he was power-crazy and egotistical but I never swore at him." Mickey Arthur on former Cricket South Africa president Norman Arendse. Arendse had laid a complaint against Arthur calling for his axing as a selector

Freedom Front Plus leader Dr Pieter Mulder presented a large colour photograph of Nelson Mandela in his Springbok rugby jersey to Khompela. "That the honourable Komphela looks at this photograph of Mandela dressed in a Springbok jersey and realizes that this is the jersey on which he wants to puke," he declared in a motion to Parliament.

"Has Butana Komphela become the Julius Malema of sports?" wondered *Citizen* reader Nhlamulo Mondlane. "For him to say he will take all the stadiums belonging to rugby clubs leaves a lot to be desired. Someone must bring him back to earth because he thinks he is God. I bet he has an H or GG symbol in one of his matric subjects."

As if that wasn't enough, Sports Minister Makhenkesi Stofile made an arse of himself when he declared that SARU owed money to the government for the use of the Springbok emblem. "I can give you the registration numbers," Stofile said. "We own the emblem. It was registered for the small Bok, the big Bok, the Bok jumping to the right, the Bok jumping to the left ..."

Then some trademark lawyers piped up that, actually, SARU owned the rights to the Springbok—not the state. The government had registered the trademarks, but because SARU already owned them, it was invalid. And in any case, they hadn't paid the renewal fees.

"Flowers, of course, wilt, lose their petals, and their stems droop. A bit like Bafana Bafana, who unify the nation by losing nearly all of their matches. Vomiting on them would be like kicking a man when he's down." John Scott

The adventures of Pete Helium

"There's little difference between winning and losing, except that one feels better after winning." Peter de Villiers

When Peter de Villiers, aka Div, aka Twakkie, was appointed as the first non-white coach of the Springboks, SA Rugby president Oregan Hoskins said, "I want to be honest with South Africa and say that the appointment was not entirely made for rugby reasons."

Former Springbok captain Corné Krige predicted that South African rugby was in for seven years of drought. Andy Capostagno reported that the players' nickname for de Villiers was 'Pete Helium' because his voice "sounds like most ordinary people after inhaling a lungful of the gas" But, he wrote, "it might as easily refer to the lighter-than-air rugby ideas that emanate from the man."

But what makes Peter de Villiers really special—at least, for the purposes of this book— is that he is quite possibly the most quotable man in South African sporting history.

"We played kak." Springbok coach Peter de Villiers after the Boks lost to the Wallabies in Durban

Even the Australians are entranced. Aussie journalist Greg Growden reported that colleagues told him that de Villiers' press conferences were hilarious, if confusing. "Watching him you can only think of cuckoo clocks and ticking bombs," Growden wrote. "Tick, tick, tick. How long before the final explosion?"

Dubbing de Villiers "the most eccentric coach in Springbok history", Clinton van den Berg reflected, "He may not know his scrum cap from his kneecap, but his contribution to rugby's lexicon is, as he might say, moerse impressive."

Asked about his team selection plans by a Welsh journalist prior to the Bloemfontein test, de Villiers suggested that he might "pull a rat out the hat".

Before the start of the Tri-Nations, he said, "I have such a wonderful bunch of guys to choose from and there is pressure on all of them to perform. But even if you're playing a game on the moon, if you have the skills and you play well, you will win."

"Thanks for that information." Peter de Villiers, in response to a long-winded question from a New Zealand reporter

The issue of race surfaced, inevitably. When former All Black Craig Dowd—who happens to be a Maori—called de Villiers a "puppet" and questioned his ability to do the job, South African Rugby chairperson Mpumelelo Tshume called on him to issue an apology: "Mr Dowd's comments are not only deeply and personally offensive to Peter de Villiers and SARU but also comically ill-informed on the affairs of South African rugby. We trust he will show rather better judgment in having the good grace to apologize to Peter de Villiers and to the South African rugby community for the profound offence and hurt he has caused."

"It's quite stupid to make a call like that," de Villiers responded. "I don't know Craig Dowd. The closest I got to him was on TV in my sitting room. I don't know if he ever saw me or knows me. What's his agenda? If it is racism or not, I've found out that in South Africa it's a big thing, racism, but in other countries, especially here and in Australia it is big too, really big, so maybe you can ask him that."

"Maybe it is time de Villiers' supporters face reality—when we criticize de Villiers we do not see skin colour, we see his inadequacies as a Springbok coach," argued Gavin Rich.

"I don't care if our coach bonks the entire West Coast cheerleading team, he must be judged strictly on his merits as a rugby coach." Michael Trapido on the possible existence of a Peter de Villiers sex tape

Martin Williams christened de Villiers 'Snor' and dismissed him as "this feeble joker". "If Peter de Villiers's moustache isn't distracting enough, worse damage is done when he opens his mouth," he wrote. "Never mind the strange voice pitch, although we may wonder how he barks instructions to two metres of towering testosterone."

De Villiers, he argued, was "cringeworthy". "Everyone's being far too polite. The Springbok coach is stupid, embarrassingly so. He talks too much and, if you can bear to listen carefully, a lot of it is nonsense."

While preparing for a Wellington test in New Zealand, de Villiers explained how he would motivate his team. "I'll tell them talk is cheap and money buys the whisky," he said.

After the Springboks lost 8–19, de Villiers was philosophical. "You win some, you lose some," he reflected, before complaining about the All Blacks' scrum tactics. "We just have to become illegal sometimes, too," he said. Asked why he'd substituted C. J. van der Linde, he replied: "He was hit in the larynx and that's why he had to come off. He was sounding like me."

"You won't believe me but I haven't read a newspaper in two years and I'm not about to start now." De Villiers responds to a report in the London *Observer* that his first team would include ten non-white players

When All Blacks boss Graham Henry criticized the Boks for late tackles on Dan Carter, de Villiers offered these words of wisdom: "I know dancing is also a contact sport, but rugby is far from dancing. If you want to run with the big dogs then sometimes you have to lift your leg." Asked how he felt after the Boks' first loss under his tenure, he said coaching the Boks would always be pressure but at his age nothing was new anymore. "When you're over 50, you're not so new anymore, you can ask my wife about that ...," he said. Before a clash with the Wallabies in Perth, he told the media, "What we try to tell them is when you point your finger into the sky, don't concentrate on the finger because you'll miss all the heavenly glory out there. Concentrate on the heavenly glory that you can bring and make yourselves so fulfilled."

When he was asked how the Springboks had celebrated a recent win over the All Blacks, de Villiers said, "We went wild, wild, wild—some of the guys went wilder than that. South Africans are normally great people and we'll take the bitter with the sweet. It's only the guys who don't feel part of that bitter or that sweet that will always moan and groan and say: 'Why do they go so wild?' Join in; we've got enough stuff to share with you."

After the All Blacks hammered the Boks 19-0 in Cape Town, he said, "I believe we're developing a style here that the whole world will fear."

When the Boks started losing again, de Villiers explained, "I was appointed to make rugby decisions. I promised to be honest and focus on rugby. We never said it was going to be a perfect world. If you look at the Bible, Joseph started out in the pit and ended up in the palace. There was a moerse lot of kak in between,"

> "I've never had a fallout with Peter de Villiers." Cheeky Watson denies allegations that he referred to the Springbok coach as a "baboon who does not know what he is doing"

When rumours of a sex tape featuring de Villiers surfaced, the coach threatened to "give [the job] back to the whites ... I knew there were still people who do not want a black coach; I just never knew the extent people would go to discredit me," he said.

In his defence, de Villiers told the *Sunday Times* he would not have had time to engage in illicit behavior; was too tired anyway, and didn't even watch pornography in overseas hotels. "If you go through my hotel accounts overseas, where you know they have channels where you can look at that [pornographic] stuff, hey—you can see I never ever entered one of those movies: I don't even bother to do it in my room, so why would I go out looking for that kind of stuff ... and risk my family?"

Hayibo.com reported that South Africans "begged" the media not to show them the tape: "human rights groups fear that millions of citizens could be 'deeply scarred' by seeing footage of 'a stocky middle-aged man with a handlebar moustache putting the moves on a woman in the back seat of her station-wagon".

David Moseley suggested that Thabo Mbeki would make a good replacement for de

Villiers. "Mr Mbeki is black (but like black, black. Not coloured black. So that's at least three points for transformation), he's used to leading a team that doesn't want to listen to him and surely being an ex-president will exclude the usual political fiddling with Bok selection."

> "The ball didn't always get to the wings. We could not throw the ball around willy-nilly and if that happened people would have said I was stupid not to stay conservative." Peter de Villiers

After the Springboks defeated the Wallabies by 53 points to 8, de Villiers said, "The same people who threw their robes on the ground when Jesus rode on a donkey were the same people who crowned him and hit him with sticks and stuff like that, and were the same people who said afterwards how we shouldn't have done that, he's the son of God. So that's exactly what we do. You have to look at history is repeating itself, and I'm not saying that I'm God." Sighs of relief all round.

If comparisons to God and Joseph were not enough, even Princess Di got dragged into it. "Criticism appears in newspapers everywhere. People don't just want to hear that the world is good. They don't like progress. People prefer to write about things that will sell newspapers," he told a press conference at which he also referred to English flyhalf Danny Cipriani as 'Capriati'. "Some years ago Di died tragically. People made a big deal out of the rumours and never said 'shame'."

> "One thing you can be sure of when attending a Peter de Villiers press conference is that he'll always give you something to write about," observed Carly Weinberg

> "World champions? Yes, but it proves the standard at last year's tournament was the lowest in its history." New Zealand journalist Wynne Gray assesses the Springboks in the New Zealand *Herald*

After the Boks' less-than-impressive performance against the British and Irish Lions, Div suggested that criticism of Ricky Januarie's game was motivated by racism. Januarie made one mistake on Saturday, said de Villiers, "but so did other players."

"What I have learnt in South Africa is the following: if you take your car to a garage to be repaired and the owner is black and he doesn't do a good job, you will never take it back there again. But if the owner is white and the garage makes a mistake, people say, never mind, he made a mistake and will take it back again. That is how some people live their lives in this country. I respect people and their opinions but I don't have to listen to them," he added. As for worrying about the opinions of others, de Villiers said, "I like doing my own thing and I don't care what other people think. Their opinion is just that, an opinion. I can't listen to 43 million people's opinions because then I won't know where I am."

De Villiers also said that people were not giving the Bok victory the appreciation it was due. "The one thing that people appear to forget is the result. We won the test. We waited 12 years to win this match and we did it. We are very, very, very satisfied with it. We never said we were going to beat them by a lot of points, we will win with one point and be satisfied."

"We are very organized at the moment, we don't want to become a fruit salad, so 15 will be Ruan's number and 10 will be Morné's number." Div prior to the 2009 Tri-Nations match against Australia in Perth

"SuperSport's unashamed bias in rugby commentary is typified by the bland and bombastic commentator Hugh Bladen, who acts as a sort of glorified cheerleader as he yells out encouragement from behind the microphone. All that he's missing is a skimpy skirt and a pair of generous boobs, although his banal comments act as boo-boobs quite on their own." Derek Daly

Luke the Puke Watson

"The buffoons who run rugby at Newlands thought that by hiring Rassie as their coach, they could turn a smooth sauvignon blanc into a potent mampoer that would be strong enough to win the Super 14." Archie Henderson

Luke Watson became the most hated man in Pretoria after he reportedly told an audience at the University of Cape Town that he wanted to vomit on the Springbok jersey and that rugby was "run by Dutchmen". Watson later rebutted the claims. "How could I possibly be accused of an anti-Afrikaans attitude when my maternal grandmother is a van Rensburg, my paternal great-grandmother was a Schoeman and my aunt is a Swanepoel?" he said. But the damage was done, and soon he was universally known as 'Luke the Puke'.

When Watson played at Loftus, Blue Bulls fans brought along banners reading "Welcome to Loftus, the home of 50,000 Dutchmen!", "100% Dutchmen", "Luke Watson jou moer" and "Luke, we also want to puke when we see you".

In a reference to the Joost van der Westhuizen sex video scandal, one banner read "Luke, you wear Polo socks and holey underpants".

"Yeah. Let's jump on the bandwagon folks," reflected Siyabonga Nthsingila. "Boo Luke. Show the doos what for! Jeer him like he stole overexcitement from Noeleen," Still, he thought it was pointless to debate whether Watson was "a doos or a hero". And booing him at a rugby match was just not on. "Suffice to say, I think the behaviour of the supporters at Newlands was some way below par. The fourteen guys on the pitch with Luke do not deserve to be subjected—they are on the pitch with him, it matters to them too—to that kind of nonsense. If you don't like Luke, leave it for online forums and radio phone ins. Boo him at the mall if you like. It has no place at as great a cathedral of SA rugby as Newlands."

Death, taxes and Sepp Blatter

"There's also talk of 30,000 fans from Holland descending upon us. Great. More Dutchmen. Luke Watson will have a stroke." Ben Trovato on numbers projected for the 2010 World Cup

"It turns out there are three eternal certainties: death, taxes and the idiocies of Sepp Blatter," reflected Carlos Amato. "Only the four horsemen of the apocalypse could get the unloveable FIFA boss to shut up and, they would need to gallop directly into his office and convince him in person."

"Roll out Plan B Mr Blatter!" thundered Jon Qwelane. He felt that 2010 was a horrible waste of money, money that could be put to better use elsewhere: "In the meantime billions upon billions of rands have been poured into building these one-day wonders while the vast majority of South Africans go wanting, and the delivery of services is absolutely zilch," he thundered. "South Africa wanted to impress the world by staging a World Cup we did not need; we needed jobs, houses, first-class health facilities, good education, non-cut-throat food and petrol prices, and not a World Cup we could hardly affo·d."

There was drama in the Local Organizing Committee. Reports that communications head Tim Modise couldn't cut it began to circulate. Danny Jordaan had torn a strip off him, according to one staff member: "The way Danny spoke to Tim—God, I have never in my whole life heard a man speak to another man like that. He humiliates him in meetings in front of other staff members."

Even those sympathetic to the formerly popular broadcaster said he was "way, way out of his depth".

Modise later resigned and returned to the SABC.

For his part, Ben Trovato was concerned about the prospect of English football fans arriving in South Africa for the World Cup. "They are a species unlike any other," he wrote in a letter to Danny Jordaan. "If you mated a wildebeest with a warthog, you would get an English football fan ... Most of the money spent by the Brits will go on undersized crayfish, bail and lawyers' fees."

As for Australian fans, "Those smug bastards don't even have a soccer team, do they? As far as I know, their idea of football involves running around in sleeveless T-shirts and tight shorts batting the ball about like a bunch of poofters."

> "Free State Stars are about as fashionable as MC Hammer's luminous parachute pants, but you have to respect their grit, if not their style. Week after week and month after month these ill-mannered plaasjapies make the glamour boys sweat and fret." Carlos Amato

After calls were made to nationalize Bafana Bafana in an attempt to improve their performance, David Kau asked, "Hasn't it become clear that if you want to completely destroy something and lose money on anything—hand it over to the government?

"If you want to see soccer players queuing to get on the field because the referee hasn't come back from lunch, or waiting for two hours after kick-off time for the new coach to arrive from another coaching job, and potholes on the soccer field—go ahead and have the national soccer team nationalized."

"You have got to hand it to the South African Football Association for being known as the most pathetic organization in our country." Lesiba Langa of *The Citizen*. Even Home Affairs was better than SAFA, he said

One player attracted more of the wrong sort of attention than all of the others combined.

In his youth, Benni McCarthy sang a hit song with TKZee that declared "Benni's in the area!" "Nowadays Benni's in the cafeteria," observed Tsamaya of the *Sunday Times*. During a friendly against Australia it appeared that Benni "had consumed one Gatsby [a giant Capetonian chip-and-polony roll] too many during the off-season. Benni's voluptuous boep was attempting a long wobble to freedom from the confines of his figure-hugging shirt."

When Benni got out of friendlies against Norway and Portugal, he claimed it was due to a hamstring strain.

Hogarth wasn't buying any of it. "On previous occasions the bloated Mampara told us that he had family problems, that the football authorities were not being nice to him, that this or that ligament was not in order and ... and ... and ..."

What would his next excuse be, Hogarth wondered. "That the dog ate his togs? That he lost one of his diamond ear studs and he can't play when he's unbalanced in the bling department? Grow up, Mampara, grow up."

Lungani Zama said that somebody needed to "have the balls" to tell Benni that he is past it, "and he no longer needs to worry about missing his nanny shifts or trying to wobble to his Bentley in order to catch the next flight to tiny Johannesburg. He can have the bright lights of Blackburn, for good.

"There are enough young, hungry—well, we are all underfed compared to Benni, it seems—strikers trying to make their mark on the world stage. Give them a go, and let Benni wobble his way to anonymity."

"The last time Pirates won an official trophy Bin Laden had only released one DVD and his beard was still black." Ndumiso Ngcobo

Putting the bunny where it belongs

"Apart from when they play South African sports teams, Australians don't often feel too threatened. Even the seedy parts of their big cities have newborn lambs bounding happily in the streets, nibbling quietly on lush trailer park lawns." Marketing website Cherryflava

Test cricket, says Ben Trovato, "is about as exciting as watching the Sri Lankan team not getting shot at."

Those who watched South Africa's miraculous win over Australia at the WACA in January 2009 would no doubt beg to differ. *Citizen* reader Brett Chatz, for one, experienced "sublime euphoria, unbridled ecstasy" and "nirvana". "Our boys finally put the Australian bunny back where it belongs—in its little cage," he wrote.

Sports Illustrated editor Steve Smith was impressed that the Proteas took a more mature view of the victory. Former Australian batsman Mark Taylor suggested to man of the match A. B. de Villiers that this was the highlight of his career.

"Hmmm," said AB, "actually I've had a few important knocks this season ... against India and one against England ... so, ja ... it's tough to say."

"I swear Taylor actually took a step backwards he was so stunned by the answer," observed Smith. "Here was young de Villiers, having just whipped the glorious, all-conquering Australians, and he wasn't treating it like the greatest victory of his life."

"Bangladesh would battle to beat my local ski-boat on a bad day. To hear how well they played against these palookas is really pathetic." Pat Symcox puts South Africa's 2–0 win against the test minnows into perspective

Former Australian cricketer Jeff Thomson tore a strip off Australia's bowlers after their one day loss in Adelaide on Australia Day.

"From what I saw of the Australian attack the other day, what they bowled was absolute crap. Every one of them was terrible. I don't know where we go from here. We took two wickets. It looked like South Africa was playing a third-grade club attack.

"I'm not the only one who thinks that. What I saw the other night was just gun-barrel bowling. There was no creativity. Nobody likes bowling on a flat wicket with no swing, but that wicket [in Adelaide] the other night showed how wanting our bowling attack is.

"They better not be taking that refugee from Queensland that plays in Sydney. Nathan Hauritz should be called Nathan Horror. Does he spin the ball?"

"[South Africa's] fast bowlers couldn't hit a cow's arse with a banjo." Martin Johnson of the London *Daily Telegraph* on South Africa's ineffectual fast-bowling on the first day of the Lord's test

Chapter 12

Even God Votes ANC:
Religion

"It is an unequivocal biblical declaration that if God is for us, who can be against us." Jacob Zuma

In December 2008, two men were arrested after having been rescued from a 50-metre radio tower in Lenasia which they had climbed to be "closer to Jesus" on Christmas.

"When we arrived at the radio tower at 07.00, we found two men, aged 28 and 30, sitting on the tower from the night before for almost 20 hours with no water or food," said an ER24 spokesperson. The men refused to climb down, so paramedics and members of the fire department climbed the tower to speak to them. On the way, they found that one of the men had spread salt along the tower's ladder in order to "protect them". After two hours of negotiating, the men climbed down with the aid of a sky lift, and spent the rest of Christmas in jail.

Jesus isn't planning on returning any time soon, is he?

"People who love God must not play with their votes, they must vote for the ANC." Jacob Zuma

Their behaviour was particularly hard to explain in light of the fact that, in South Africa, the easiest way to get closer to God is to join the ANC.

In February 2008, Jacob Zuma declared that the ANC was the only political party to have been blessed by church leaders during its founding, and therefore the only organization that could legitimately rule South Africa.

Leaders of the Apostolic Faith Mission were not impressed. "We believe that Mr Zuma should stick to politics and leave out God in his campaign speeches or at least keep his comments to his own personal faith," they said.

Max du Preez pointed out that the National Party also thought that they were God's electoral choice. He was sure that Zuma would take the nation into his confidence and explain that Hansie Cronjé's Devil had prompted him to do those deals with Schabir Shaik. But what ultimately mitigated against divine support for Kangaman, argued Du Preez, was a failure to meet heavenly standards. "The ANC president should know one thing," he wrote. "The God most South Africans believe in is far more ambitious than to want Jacob Zuma to run our country."

JZ then reiterated his assertion that the ANC would rule until the second coming of Jesus. "Did JZ really say the ANC would rule until Jesus comes back?" wondered a *Citizen* reader. "Silly, but politicians do say the oddest things. Let's hope Jesus gets here fast. Bit worried though about him having his bags nicked at OR Tambo."

The satirical website Hayibo.com speculated on what might happen if Jesus did return. "Having told his supporters in October that the ANC would "rule until Jesus returns", party president Jacob Zuma has admitted that he is concerned by the claims from various fundamentalist Christian groups that the Messiah is likely to return some time this year, ending ANC rule before the 2009 election, read their report.

"Obviously at this point we need to consider Jesus a serious threat to ANC hegemony," said senior Zuma advisor, Rapture Ngwenya. "We also need to question whether the picture that has been painted of him in the white-run media as a Redeemer and a Prince of Peace is accurate," he added.

"After last weekend's claim by Jacob Zuma that the ANC is exclusively endorsed by God, party theologians have confirmed that opposition leader Helen Zille is "probably the Antichrist". Speaking to media at Luthuli House, a spokesman said that as leader of the opposition, Zille was "fomenting a direct assault on God by Satan's minions", as reported on Hayibo.com.

In December 2008, Ace Magashule likened the persecution of Jacob Zuma to that of Jesus. "Jesus was persecuted," explained Ace who, based on this demonstration of intellectual prowess, was presumably named after the mielie meal. "He was called names and betrayed. It's the same kind of suffering Mr Zuma has had to bear recently, but he's still standing strong. He's not giving up."

By now, Patricia de Lille had had enough. Pointing out that Jesus was never charged with corruption, she called on the ANC to "stop using Jesus Christ, the Bible and Christianity in general to garner votes from the poor and the vulnerable". She added, "Adultery, the machine-gun song and Zuma's failure to condemn war talk and hate speech by the ANC rank and file are examples of why it is insulting to compare Zuma with Christ."

Echoing her sentiments, ACDP leader Kenneth Meshoe urged the ANC to stop the comparisons. "Their habit of joking about and using the name of the Lord in vain is tantamount to blasphemy, and must be condemned in the strongest possible terms," he said. He was furious about the comparison of the "unrighteous and unholy" Zuma with Jesus. He warned that the ruling party's claim that it would rule until Jesus returned was arrogant, and "will cause them to lose the privilege of governing South Africa".

His criticism fell on deaf ears. Mpumalanga roads and transport MEC Jackson Mthembu said ANC members who had defected to COPE had never been loyal to the ANC. Quoting from the Bible, he said: "They went out from us but they were not of us; for if they had been of us, they would no doubt have continued with us; but they went out that they might be made manifest that they were not all of us."

(In response, others might be tempted to quote from Matthew 24, verses 4 and 5: "And Jesus answered and said unto them, Take heed that no man deceive you. For many shall come in my name, saying, I am Christ; and shall deceive many.")

> "Msholozi is a burning bush which will never be consumed." Eastern Cape representative attending an address by Jacob Zuma to religious leaders

At a gathering of religious representatives, the ANC's chaplain general Reverend Vukile Mehana told Zuma he must feel "safe". "You must know that you are safe. As we prayed for your predecessor, we will continue to pray for you. Don't shake. The God, your ancestors, are here."[1]

A representative of the Eastern Cape said that God's work was in evidence during the Nicholson judgment, which had resulted in Thabo Mbeki being relieved of his duties. "He [Zuma] was being burnt from all sides but the leaves became greener and greener." The same man also said that religion was the "midwife" of the ANC. "We are here as the religious leaders, as the midwives, to protect the ANC who is the baby," he said.

Closer to the elections, Zuma reiterated his view that God votes ANC. "When you preach in your churches, just explain to the congregation—in a paragraph—about the ANC," he

---

[1] Bit of hedging of bets there surely?

advised the clergy. "We in the ANC know God. When the ANC was born, it was baptized. We have respect, we are beautiful, we conduct ourselves in a good way ... I believe no one can argue South Africa is not based on the principles of God."

> "100% JC! Turn or Burn! Helen Zille is the anti-Christ! The end is not nigh! Jacob the Baptist for President!" Max du Preez imagines ANC election posters in the wake of Jacob Zuma's claims that God supports the ANC

At least we know that—according to Ray McCauley at least—Jacob Zuma is not "a devil with two horns and a tail" (although that strange bumpy bit on his skull has had a lot of us wondering). This was after McCauley invited the putative president to address a Rhema congregation prior to the elections. "Rhema believes the visit by Mr Zuma and his delegation gave the church an opportunity to minister in a significant way to the leader of the ruling party and his colleagues," said Rhema spokesperson Vusi Mona. He added that the number of those congregants who walked out during Zuma's address was "statistically insignificant".

> "McCauley's Jesus-on-steroids schtick is such powerful muti that it is hardly surprising he has wormed his way into the Love Pants inner circle as the leader of some 'inter-faith leadership' organization, a bunch of frauds and charlatans who are now apparently 'working with government' in matters of crime, corruption, moral regeneration and orphans." Andrew Donaldson

Bantu Holomisa then asked Rhema for the same opportunity. He was furious when Rhema said no, they would not allow him to speak to the congregation—but they would announce his presence. "Frankly, it begs a question about the integrity of some church leaders who decide for their congregations which political parties they should support or be exposed to," complained the former leader of the Transkei.

Citizen readers were not impressed. "Brother Ray, you have some repentance to do," commented one. "Rhema: Pick and Pray," snorted another. "How anyone can sit through a Ray McCauley 'preach', is beyond me. My hat off to Bantu Holomisa for klapping this R100-million-a-year clown."

Given his comments about JZ's horns and tail—or lack thereof—it is worth remembering that, as the spiritual adviser to the late Hansie Cronjé, Ray McCauley knows all about the Devil and his ways. Perhaps Pastor McOily would have agreed with the reader of the *Sunday Sun* who said that COPE's departure from the ANC reminded him that Satan "was kicked out from heaven through his arrogance to go and start his own kingdom". Furthermore, said the reader, the leaders of COPE had "Satanic interests".

One also wonders whether former Rhema employee Carl Niehaus, who was outed as a fraudster and serial spinner of yarns, had 'Satanic interests'.

As Max du Preez mused, "Perhaps the devil made him do it."

"The only person known to have paid money to see *Hansie: The Movie* says he was tricked by Satan. Hempies Smit, 28, of Brakpan, says he had no intention seeing the film about former cricket captain Hansie Cronjé, but was overcome by demonic forces at the box office. Smit is believed to have seen the entire film and is currently in a critical but stable condition." Hayibo.com

Satan gets into people

The Devil still got blamed for all sorts of things. KwaZulu-Natal Transport MEC Bheki Cele had launched the 2007 December holiday road-safety campaign by declaring that motorists were aware of the rules of the road. "But Satan gets into people," he noted. "They refuse point-blank to do the right thing."

(While we're on the issue of road safety, Afrikaans singer Dozi was convinced that being arrested for drunk driving after skipping a red light in Mossel Bay was a sign of divine intervention. "It was probably God's way of telling me not to drive further," he said. To drive the point home, the Almighty also ensured that Dozi spent the night in jail.)

Xolani Nyaba told the North Gauteng High Court that the devil was to blame for the fact that he kidnapped, raped and robbed Catherine Ivy Flietoor. "I was possessed by the Devil. I feel very bad about what I had done, which is why I pleaded guilty."

In a similar vein, the Krugersdorp matric pupil who walked into school one Monday morning and slashed a fellow pupil with a samurai sword claimed that the Devil had told him to kill three people that day (he only managed one). Fingers were pointed at the killer's favourite band, the heavy metal group Slipknot. They were responsible for the boy's murderous thoughts, argued religious leaders and readers of *Huisgenoot*.

Chris Roper was not buying the argument that music makes people kill. "With community leaders as dumb as this, it's no wonder kids go crazy," he reflected. "Dysfunctional kids will always find a reason to be screw-ups. Charles Manson claimed to kill for God, and George Bush does it for Democracy. Satan does not in fact write music, although he does on the odd occasion do backup vocals for Celine Dion."

> "Some of these people want to tattoo the Ten Commandments on my testicles while I'm eyeing their daughters." Steve Hofmeyr—who is not a churchgoer—on his audience

The Almighty was forced to take credit for some unpleasantness. Julius Malema, for instance, never went to school to learn how to be a politician; his talent was given to him by God. Or so said his aunt, Maropeng Mashatole. "I think if it was not politics, he would have been a priest. He loves his own voice," joked a friend.

So now you know: Julius is God's fault.

God also took credit for killing off a couple of joggers, at least according to Hansie Louw, the former leader of the African Christian Democratic Party in the Western Cape. Louw warned South Africans that God would take out His wrath on silly people who ran ultramarathons on Sundays. "Last year two athletes died during or after Comrades," he pointed out. "Was this a message from above? How many athletes will run with this type of threat?"

Oddly enough, the Almighty did not seem too concerned about rugby,[2] cycling, cricket, horse racing, golf or soccer on Sundays, but perhaps He never did buy into the jogging craze. Indeed, if He were to show His power and do a bit of judicious scaremongering, He could do worse than pack Robert Mugabe off to the hereafter. "Only God, who appointed me, will remove me—not the MDC, not the British—only God will remove me!" said Uncle Bob.

Hint, hint.

"Mr Mugabe's actions and those of his generals, their wives, his thug supporters and

---

[2] Springbok coach Peter de Villiers certainly believes that the Almighty takes a very keen interest in the outcome of Springbok rugby matches. As he has said, "I've got nothing to prove. I believe in myself, the players and God."

the so-called 'war veterans' are offensive in the eyes of God. Judgment awaits," declared Cardinal Wilfred Napier, speaking on behalf of the Southern African Catholic Bishops Conference. Later, Uncle Bob himself blamed God for the car crash that killed Susan Tsvangirai. "It will take him time to recover from this shock. I plead with you to accept it, it's the hand of God," he told mourners at her funeral.

At the time of writing, Judgment for Uncle Bob is still awaiting, and we're all rather hoping it will hurry up.

> "If no one has any ideas to salvage the situation, I'll be convinced the devil must have found refuge in SA." A reader of *The Times*, in response to the wave of xenophobic violence that swept the country in May

Christian Afrikaans Sheep

People who wished to worship the Devil—as opposed to merely blaming him—had their defenders, notably Deon Maas. "Satan does not necessarily represent evil; it is just a different philosophy," Maas argued. "You still pray, but only to another god. If Muslims think they are having a hard time, they should look at Satanism. They really have a bad deal."

He wrote this in *Rapport*, which of course is a Sunday paper with a readership that believes very firmly in *Godsdiens*. So some people complained. Others started Facebook groups campaigning for boycotts of the newspaper. The editor folded and Maas's much-hyped column was pulled.

Later Maas said, "I am disappointed and sad about what happened. I have been humiliated in public. But I still believe that the whole *Rapport* campaign was initiated by a small minority and that *Rapport* did not have the balls to stick by me." He added that the Satanism scandal was in fact not the most heated he has generated: that honour went to a game on his website in which players would score points every time they knocked over a cyclist.

Maas had plenty of support from other commentators. Writing on thoughtleader, Riaan Wolmarans declared: "I hate sheep. Afrikaans sheep, to be exact, and more specifically, Christian Afrikaans sheep."

Professor Pierre de Vos thought that, if anything, being a Satanist would be rather dull. "I would not mind the post-midnight gatherings," he wrote, "the listening to Cora Marie or Bles Bridges backward to hear messages of support, the incense and the candles, or the fetching young men in black looking morose and comically trying to feign evil looks." He was convinced, however, that weeks of rituals "to a non-existent being" would become boring: "Soon going to the Satanist gathering would be no better than attending an NG Kerk sermon in Christiana or a Julio Iglesias concert in Boksburg."

Zapiro weighed in with a list of deities and legendary figures, including Santa Claus, the Tooth Fairy, Allah and Humpty Dumpty. "Can you provide proof of the existence of any of the above?" the cartoon challenged readers. Why should a newspaper columnist have been fired for writing that people should be allowed to believe in Satan?

(Technically, of course, Zapiro was wrong on that score, because the sort of people who complained about Deon Maas believe wholeheartedly in the existence of Satan. They just don't think it's acceptable to worship him.) "I do these things because I believe in freedom of expression," the cartoonist said later, in the wake of complaints about his depiction of Allah in particular.

> "That so many Stellenbosch students leave their baloney detectors outside the classroom—is no good advertisement for what should be one of Africa's leading universities." George Claassen of Sceptic South Africa on a fundamentalist Christian cult that was the source of controversy at Stellenbosch University[3]

"God is not petty!!!!"

The following February, 5FM DJ Gareth Cliff—a man with a history of heresy—found himself in trouble, again, and, in the process, emerged from the belief closet to declare himself openly atheist. Cliff was commenting on an incident in the Sudan in which a British teacher became embroiled in controversy after she permitted one of her classes to name a teddy bear mascot 'Mohammed'. "If God is great," Cliff asked his listeners, "why

---

[3] Apparently, Shofar members walk out of zoology lectures when the subject of evolution comes up (which tends to beg the question: why are these students doing studying university-level zoology in the first place?)

would he be so easily offended by what a mortal man says? If God has such an ego, then he must be petty."

Inevitably, a Concerned Listener from Pretoria then wrote to him to complain. Demonstrating the inverse link between number of exclamation marks and intelligence, Gerda-Mari Povey wrote, "You know what, Gareth, I love your show, but this morning u shocked me!!!! just wanted to say, God is not petty!!!!! I pray that something drastic will happen in your life that will allow you to experience the loving kindness and mercy of God."

Stung into action by what one can only assume was the intemperate use of punctuation, Cliff wrote back: "Stop sprouting nonsense. There is no god. There is no tooth fairy and there is no Father Christmas."

Having had time to think about that first response, Cliff then mailed Povey again, explaining: "I will never agree with you just as you find my lack of belief so distasteful. The difference is that I concern myself with people and try to be a good and hopefully moral person. I don't need blessings or permissions or prayers. I'm a happy guy."

The SABC defended Cliff against complaints that he had made blasphemous comments on air, arguing, "We are dealing here with the classic example of people who hear not what is actually said but what they want to hear. We are satisfied that the presenter did not say: 'If God wants to be petty, leave him to be petty.'"

The Broadcasting Complaints Commission of South Africa found in Cliff's favour and concluded that his remarks were not blasphemous—though one is tempted to wonder whether, even if Cliff had blasphemed, this should be worthy of censure.

Fools stealing church money

"… politicians are lying, opportunistic rubbish. Hand in hand with them are the pastors, priests and other religious child molesters who control the flock through fear and lies." Charl Pretorius

Being a member of the clergy is of course no guarantee of spotless behaviour.

Terry Hogan, who was retrenched from Rhema for her "negative attitude" and "disdain towards the church", said of her former employers: "They've got an absolute cheek to call themselves Christians. If that's what being a Christian is about, I have to question my faith."

Gideon Cogzell, who worked as a volunteer for the church, was excommunicated after he asked about what was being done with the congregation's tithes. Rhema management said it remained "committed to pray" for him although he had "rebelled against and refused to accept all Godly counsel and advice".

In the mean time, Ray McCauley published a book on spirituality and life called—to the surprise of absolutely nobody—*The Bottom Line*. Rhema's last audited figures included an income of over R100 million, so the pastor clearly knows what he is writing about.

Fred Khumalo wondered why people tithed so much of their income to Rhema and was provided with an answer by a friend of his wife. "Fred, I go to Rhema and I give them a tenth of my salary because I want to," she explained. "I am not buying salvation. I go to church because I enjoy it. It's a social occasion to me." Fred, she argued, had his jazz CDs and his whisky. "So why can't I enjoy going to church, even if I have to pay for it?"

At least the Rhema top brass could only be accused of spending the congregation's money on lavish lunches and designer apartments in Umhlanga. The *Daily Sun* reported that five people—including a Zionist church bishop, a priest and a Swazi who posed as a Zionist priest—were charged with the muthi murder of the unfortunate Khanyasile Mama.

The same paper also reported on the pastor of the Faith Mission Church in Mamelodi West who shot his wife and mother-in-law before crashing his car while fleeing the scene. The church subsequently explained that the man was not a pastor, but a "spiritual leader". "We are very shocked about the incident and we are praying for both families for a speedy recovery," said the real pastor. "We want them to be well and come back to church to praise God."

"Teach your kids Santa Claus is dead and Jesus is alive." A Christian Group in Cape Town to parents prior to Christmas in December 2008, saying that Father Christmas was "the new pagan god of materialism"

Then there were the shenanigans at the International Pentecostal Holiness Church—one of South Africa's perhaps less well-known religious institutions—which came to the attention of the media after the founder's son claimed his brother-in-law threatened to kill him. Glaton Modise and Bobo Bethuel Modise had failed to see eye to eye in the past, notably in the year 2000 when Bobo led a splinter group, the International Comforters Holiness Church.

Glaton Modise said that his brother-in-law had sent him insulting SMSes. "He sent me SMS messages calling me names. 'You have failed Standard 1 eight times', the messages said," he told the court presiding over the case. Other messages apparently read: "You are cruel, you donkey", "Fuck you", "You have an evil heart bastard" and "You are a fool and steal the church money".

Bobo Modise's lawyer said that Glaton was merely coming up with a pretext to prevent his brother-in-law and sister from inheriting what was rightfully theirs, as the church's founder had left millions in his estate.

The rival Universal Church of the Kingdom of God also had its share of bad publicity. Several pastors employed by the UCKG claimed that not only had they been left destitute after making millions for the country's fastest-growing charismatic church, but they had been forced to undergo vasectomies so that they would have no "baggage".

"When people warned us that these Brazilians were here to make money we did not want to believe them. But now we know. They brainwashed us into believing that God would take care of us, but when they kick us out we have nowhere to go," complained one.

A UCKG spokesperson confirmed that pastors are given the option of getting the snip for God. "There are countries where pastors are, where conditions may not be as favourable for a pastor with children, and for this reason pastors are advised of this possibility and the challenges they may face," she said. "No pastor is forced to undergo a vasectomy. Those pastors who have undergone this medical procedure have done so of their own accord."

"After 15 years, we have now seen the outlines of an evil society." Mosioua Lekota, who apparently saw the light after leaving the ANC

Heaven Forbid

As the elections neared, South Africa's politicians suddenly started spending a lot of time in church. Jacob Zuma told the congregation of the New Covenant Fellowship International Church in Rustenburg that it was important that churches pray for the government. "We need constructive criticism," he added. "Why don't you speak so that we can see when things go wrong?"

By this time, Zuma had apologized for saying that the ANC would rule until the second coming of Jesus, but that didn't stop him from calling on the big man in the sky to back him up. After the NPA dropped corruption and racketeering charges against him, Jacob Zuma accused the judges of the Constitutional Court of acting "as if they were almost like God".

This was, of course, completely unacceptable: everybody knows that only JZ himself is almost like God.

When he wasn't asking churches to pray for government, Zuma was warning his supporters against the depredations of witches. The worst kind of witches, he said, where the enemies who were closest to you. "In Zulu we refer to a form of witchcraft called *ukuphehla amanzi* where your enemy would mix dirt from your body in a calabash and stick a spear into the mixture ... this would cause you sharp body pains. When a witch is a family member, we know that it's more dangerous than an enemy from outside," said Zuma, explaining in a mix of Xhosa and Zulu to a crowd in the Eastern Cape.

On Easter Sunday, the president-in-waiting hedged his bets, attending the International Pentacostal Church in Zuurbekom in the morning and a Muslim service in Mayfair in the afternoon. ZCC member Mbhazima Shilowa and fellow COPE leader Mosioua Lekota were in Moria, while Mangosuthu Buthelezi attended an Anglican service in Mahlabathini.

"Electioneering? Heaven forbid!" the *Sunday Sun* cackled.

A week later, Mpumalanga ANC leader Yvonne 'Pinkie' Phosa told a crowd in Elukwatini, some 120 kilometres from Nelspruit, that the ANC enjoyed the powers of both Jesus Christ *and* Moses. "No matter what happens, the other political parties don't have vision," she explained. "They are unable to see that, at the moment, the ANC is in possession of the wisdom of Christ and the stick of Moses." She told the crowd that when the ANC implemented its five-point plan, its supporters should be like the disciples of Jesus. "As we emerge from the Easter, we are sprinkling the blood of Jesus Christ into the body and soul of the ANC ... If you go with Jesus Christ nothing is impossible. We have seen Jesus's miracles. He could not fail on anything. Now, He is with the ANC."

Indeed, it would appear that not even a miracle could prevent an ANC victory.

One *You* magazine reader disputed Zuma's claim that God was on the side of the ANC. "Well, you are so wrong," declared the reader, a week before the elections. "Your ignorance and opportunism scream from the mountaintops." God, pointed out the letter writer, said you should not steal, lie or commit adultery. "Through the mouth of the great prophet

Jesus, God also counselled us to uplift the poor, have compassion and oppose greed and tyranny." And to conclude: "No, Mr Zuma, God has never been on the side of smug, arrogant, greedy and corrupt people who violate those fine principles in their everyday behaviour."

Self-confessed non-practising Christian Fred Khumalo reckoned that God was onto all these politicians. "I think he can spot an opportunist a mile away. After all, God created us. We can't lie to Him, we can't fool Him." He added: "We have perverted religion into a pliable commodity that is meant to suit all seasons."

Amen.

"Dear God
Sorry to bother you again, but you did such a splendid job with that Rainbow Nation miracle in the early 1990s, we'd really appreciate it if you could glance our way again because things are looking decidedly dodgy." Chris Moerdyk.

How about "Behold, I have played the fool" (I Samuel 26 v 21) for Julius Malema?
I prefer "What will this babbler say" from Acts 17 v 18.

"Be sure your sin will find you out."
Numbers 32 v 23

"Multitudes, multitudes in the valley of decision." Joel 3 v 14

Chapter 13

Let's Hunt Down the Kwerekwere:
Ethnic Insults and Xenophobia

"We humans discriminate against each other on the basis of skin colour, gender, metabolism, age, dental structure and so on. Of course we use teeth as a discriminator alright. Hands up anyone whose partner has a passion gap. I thought so." Ndomiso Ngcobo

When Minister of Labour Membhathisi Mdadlana acted dumb, he wasn't pretending. Demonstrating watertight logic in response to the inclusion of Chinese South Africans in BEE legislation, he argued: "I hope that they would make sure that they implement and comply with the Labour Relations Act and the Basic Conditions of Employment Act much, much better now that they have decided to classify themselves as coloureds as in the past." He continued, "One would not expect a coloured person to ill-treat other coloureds, or black people to ill-treat blacks."

"They say they can't speak English. Chinese pretend to be dumb, when they are not. We know they are not. Chinese are very clever people. Therefore, if they are coloureds, they can't now say 'I can't speak the South African languages.'" Minister of Labour Membathisi Mdadlana

Mdadlana's logic was surely foolproof. And yet, based upon available evidence, coloured people are more than capable of ill-treating other coloureds, or black people of ill-treating other people who happen to be black, and from the wrong side of the continent. Just ask the thousands of people who fled their homes as xenophobic violence swept the country in 2008. This was a time when being a Shangaan wasn't just a joke. It could get you killed.

"We will burn the Shangaans if they don't go back," a man arrested for burning shacks on the East Rand told the media. "We will fight for this country. We will keep on going, they can't stop us. I will be proud to meet the man who started this," he said of the violence that had flared up in Alexandra Township and than spread across the land. By the end of it all, 62 people were dead, hundreds injured, and thousands homeless.

"It's better to go home than to die," said a Malawian man who escaped death by stoning.

Victims of the violence reported that crowds of Zulu speakers were telling Shangaans and Pedis to "Go home to Limpopo". A Pedi resident of Johannesburg told the media, "I don't know how this is going to end. They just take your things and they beat you up."

A Zimbabwean woman who had worked in South Africa since 1991 observed, "They [the attackers] are not educated. They have only a little and they think we are here to take it away. Mugabe will be so thrilled when he sees this ... what should we do? We don't have any place to run to."

Professor Loren Landau, a migration researcher from the University of Witwatersrand, coined a motto for the counter-movement: "The nightmare is a wake-up call."

"Chief, they are running a war here." Johannesburg police officer to his superior, after coming under fire by crowds rioting against the presence of foreign nationals

Now came the really important part: figuring out who to blame.

Essop Pahad—"that cadaverous mugger in the Presidency" as Hogarth described him—had his theories about who was responsible. South Africans were targeting Zimbabweans, Mozambicans and even Shangaans because white rightwingers had persuaded them to turn upon their brothers and sisters. "We need to understand that xenophobia has historically been used by right-wing populist movements to mobilize particularly the lumpen proletariat against minority groups in society," he intoned. "Political mobilization on the basis of xenophobia poses grave threats to progressive forces in our society and to our democracy."

Hogarth deemed Pahad Mampara of the Week and dismissed his theories on the causes of the xenophobic attacks as a "convenient excuse by second-rate government to explain lack of decisive response to national crisis".

Whether the downtrodden residents of South Africa's townships and informal settlements thought of themselves as the "lumpen proletariat" is not clear.

Perhaps they would have been happy to take Pahad's word for it.

President Mbeki had a good excuse for not visiting sites of xenophobic violence, as Hayibo explained. "Mbeki has spent a total of 19 days in South Africa since 2002, and according to a presidency spokesperson most citizens now believe him to be a foreigner," the report noted, before quoting a source who opined: "We must be pragmatic and concede that most of our citizens think that Mr Mbeki is a hybrid Shangaan-Belgian, dividing his time between the Rift Valley and The Hague."

> "I ask myself if there was a French guy in that taxi who didn't know English, let alone not having the necessary documentation, would he be labelled as a kwerekwere? Would he be dragged by his trousers to get inside the police van? Do police harass Chinese, Pakistanis and Portuguese in the CBD similar to the way they do to those with darker skins?" Tendayi Sithole, an intern at the Freedom of Expression Institute, comments on the xenophobic violence

Allan Boesak blamed the ANC, accusing the party of entrenching racial hatred. "The ANC has succumbed to the subtle but pernicious temptations of ethnic thinking, has brought back the language of ethnicity into the speech of the movement and has, as government, brought back the hated system of racial categorization," he said during a lecture in Cape Town in July 2008. He also argued that affirmative action had in some cases "taken on new forms of racial exclusion, ruthlessly and thoughtlessly throwing overboard the solidarity forged through years of struggle".

"That is why, before we know it, we begin to accuse and slander, to maim and kill in a xenophobic frenzy so utterly strange to the deepest heart of our people." Boesak—somewhat ironically—given past his prior conviction for fraud—said the poor people in South Africa had been betrayed by those hungry for power, warning that the situation was like a "time bomb … real and ticking". "Today, everywhere we look; it takes but the merest provocation for the ghosts of racism to rise and haunt us, because we have buried them in graves too shallow and too close to home."

> "Here, hordes of jolly South Africans are blikseming anybody who looks vaguely alien, and if they can't find enough of those, raping their countrywomen to keep their hand in until a suitable foreign devil comes along." Chris Roper

After the chaos had died down, *Sowetan* columnist Nthabi Moreosele reflected that nobody would admit their involvement in the violence. "I am not comfortable with the idea that other people see me as a monster," she wrote. "Already the cover-up has begun. I have not met a single person who was involved in the atrocities. Just like apartheid, no one wants to own up."

Arguably, reflected the *Sunday Times*, this was "the most grave, dark and repulsive moment in the life of our young nation".

David Kau offered his own unique take on the issue, announcing that he was thinking of a line of T-shirts for 2010 soccer fans, featuring slogans such as, "I don't own a tuck shop", "I won't do your garden for half the minimum wage", "It will take me weeks to braid your hair", and a limited-edition one that says, "Just because my name is Lovemore and I'm from Malawi, it doesn't mean I'm here to work as a butler!"

> "If South Africa cannot resolve to exorcise the demon of xenophobic treatment of fellow Africans from its society and government departments, they have but two options: the first is to impose prohibitive visas to restrict 'the undesirables', failing which they should close the fucking border and spare fellow Africans this inhumane treatment." Jeremiah Kure, thoughtleader blogger, writing about his experiences at the Musina border post

Killing the monster

There were cases, though, where even David Kau found it difficult to laugh. At one of his corporate gigs, an Afrikaner client told him a joke that a barman had told him. "What's the difference between a kaffir donkey and a baas donkey?" "The owner."

"I was most offended that it wasn't a funny joke, if it was a joke at all," he said.

Irvin Khoza of Orlando Pirates was not joking when he accused a black journalist of "thinking like a kaffir". Impatient with questions from the press about a rift between him and fellow 2010 committee member Danny Jordaan, Khoza explained at a press conference, "I am going to use a strong word, and the media will forgive me for this, but people must stop thinking like kaffirs. I told him to stop thinking like a kaffir because you are misconstruing something that is not there." Not everyone understood where he was coming from. In the wake of a storm of protest, the Iron Duke defended himself, saying,

"I know the word has another meaning, but in the context in which I used it, it refers to dubious character and unreliability." The journalist in question was being "willful", he said.

Andisiwe Makhinana was not convinced. "People who suffered the insult decades ago still rage at the insult," she wrote. "It carries a weight so enormous; it causes grown men to flinch." Obviously Khoza hadn't heard of black-on-black racism: "Essentially, it is as bad, as damaging and blunt as any other form of racism."

Fikile-Ntsikilelo Moya thought that Khoza had a point, but suggested that perhaps he should have substituted the phrase "onyela batho otshaba makgoa" ("you shit on blacks, but are afraid of whites"). "Stripped of its colourful language, it accuses one of behaving like a kaffir," he explained. "Like the African-Americans who last year symbolically buried the N-word, I hope that we will one day soon bury the K-word. But first we have to stop behaving like kaffirs and tell our own people when they delay us killing the monster."

> "We all, even myself ... my chommies and I have beaten up a couple of kaffirs. You are young, that's what you do. In those days your dad told you that's kwaai. The only reason this is an issue is because it's a kaffir who died and it was a white laaitie who hit him." Pumas fan J.R. Nagel comments on the presence of convicted murderer Gert van Schalkwyk—one of the Waterkloof Four found guilty of murdering a homeless man—in the side

And the monster still appeared to be alive and well. During a match in the UK, Australian tennis player Brydan Klein was fined €10 000 for using the K-word on his South African opponent Raven Klaasan. A Meyerton man and his three-year-old nephew were assaulted on their way to a phone booth by two young white men who told them: "We do not want kaffirs in our town anymore. We are going to kill you."

Workshop manager Anton Anderson of Wilgeheuwel in Roodepoort spent five days in jail on a charge of crimen injuria after he used the K-word on his neighbour; earlier he had attacked a woman and smashed her windscreen after she visited the complex where he lived. Anderson denied he had used the K-word and said his neighbours had a vendetta against him.

The K-word was also liberally used in an amateur rugby match one July afternoon between Wanderers Rugby Club and Eldoronians, which also involved references to maternal genitalia, threats with knives and a brawl that left one player in hospital. Wanderers coach Bokkie Keulder said that his players were racially abused. "Throughout the game they were using words like 'your mother's poes' and they kept calling our vice-captain who is black, 'a black fat fuck'." In turn the manager of the Eldoranians, Reynald Isaacs, retorted that his players were called "hotnots" and "kaffirs".

The game was stopped 15 minutes into the second half when a fight broke out and an Eldoronian player suffered concussion. Keulder said he went onto the field to stop the fight and was threatened and spat at. "They said, 'We are going to kill you, you're not going to see tomorrow,'" he said.

The Eldoronian players, he claimed, threatened the Wanderers players with knives which they had obtained from spectators. Later they stood outside the Wanderers change room, challenging them to come out. Keulder, who called the police, said, "Luckily they didn't know there is another door that leads into the club."

Isaacs denied that his players had knives, saying it was "cheap sensationalism". "If players did have knives, why didn't they point them out to the police?" he wondered, though he did admit that some of his players had brandished pieces of pipe "to protect themselves".

The Golden Lions Rugby Union said it was investigating and that any players found to be guilty would be suspended.

> "I told him I was transporting a corpse and relatives but he showed no mercy."
> Funeral parlour worker who said a police officer called him a kaffir

Khadija Bradlow, who followed the story in both the English and Afrikaans press, wondered why the word 'hotnot' was spelled out in full in some publications, but not others. Citing the history of the word, Bradlow reflected: "Whatever it meant then, there's only one thing it means now. And it involves missing front teeth, a tik pipe and that man or woman dik gesuip [drunk] at the kerb."

But to legislate against the use of a word like 'hotnot' made no sense, she argued, and there was a risk of becoming too "precious". Besides, "A word like hotnot says more about who utters it than about who is on the receiving end. Offensive? Maybe. Illegal? Ridiculous."

That distinction, between offensive and illegal, came to the fore in a Broadcasting

Complaints Commission ruling in response to a number of complaints—all of them from white listeners—after Arthur Mafokate's 1995 kwaito hit 'Kaffir' was played on 5FM. The BCCSA fined DJ Fresh R10,000, with Professor Kobus van Rooyen arguing that the word represents "one of the elements of apartheid which degraded a whole nation of black people. The broadcast of the song flies in the face of the constitutional founding values of dignity and equality".

Chris Roper thought the ruling was ridiculous, amounting to making it illegal for anyone but racists to use the K-word. Instead of using the song as an opportunity to teach children about apartheid, "Let's rather let them believe that their parents fought and died so that they could have equal access to BMWs. Let's have them believe that a dompas is something the Stormers do, and that forced removals are what you do when you want to make space in your belly for more beer."

> "When you get locked into the idea of minorities you think like a minority ... It divides people. We must see ourselves as one group," ANC Secretary-General Gwede Mantashe, addressing a coloured community in Durban

Themba Keswa wrote to the *Sunday Times* about the "shame" and "crime" of the white mispronunciation of African names. "I shudder each time I listen to white newsreaders on radio and television committing the same crime with our black surnames every day."

Readers were not impressed. "Hey, Themba Keswa—get rid of that chip on your shoulder! Blacks massacre my language every day," retorted Beverley Scott of Port Elizabeth. "And they mispronounce the names of many whiteys all the time. How about extending us the same understanding?"

Lynette Rens of Johannesburg was incensed: "When all darkies speak perfect English, you can complain about whiteys not pronouncing an African name correctly. So please don't demand special privileges."

> "A friend of mine was running to catch the train and he screamed: '*Hey Kaffers, hou die deur oop vir my!*' A couple of black guys at the door were not amused." Mitchells Plain resident Shawn Kaffers on his unusual surname, as quoted in the *Sunday Sun*

"We have substituted practically every vision in this country and every policy for racial percentages; we've gone for demographic bean-counting as the essential pillar of current policy." Tony Leon

It's not all honky dory

Was there an equivalent of the K-word for whites? No, argued *Citizen* columnist Hlengiwe Mnguni, who said that 'mlungu' was purely descriptive. She understood why white South Africans would dislike the word, she said. "However it always comes down to this sad South African question: When will white people learn to speak black languages? Not just for their own sakes so they can tell when someone is skinnering about them, but also to release me, so I can say 'mlungu' whenever and wherever I please."

"The word means 'white scum' and is far more derogatory than the K-word, which means 'unbeliever'," retorted one Wally Hemmings, apparently an expert on etymology. "The word should be treated as hate speech, as is the K-word. But then, of course, it is only whites who are racist."

The blogger Juno was thoroughly sick of generalizations about whites. "To the Christine Quntas and other pontificators, 'commentators' and dunderheads whose racist dribblings stain our newspapers, and to the editors who give you space, fuck off," she wrote. "Really, fuck off. Say something useful and intelligent in your columns, or go away. And don't you dare presume to know what *I* think."

Star reader Mariano Castrillon was not a fan of Qunta either. "Her articles are so wonderful, so predictably racist—or anti-white anyway—that I use them at home to teach my children how to be politically correct at all times," he wrote. In fact, the solution to the problem of too many whites in management was obvious: whites should not send their children to university "because that would be conducive to taking the place of a black person in the workplace after graduation". If white women had ten children each, they would not be able to afford to send them to school, so the problem would be solved.

Sunday Times columnist Pinky Khoabane argued that white students who studied in South Africa and then took their skills elsewhere were "plundering the resources of our country".

"Does going to university and studying for a degree automatically make you a plunderer?" wondered Cape Town reader Ron McGregor. "Are you automatically a plunderer just because you are white, even if you are just a regular middle class oke? With such attitudes, white South Africans are constantly reminded that they are not welcome in the land of their birth. Perhaps we should all go now and leave Khoabane and her ilk to plunder the resources all by themselves."

Cape Judge President John Hlophe refused to reconcile with former Chief Justice Pius Langa: "I will not shake the hand of a white man." Hlophe later claimed his remarks had been distorted, saying he came across as a "careless Zulu".

Chris Roper reasoned that Hlophe probably had a perfectly valid explanation. "To say that you wouldn't shake hands with a black man who is looking a little pale, isn't an entirely unreasonable standpoint. After all, swine flu is rife, and if anybody's going to catch it, it'll be Zuma appointees, a fair few of whom are known for feeding from the trough."

One of Roper's readers, Bongane Makwakwa, was appalled. "As a civil citizen I can say whatever I want about any ethnic group, but the last thing we need is a person who wants to be appointed as a judge to the highest court in the land to articulate such pathetic statements ... it's disgusting.

> "Black racism is no less real than white racism." Eusebius McKaiser, who argued that to recognize John Hlophe's remark as racist was a matter of "fully respecting his humanity and holding him morally accountable"

Ben Trovato suggested that whites could find gainful employment as stand-ins for non-functioning traffic lights. "Here's another job in the extremely informal sector: with so many robots out of order, white people can stand at intersections and hold up placards saying 'red' or 'green'. This is not a job for darkies because nobody can see them at night. It has nothing to do with racism. Besides, it doesn't pay so only a drunk whitey would do it." Trovato also thought it was inexplicable that there are eleven kings in South Africa, but no white king. "Thousands of foreigners are coming to this country next year and they are going to want to know who is the King of the White People. We can't simply scratch our heads and say, 'Well, there's Lolly Jackson ... '"

Trovato suggested that he would make a good monarch, and proclaimed himself "King Benjamin Trovato the First, Supreme Ruler of the Caucasoid and Slapper of the Meek".

Julius Malema, whose ongoing struggle against severe retardation has captured the hearts of South Africans, hit the headlines again when he accused Helen Zille of trying to turn the Western Cape into a whites-only enclave, and said "more blacks and Africans" should migrate to the province from the Eastern Cape. Hayibo reported that Malema, an "ambassador for children with severe learning disabilities", had been advised by doctors to use his brain properly.

Malema also opined that ministries in the economic cluster were all given to "minorities", while blacks were put in charge of security: "If you look at the security cluster, it's all Africans. Are we being reduced to security?"

"Forget the validity of the implied accusation," interjected Chris Roper, "forget the straight line delivered to a million racists worldwide who are dying to answer, 'Well, set a thief to catch a thief', or 'If you want to screw up the economy, get the white man for the job'."

> "As a darkie myself, I am really sad of the day I voted ANC. Us Indians have always been in between the witous and the darkies and have never had an entity of our own, but seriously, under the Nats, we all had a better life." Comment, Dispatch blogs

While the ANCYL welcomed the appointment of ex-communist Gill Marcus to head the Reserve Bank, it would have expected "an African child to occupy the position". After all, if black youth saw that whites were in positions of strategic economic influence, their horizons would be limited. "The youth will think, because Marcus is white, they [whites] are born like that; there's no way I can be like that."

"Who died and gave Malema the power to declare the ANC a single race party?" fumed blogger and ANC supporter Michael Trapido. "I believe that the party shed its blacks-only image quite a while ago and currently represents all races and cultures in South Africa. If that be so, are the whites targeting only the blacks within the ANC?"

S'thembiso Msomi of the *Sunday Times* argued that poor children in the coloured and Indian communities were as much in need of role models as "African" children. "But, then again, it should not be a surprise that the youth league leader would ignore this important fact," he observed. "Have you seen the league's membership profile lately—especially at leadership level? For an organization that espouses 'non-racialism', its leadership structures are dominated by one racial group."

"Just how stupid does Malema think black kids are?" wondered Chris Roper, who suggested that perhaps it was more likely that black kids would look at the ANCYL's investment arm, in the news for corruption and financial mismanagement, "and decide to aim a little higher than just being a corrupt, financially compromised official. Like president of the country, possibly."

> "Sideshow Malema is a racist bigot. There is no polite way to say it." Comment, thoughtleader

Affirmative, sir

Reflecting on how things had changed over the years, Max du Preez told an audience at a literary festival, "People were no longer hiring people with Afrikaans and penises." Affirmative action continued to be a bone of contention, no pun intended. When Helen Zille defended her all-male provincial cabinet, she said she was interested only in who would do the best job. "Quotas take precedence over all matters in South Africa," she complained. "We don't believe in shell state s. It's all style, pomp, glitz and glamour ... perks for families has nothing to do with the job ... We had to look at who would do the best job."

So it was only natural that a radio station that targeted black youth should launch a search for a white male DJ to join its lineup. YFM said it "fervently believed in affirmative action", rejected "tokenism" and was looking for a "hot white boy". 21-year-old Jon Hooper, a UK-born Setswana-speaking baker from Pretoria won a 12-month contract with the station.

"Hooper, who was raised and educated in Pretoria, found that he naturally gravitated towards the young black children in his area," explained the YFM press release. "As these friendships developed he began mastering the language, until he grew to become a fully fledged member of the black community."

(As opposed to all the English-speaking black South Africans who have grown to become fully fledged members of the white community, one supposes.)

> "For me black suffering has no hierarchy; to be forced into a white friendship is as repugnant as being instructed to eat white piss and shit." South African writer Andile Mngxitama in a discussion with *M&G* editor Ferial Haffajee

The possibility that all South Africans might live as fully fledged members of the same community seemed within reach from time to time, however, such as when Julius Malema surprised everyone by visiting Orania in March 2009. Carel Boshoff Jnr, president of the Orania Movement, helpfully informed the media that there was no "shoot out" or "search for control" attitude during the meetings with the ANCYL delegation. For his part, Malema was surprised that they had actually let him in. "We thought well-armed Afrikaners would stop the blacks," he said. He liked the fact that everybody in Orania worked together, but expressed the desire to reintegrate the community back into South Africa. Before he left, he hung up four ANC election posters beneath those of the Freedom Front on the main road through the town. Boshoff joked that Malema should not expect too much success in Orania.[1]

Hayibo explained that Malema had actually tried to programme his GPS to take him to the Oranje Minimart in Hillbrow where he wanted to buy a packet of Nik Naks. "The leaders of the whites-only enclave of Orania in the Northern Cape have lauded ANC Youth League president Julius Malema for his clear thinking on race and gender issues, saying that they and Malema have much in common, including a love of the South African soil, a passionate devotion to the well-being of their people, and an IQ of roughly 55.

"'Mr Malema also represents an increasingly insular African tribe,' said an Orania spokesman, Abraham Bittereinder. 'Both our tribes see persecution everywhere, and we both base our nationalist claims on the Bible and a concept called "freedom" which is never accurately defined so that we can manipulate it as we see fit.'"

"Stupidly revealing comments" was another trait shared by both Malema and the Orania community, Hayibo reported.

On the subject of a volkstaat, David Kau thought it might be a good idea. He for one couldn't wait for the government ad in the newspaper for a volkstaat tender: "The government is looking for a black-owned or BEE-compliant company or organization to facilitate setting up a volkstaat for Afrikaner people. The said company must have skills-transfer programmes and initiatives, and be willing to train Afrikaners from poor communities to sustain themselves with jobs previously reserved for blacks: gardening, wearing blue overalls, taxi-driving, packing groceries at Pick 'n Pay and domestic work, including walking white kids to and from school. Must be able to adjust to living in a back room and going home only when there's a funeral."

---

[1] As it turned out, the joke was on Boshoff, after three residents of Orania voted ANC. "I am hoping that these three ANC votes were cast by munt civilian IEC volunteers," wrote one blogger.

"My iron also shoots whites." Allegedly drunk policeman to a man at the scene of a motor vehicle accident in Delmas

Talking kak

"I shall not permit you to talk to me like whites used to talk to blacks." South African Reserve Bank governor Tito Mboweni to Bank shareholder Mario Pretorius. Pretorius later demanded an apology from Mboweni

Farmer Derick Steyn of Meyerton—evidently a hotbed of racism and rival with Delmas for the status of the armpit of the Transvaal—scored a front-page story in the news after assaulting his domestic worker.

"He threatened to shoot me if I did not open," reported Thembi Ndlovu. "As soon as I let him in he smashed my phone saying I was trying to call my black kaffir mother. He continued to hit me with his fists and kicked me all over my body." Steyn was unrepentant, telling *The Sowetan*: "You people are clever, ja! Bring all that information to court and it will be investigated. I think you are talking kak."

Speaking of kak, black police officers at Badplaas police station complained that certain toilets were reserved for whites. Black officers were instead required to use a toilet that doubled as a chicken coop.

"As for me, I'm even afraid to come into this toilet at night because chickens are not my friends, I'm scared of them," said one.

Afrikaans singer Fredi Nest—apparently known as "South Africa's Chris de Burgh"—found himself in a bit of a gemors after it emerged that the chorus of one of his hits went "Net in Afrikaans/ nie in Engels/ Nie in bobbejaan nie/ Net in Afrikaans". Nest denied that there were any political or racial overtones to this. "It's not a political song at all. I used bobbejaan because it is the closest animal to humans," he said. "I wrote the song because I'm standing up for my language and my culture."

"To think that he puts his singing on the same level as Chris de Burgh's—what a cheek!" one *Sunday Times* reader wrote. "It's people like him and many other Afrikaners who messed up this country and still think they are the 'salt of the earth'."

"This Afrikaner bobbejaan must be so ignorant if he believes what he is 'singing' about is not racist," wrote another.

Fellow Afrikaans musician Lee Vaughan said that he thought the lyrics might cause trouble and warned Nest. He suspected that Nest was just naïve. "Unlike people like me, who have attended English schools and have been exposed to various cultures," he said, "some Afrikaans musicians view things differently."

> "Breeding grounds for racists who still see Africans as nothing else but savages." South African universities, according to SASCO

Political analyst Steven Friedman was concerned about the way 'black' public personalities were reduced to buffoons, "much as smiling minstrels were in the days when prejudices were expressed more directly because they were the law." Peter de Villiers was a particularly good example of how apartheid-era prejudices were still in circulation—only this time, camouflaged as common sense. "Fifteen years after apartheid formally ended, it is time for those whites who never tire of accusing others of 'playing the race card' to realize how often they do it themselves—without even noticing ... what I cannot help noticing is how common it is in our society for black people who cross boundaries, which whites create, to be reduced to figures of fun.

"And which sort of racial prejudice should worry us more," asked Friedman, "that of black professionals and politicians who react to bigotry in self-serving ways or those of bigots whose prejudices are so deeply rooted that they manage to convince themselves and others that they are not prejudices at all?"

> "He is the type of person South Africa does not need within its borders." Pallo Jordan on David Bullard. He was responding to the article that got Bullard fired from the *Sunday Times*

Perhaps not surprisingly, David Bullard could not agree with Friedman. As he saw it, "what we should be doing is politely averting our eyes and pretending the emperor, if he is black, is fully clothed". Friedman, he argued, seemed to imply that black South Africans were not "sufficiently psychologically developed to be able to take a joke". "Calling someone a 'racist' in this country is normally the first resort of those who either cannot or refuse to debate important issues in public. So, am I about to change my ways and treat black South Africans as if they were retarded children? The answer to that is no. The reason for that is simple. It would be racist. I can't think of anything more insulting than being regarded as being so pathetic that someone from another race has to make excuses for my very existence."

Political analyst Aubrey Matshiqi found it all rather amusing. Noting how, in a debate over the issue between Friedman and Black Consciousness expert Andile Mngxitama, the latter had argued that blacks could not be racist, he reflected, "This makes me happy because, from now on, I will be racist but safe in the knowledge that I am a perpetrator of something blacks are incapable of.

"What is the point of being black, I ask, if one cannot be racist?"

Reflecting on Friedman's article, Jeremy Gordin suggested: "The way I see it is that, even if de Villiers were a Jewish sage, he'd still be a bozo."

"The perception that African people are dangerous is not true." Township residents Johan Jonker and Edna van Rooyen, who happen to be white. They live in an RDP house in a township outside Polokwane

Poker face: using the race card

"Can't blacks achieve and be what they are without some creepy-crawly bigots belonging to latent international white supremacy dehumanizing and debasing them?" Letter to the *Sunday Sun* in response to the Caster Semenya controversy

Was Caster Semenya a latter-day Saartjie Baartman? When embarrassing and insensitive questions were asked about the 800m champion's gender, Athletics South Africa president Leonard Chuene said it wasn't because the powers that be were wondering, a little, about her facial and underarm hair, deep voice and an extraordinarily muscular build, it was because her critics were racist. "It would not be like that if it were some young girl from Europe ... If it was a white child, she would be sitting somewhere with a psychologist, but this is an African child ... People think we come from the bush in Africa and live like animals," he said. "We're not going to allow people to destroy children."

The South African Football Players Union (SAFPU[2]) blamed Australia, saying that our antipodean cousins were targeting South Africa because FIFA had awarded the 2010 World Cup to South Africa: "It shows that these imperialist countries can't afford to accept the talent that Africa as a continent has."

Later Chuene blamed racist South Africans for the rumours, saying, "This is about racism. These rumours come from South Africa. Why did these people write to the IAAF? These are the same people who don't want 2010 [next year's FIFA World Cup], the same people who bring black people down and the same people who refuse to believe that Africans can make it on the world stage."

Butana Komphela of the Portfolio Committee on Sport and Recreation said a complaint would be lodged with the UN High Commissioner of Human Rights over the undermining of Caster's rights and privacy. "It is a very gross action that gives an impression that the IAAF only recognizes good things when they are done by men," he said, and added for good measure that white female athletes who looked like men were not tested: "Just because she is black and she surpassed her European competitors there is all this uproar."

Somewhat mysteriously, the Young Communist League said the controversy over Semenya represented "a mentality of conforming feminine outlook within the white race". "The Williams sisters were never subjected to such public humiliation as is done by the international athletic body. Is it because they are of American descent?" they added.

One reader of *The Times* of London's website offered a simple solution. "Why doesn't someone just give her a car and ask her to park it?" he—it must have been a he—suggested. "If she can, then ban her for life!"

"And that is why they start this racist attack on this beautiful woman, well-built, well-relaxed, and even her appearance you can see that this is a beautiful woman coming from this beautiful country in the southern hemisphere of Africa." Julius Malema, who knows all about 'well-relaxed' women, weighs in on the reasons behind the questioning of Caster Semenya's gender.

The case of poor Caster suggested that, even if it was a little battered and somewhat worn, the race card proved as reliable as ever. KZN Transport MEC Bheki Cele turned a legitimate road safety concern into a race issue. "All of a sudden there is a hullabaloo about

---

[2] There are surely some smart alecs out there who might be attempted to observe that SAFPU is an appropriate acronym for an organization that talks such kak.

blue lights," he said in response to criticism by other road users. "I suggest it is because some people are aware that in the blue-light car today, there is a darkie inside there."

Membathisi Mdadlana said that only a racist could say that his comments about Chinese South Africans indicated a certain tendency to stereotype and generalize unfairly. "If you are racist, don't dump it on me," he said. "I've never been a racist and I will never be a racist. It came by three boats, *Dromedaris* and *Reijer* and others. I've never been a racist, that's why I joined the ANC."

"Speaking to journalists at the Union Buildings, government spokesman Bokkom Kiewiets said that Mdladlana could not be blamed for any racial stereotyping, as he had 'the mental capacity of a golden retriever'," the satirical website Hayibo.com reported.

Still, you do have to give him credit for doing something that most white South Africans can't—naming two of Jan van Riebeeck's ships.

Bantu Holomisa accused Essop Pahad of using the race card when the latter told an audience in Beijing that many white South Africans did not support Bafana Bafana and did not want South Africa to host the World Cup.

"They don't even care that the Soccer World Cup will take place in South Africa," Pahad told a press conference in Beijing.

Holomisa said Essop's comment was "ridiculous ... He badmouths our country and its citizens". "His statement is utter rubbish; white people vote in large numbers for his party, whilst his party and their government have promoted numerous white people into leadership positions," said Holomisa.

The explanation for Pahad's statement was obvious. "He has realized that he's about to be removed from his posh position in the presidency and Local Organizing Committee, and this is just a pathetic attempt to ingratiate himself with the prospective new president and his supporters, who seem to value wild militancy highly," said Holomisa.

"There is simply no evidence to suggest that any group of South Africans is against staging the 2010 Soccer World Cup in South Africa," said the DA's Ian Davidson. "Thankfully, Pahad himself will no longer be in government when the tournament kicks off. It is clear that he is ill-able to make it the successful event that we know it will be."

"All that Mbeki's government has achieved is to replace 'blacks out' with 'whites out'." Donwald Pressly

As a result of Pahad's comments, The Afrikanerbond laid a claim of hate speech with the Human Rights Commission, charging that Pahad had made use of "cheap politics" by abusing his opportunity to showcase South Africa in China. It said Pahad had broken the rules of a tolerant society "on an international platform, harmed the image of South Africa irreparably and promoted hate-speech".

The UDM said there were several ministers who resorted to "war-talk or playing the race card to appease the new faction controlling the African National Congress".

Minister of Minerals and Energy Affairs Bulelwa Sonjica brandished the race card when she told a crowd at a meeting about proposed mining at Xolobeni on the Wild Coast that a white man could not have their interests at heart. "He is a white person," she said. "Today Spoor says he is fighting for people's rights, but where was he when Joe Slovo [former South African Communist Party leader] was fighting for people's rights and was imprisoned for that? I ask myself: 'How much does he get for dividing our community? What is his agenda for not wanting progress in our community?'"

The person in question was Richard Spoor, a respected lawyer who worked with trade unions during the 1980s.

> "Bullard's sin was to treat blacks as adults. He laughed at the crimes, follies and ignorance of black men in the same way he laughed at the crimes, follies and ignorance of white men." Andrew Kenny writing to *Business Day* to defend David Bullard after the latter was fired from the *Sunday Times* for the column in which he tried to imagine what Africa would have been like without colonialism

Julius Malema claimed that the Sonke Gender Justice Network was serving a "white agenda" after the NGO laid a complaint with the Equality Court about remarks he had made about Jacob Zuma's rape accuser. "We will never apologize to some Mickey Mouses who want to put pressure on us," he declared, saying that Sonke represented "the whites who are opposed to African leadership. They want to rid and embarrass the leadership of the movement."

To the applause of onlookers outside the court, he said: "We are in court because the whites who are sponsoring this organization, they want to make sure they embarrass the leadership of this movement. An agenda must be exposed. This is a case of those who are refusing to accept the leadership of the ANC."

Cape Judge President John Hlophe—aka the slippery hlophe, according to Chris Roper —accused Chief Justice Pius Langa and his deputy Judge Dikgang Moseneke of "serving white interests" and that Acting Deputy Chief Justice Kate O'Regan was actually running the Constitutional Court.

"By the way, who else believed blacks couldn't think for themselves? Hendrik Verwoerd, Eugène Terre'Blanche, Jim Crowe, Strom Thurmond spring to mind," observed Hogarth, who honoured Hlophe as Mampara of the Week.

Butana Komphela continued to battle with Julius Malema for the title of South Africa's least tactful public figure. SASCOC (the SA Sports Confederation and Olympic Committee) was "full of whites and Indians who don't understand transformation and lack vision".

These comments were slanderous and racist, said SASCOC's Moss Mashishi, who said he was going to lodge a complaint with the Human Rights Commission. "SASCOC is an organization dedicated to implementing meaningful transformation in sport," said Mashishi, "and the wild allegations against a body made up of officials who have worked tirelessly towards this objective only demonstrate the ignorance of the source from which they emanate."

> "I think that it is profoundly racist to play the race card as nonchalantly as it is often being used today to denigrate people, to deflect criticism and to stifle debate. This has become something of a national pastime." Professor Nithaya Chetty, during an address on academic freedom at UCT

Afrikaners is pieperig

When latter-day Afrikaner hero Steve Hofmeyr wasn't in the news for having affairs ("Steve se dis mos net seks", according to the headline), he was talking about what it was like to be a boer through and through. "It's genetic. If I have to call myself a South African I have to work too hard, while if I call myself a boer, I immediately know what I am … I don't believe that this frenetic globalisation is either natural or good. How fucking boring if we all have to be the same … But I'm also gatvol of race. I was just about to forget skin colour when the ANC came along and rubbed everyone's face in race."

But it didn't always make sense, not when Julius Malema was putting up ANC posters in Orania and other white people were rude about each other. Like the time when

AfriForum launched a complaint to the Equality Court about Luke Watson's use of the word 'Dutchmen'. "The problem with South African rugby," he reportedly said, "is that it is controlled by Dutchmen."

AfriForum's leader Kallie Kriel said, "Watson's deep-rooted ethnic prejudices against Afrikaners should be addressed with the same rigour as is the case with other incidents of racism in the country."

"And there was a time when Dutchmen didn't run to the Equality Court when you called them names," Andrew Donaldson reflected. "No, they came round to your house, rang your doorbell and asked to speak to you outside in the street. Then there was a bit of what-for, and any confusion about clutch plates, spanners, planks, spiders on rocks and what have you was all quickly dealt with in a polite manner. And you didn't do it again. At least not in a hurry."

Andrew Donaldson thought it unlikely however, that anyone would run to the Equality Court to complain about being called about a rooinek or a soutie. "It's that superior, stiff-upper-lip thing we have. Either that, or we're just too sorry-arsed a bunch of losers to even bother with such matters."

"Crumbed mushrooms. Veggie stir-fry. Organic fucking coffee! And everyone's speaking English! I thought this was an Afrikaans festival." Chris Roper quotes a visitor to Oppikoppi

Calling someone a Dutchman could be an expensive exercise, however, as Pretoria resident Brian Read discovered. In August 2009, *Beeld* reported that Johan Paul Kleynhans was suing Read for R200,000 after the latter allegedly called Kleynhans a "typical fucking Dutchman" and a "fucking Vlok" outside a golf clubhouse in Pretoria. Read claimed that his language was justified because Kleynhans called him a "kafferboetie" and a "soutie", and countersued for R250,000.

Read allegedly asked Kleynhans, "Are you going to wash my feet as well?" and told him: "You're a fucking cunt." Read claimed damages for violation of privacy, as well as damage to his reputation and emotional well-being. The argument apparently began after Kleynhans paid a clubhouse bill of R2,000, which included a R200 tip for the waiter, one Maestro Morake. Later, in the parking lot, Morake brought Kleynhans a woman's handbag that had been left behind in the clubhouse. Read thought that Morake should get a tip for bringing the handbag; Kleynhans retorted that he had already tipped the man. It was then, Kleynhans claimed, that Read called him a "fucking Dutchman".

Morake testified that Read told Kleynhans: "You Dutchmen are all the same," that he had become aggressive and said "I'll moer you". He had also said, "Vlok, Vlok something".[3]

"I thought he was going to assault me," Kleynhans said. "Maestro had to hold him back."

"I asked someone what is Afrikaner traditional, and they're still puzzling it out. The problem is, if you go for khaki you're in trouble; you're AWB." Freedom Front Plus leader Pieter Mulder on the choice of outfit for the opening of Parliament

Assholes in all colours

Now, as the xenophobic upheavals of May 2008 recede into the past the impulse to turf out those with whom one disagrees is still there. Citing Julius Malema's calls to "kill for Zuma",

David Bullard was convinced that it would not be long before other communities were targeted, too: "When politicians can openly talk about eliminating those whose political views they disagree with you don't want to hang about to find out if they are joking. The signs couldn't be much clearer and I read into Mr Malema's comments a barely veiled threat to the white, Indian and coloured communities. After all, if you're going to have xenophobia how much easier it would be to carry out slaughter on the basis of skin colour rather than having to ask a fellow black the Zulu word for elbow."

Those who were inclined to agree with Bullard would have been disconcerted by the words of Deputy Minister of Foreign Affairs Fatima Hajaig. During an anti-war rally in Lenasia in January 2009 she told the crowd: "The control of America, just like the control of most Western countries, is in the hands of Jewish money and if Jewish money controls their country then you cannot expect anything else."

"I wish I were in the hands of Jewish money power," commented Zuma's biographer and self-described "nice Jewish boy" Jeremy Gordin. Tony Leon, then the DA's spokesman on

---

[3] Presumably a reference to the former minister of police with a penchant for podiatry, Adriaan Vlok's gesture of contrition by washing Frank Chikane's feet was in the news at the time.

current affairs, condemned Hajaig's allegations as "nothing more than bargain-basement conspiracy mongering". "Clearly, she's unsuited to a job that demands nimble diplomatic skills," the *Mail & Guardian* observed.

Hajaig later apologized, but there were those—like Cosatu's Bongani Masuku—who suggested that Jews who supported Israel should be persuaded to leave South Africa. "I have much in common with decent Jews who stand for justice. I love and honour their huge contribution to humanity and my own morality," said Masuku. "In fact, all the people who deny that occupation [of the West bank, presumably] is wrong must be encouraged to leave South Africa before they infect our society with much more racism."

"You sir, on the other hand will stay a Charrou and the bruinous are going to continue screwing your life up. Listen to the witous for a change, my larney. You may learn something yet." 'Sanjay' to 'Indian Larry' on the Dispatch blogs, during a vicious argument triggered by a report on Jacob Zuma

Perhaps it is better to accept that South Africans are race-obsessed: it was ever thus, and so it ever shall be. Without acknowledging that truth about ourselves, we would all require chronic prescriptions for anti-anxiety drugs. Max du Preez, for one, might be happier. A little over three months into the Zuma era, he concluded gloomily that the new version of the ANC was just as obsessed with ethnicity as the party under Mbeki. "The simple truth is that if non-racialism was indeed alive at some point, it is now dead. Stone dead. Deceased. It's snuffed it. It's not resting, it's not just stunned, it has passed on. Kicked the bucket." On the other hand, racial solidarity was alive and well. "Whites sit and wait for blacks to falter so they can shout: Incompetent! Buffoon! Affirmative Action! Quota System! Around the braai whites swap their stories of uneducated, incompetent blacks who had been pushed into positions of power above them. Their black counterparts also swap stories around the braai fires: of how racist their white colleagues are, of how there is still no real transformation, about whites being paid better than blacks even when they do the same job."

"When Zuma triumphed over Mbeki, there were sniggers about Zulus abandoning their taxi ranks and hostels to kick the Xhosas out of the Union Buildings. But when the Zulus got to the Union Buildings they couldn't take the boredom of having to use slow lifts and escalators ... they missed their fast taxis." Fred Khumalo

Far better to laugh at ourselves and our differences. After Highveld Stereo's Rude Awakening team devoted a show to a discussion on the difference between Joburg and Durban Indians, some listeners were incensed. They complained, among other things, about Jeremy Mansfield's mock-Indian accent, claims that "all Indians own sound systems that are worth more than the value of their car", a caller who said that Durban Indian women were classier than Joburg Indian women, and a caller who said that Durban Indians are so dark they're purple.

Fred Khumalo wondered why the word "Pakistan" was used to refer to big bums, "seeing that the natives of that Asian country are not necessarily well-endowed when it comes to matters of the behind. In fact, they are down there with the white okes in their competition to determine who has the flattest ironing-board buttocks". Khumalo said that the Zulus had names for people with flat bums: "Akusishwapha yindlovu iyashesha—his bum is so flat it's like that of an elephant taking a purposeful walk".

Law professor, blogger and gay activist Pierre de Vos argued that those who were victimized by epithets should claim them with pride. "So let us 'kaffirs' and 'moffies' get together and celebrate the fact that we are proud and out 'kaffirs' and 'moffies' who will not be intimidated and hurt by the prejudices of others," he declared. "That way we will help to pull the sting of these words and strike a real blow against racism and homophobia."

"The Isle of Man. There are no Muslims, no blacks. It's got a good healthcare system. It rains a lot, but so what? I'll get under-floor heating and I'll get a good mackintosh … I'm going to the Isle of Man, for Christ's sake." Former Anglo American deputy chairman Graham Boustred, now 84, reflects on where he would move should he obtain a UK ancestry visa

Since this chapter began with a discussion of the Chinese, it makes sense to end it with them, too. David Bullard, writing in the column that got him fired from the *Sunday Times*, speculated on what might have happened if Africa had never been colonized by Europeans: "Huge metal ships land on the coast and big metal flying birds are sent to explore the sparsely populated hinterland. They are full of men from a place called China and they are looking for coal, metal, oil, platinum, farmland, fresh water and cheap labour and lots of it. Suddenly the indigenous population realize what they have been missing all along: someone to blame."

MORE South African Insults

The column caused an uproar. Though Bullard apologized in the pages of *Business Day*, he was unrepentant, arguing later that South Africa is "not even an emerging nation when it comes to humour". He wanted, he said, to live in a country where he could make tasteless jokes with all of his friends, regardless of colour. "I can't stand all this cringing Uriah Heep white self-consciousness about race. In my book, an asshole is an asshole. And, like M&Ms, they come in many colours."

Technically, it must be pointed out, most assholes come in various shades ranging from pink to brown. But that's not the point. The point is that everyone's a shit. Some bigger than others, certainly (see the chapter on politicians). In the final analysis, as the political analyst Eusebius McKaiser reflects, everybody is capable of racism. "The question to focus our minds on—we can take a rainbow break during the World Cup—is to think through how we will eliminate this racism that persists in our social fabric," he argues.

"It is an emotionally challenging discussion, but one that need not be jarring."

"But if he wants to come with this whole 'coloureds are such-and-such' plak, we'll be happy to pick him up in a pimped-out Ford Cortina with wild horses airbrushed on the bonnet, threaten to stab him, blow tik smoke up his nose, bite him with a gold tooth, take him to church with Mommy and Granny, then watch a Manchester United game on Granny's television, and then threaten to stab him again." Hayibo. com imagines a response to Membathisi Mdadlana

"Racism will be with us for a long time and the sooner we accept that, and openly acknowledge it as a factor in our daily lives, the better. South Africans like to say we should not harp on race, but we would be living in a fool's paradise if we did not." Rapule Tabane

Chapter 14

Jacob Zuma, Helen Zille and the Wild Whore Libido

"We say things that Zuma cannot say because he is a politician. We are not politicians, we are activists. It is our job to say to Helen Zille: 'Shut up, you racist' when she starts attacking Zuma." Julius Malema, who rejected calls for him to stop opening his mouth before thinking, saying that he represented the voice of the youth

If you were to devote yourself to the study of the A to Z of South African politics, you might pause halfway through the alphabet to examine the wit and wisdom of Julius Malema. But much of your time would be spent on the letter Z, for it is there that we find the two figures who define contemporary South African politics. Jacob Zuma and Helen Zille represent completely opposite strands of political tradition and style.

Zuma is the smiling man of the people, Zille their stern headmistress; Zuma the leader of the party with which, many have claimed, Zille is obsessed. (Ndumiso Ngcobo asked if anyone had heard Helen Zille string together three sentences free of the word 'ANC' in the whole of 2008. "I bet Zille often sits in her office, admiring her Botoxed brow, calls the president's office at Luthuli House and breathes heavily for ten minutes.")

They are the yin and yang of the South African political establishment.

In a strange way but entirely logical way, they are united by Malema, their congenitally troublesome offspring, who requires both of them to fulfil his magnificent potential. With Zuma as his raison d'être and Zille as his bête noir, Malema is able to take his rightful place as the deepest donga in the South African political landscape.

This much became clear when, a few days before the country went to the polls, in perhaps his most revealing speech of the election campaign, Malema told students at Walter Sisulu University in East London, that his role was to "distract" the opposition while Zuma "sprinted to the Union Buildings". Zuma, he explained, was like a parent who would "not lower himself to his opponents' level" but instead would "send" his "children after you".

"People need to understand that the youth league says what Zuma can't say and [what he] can't be heard saying. For example, if Helen Zille takes on Zuma, saying he is not fit to govern, our task was to occupy her mind with the fact that she's a racist, colonialist with … a fake face. While she was concentrating on calling me names, thinking she was embarrassing us, Zuma was sprinting to the Union Buildings," he told the crowd.

> "We do not want a president who is above us … who is extremely advanced. You will leave us behind, and by the time you look back, we are gone." Julius Malema on Jacob Zuma

For much of 2008, South Africans were riveted by the uncertainty as to whether Jacob Zuma would sprint to the Union Buildings while wearing a prison uniform. COSATU and the ANC Youth League were having none of it. "I just want to ask those who are behind this case if they would be proud to prosecute their own president, and embarrass their own country," queried Malema.

JZ certainly inspired loyalty, with both Malema and Zwelanzima Vavi vowing to die for him. "All of these leaders have rubbished the Constitution in the political interests of their leader, Jacob Zuma," fumed Helen Zille. "His silence, if it continues, must be taken as a sign that he too has no respect for our constitutional order."

"Welcome to the age of lunacy," Lucas Ntyintyane wrote in a letter to News24. "The masters of claptrap are the new kings. They spout nonsense to make news headlines and they don't care about the damage caused by their poisonous stings to this beautiful country.

"This rhetoric should act as warning bells for everyone. Politicians are like children and need constant babysitting. For the sake of this great nation, we must do our part in calling them into order. Don't just sit and moan. Stand up and protect the constitution. Tomorrow the kingmakers will come for you."

Max du Preez said that Vavi was "so jealous of the publicity Malema is getting for huffing and puffing and making hollow threats that he is trying to out-Malema Malema to also get on TV".

"For someone who attacks ZANU-PF so often, he really sounds like a Mugabe thug. We can never take Vavi seriously again. Nzimande is an intellectually dishonest weakling," he added, saying that Nzimande was "not worth the shadow" of Chris Hani or Joe Slovo.

"No Zuma, no country." Former MK commander in uniform in the streets in front of the court in Pietermaritzburg where Jacob Zuma was appearing on corruption charges

Fred Khumalo thought that Zwelinzima Vavi's parents had named their son "the land is tough" because he was certainly living up to it with stupid statements. "Every time he opens his mouth, he sinks it—the country—into difficulties," Khumalo complained. He had heard rumours that Vavi had designs on becoming minister of labour under Zuma. "Help! The land is going to be even tougher.

"It beggars belief that this mampara—who not only misunderstands bread and butter issues that affect his constituency, but also defies logic in the campaigns that he organizes—has these ambitions of becoming a government minister at all. But the most amazing thing is that he doesn't listen to reason; he only listens to his own head."

"If I was Thabo Mbeki I would step down as President of the country and surrender power to these over-hungry hyenas led by Jacob Zuma ..." Nkululeko Mposi wrote to *The Citizen*. "Give them power even before 2009 and watch South Africa turn into a 'Banana Republic'. People, wake up and smell the coffee."[1]

"The page performed an illegal operation and was promoted to vice-president." Warning on the website of the Eastern Cape department of health, after it was hacked. Alternative suggestions for why the page was not found included: "The page is sleeping. After all, this is African time we are talking about," and "The page was considered redundant and was given a raise so it now works even less"

"Do we leave it to chance in the ANC when another energetic president wants to stay on—because he feels that he has something to contribute?" Jacob Zuma—himself no slouch when it comes to singing, dancing and partying—raises questions about the desirability of an "energetic president" like Thabo Mbeki

---

[1] Thus demonstrating that even black readers of *The Citizen* worry about banana republics. Yes, there is hope for the Rainbow Nation.

Garden boys and inkwenkwes

> "I only debate with serious political youth formations, not a group of the racist Helen Zille's garden boys." Julius Malema turns down a challenge to debate the DA Youth

As expected, the elections were nasty. Trevor Manuel had a dig at Zille while campaigning for the ANC at a rally organized by COSATU. "You know, there are some parties … you ask them about this, they say: 'Crisis, what crisis? We don't know that there's a crisis.' They'll say to you, 'We've been too busy campaigning to know that there's a crisis,' or 'Maybe our leader's gone for new Botox or something, we're too busy to consider this crisis.'"

Zille had previously admitted that she had endured Botox injections in an effort to win over the electorate. "Over the past few years I have started taking more trouble over my appearance," she said. "I now realize it is a sign of respect to the public to make the effort."[2]

One could hardly blame her. She might be surrounded by some of the most grotesque examples of male physicality to be found in any political establishment anywhere in the world, but somehow, female politicians were required to have a personal stylist on permanent call. Asked what Helen Zille's greatest weakness was, Max du Preez suggested her hairstyle: "She looks like a Boere auntie." Zapiro said she spread herself too thinly. "Either that or vanity. Enough with the Botox."

Julius Malema said that Helen Zille's dance moves made her look like she missed apartheid. "She is not original but is plastic and cannot stand in the heat. But when you look at her pictures before the makeover, she looks like an apartheid spy," said Malema of the woman who, as a journalist, revealed that Steve Biko had been murdered by the apartheid police.

Insults flew thick and fast, though Zille generally kept above the fray. It was after Julius dismissed DA deputy leader Joe Seremane as a "garden boy" that Zille lost her cool and aimed directly below the belt. Julius, she said, was an *inkwenkwe*, an uncircumcised boy.

---

[2] Yes, people, we live in a culture in which injecting oneself with deadly poison in order to freeze the muscles in one's face is a sign of respect for the public.

Shock! Horror! A white auntie using culture, usually off limits, to make comments about a black man's dangly bits. The cheek of it![3]

Matthews Posa said that it was inappropriate for Zille to refer to Malema in that way. "Malema is not circumcised, but let us not go there, let's keep it decent," he allowed, but said, "We think the call is more an electioneering stunt and must be understood in that context.

"She stooped very low in her response, very low. It means that she is not able to take the punches as we can. She is hysterical. As a leader she went below the bar with her response."

The ANC, he said, would respond to Zille's remarks in a similar fashion to "try to make her aware that if you throw mud, there's a lot of mud around".

"Anyone can throw mud."

Many wondered exactly how Zille obtained such specific information about Julius's schlong. Among them was Fred Khumalo, who decided he'd rather not know. "I'll stay in the dark, rather than in the gutter."

Zille later explained that she used the word inkwenkwe because Malema insulted an older man. "An inkwenkwe can't insult an ixhego [an elder], and that is the context in which I referred to him as that.

"Julius Malema is rude and disgusting ..." she fumed. "He called Joe a garden boy and I call him a gnome. I am sick of this rude boy. He must go get a proper job."

"One of the positives of living in South Africa: you get a president free of charge."
Internet joke that circulated after the NPA dropped charges against Zuma

Long walk to being free of charge

"What has happened to me is that certain people have thrown this dark cloud to me with the aim of demonizing me. So if I step aside, a bad precedent will be

---

[3] *Citizen* reader Homeboy Mmoba pointed out that it was only an offence to call a graduate of an initiation school an inkwenkwe. "In strict cultural language, Malema is completely out of order to reject his *inkwenkwe* status and must just go to the mountains to pay his dues. At least Fikile Mbalula will give him tips on how to survive initiation school."

created. People will know that if you hate somebody, you just throw a dark cloud and it is the end of the story." Jacob Zuma explaining his refusal to step down as the ANC's presidential candidate

Reflecting on the events of 2008, Max du Preez had felt that Zuma was a big disappointment. "He went from peacemaker and caring father figure to one who has dealings with devious financiers, who refuses to tell what he really knows about the shady arms deal, who uses thugs and tribalists to further his cause and oversees Stalinist purges in the ANC."

Helen Zille would have no doubt agreed with du Preez; she had, after all, long made her views on Jacob Zuma clear.

"Corruption is increasingly being accommodated and normalized," she argued in one interview. "The other day someone said to me: 'I don't care if Zuma is corrupt, he has done a lot for us.' People don't seem to understand that when a politician is corrupt, he is stealing from them."

Julius did not care. "If Zuma is corrupt, then we want him with all his corruption," he told a crowd in February 2009. "We want him with all his weaknesses. If he is uneducated, then we want him as our uneducated president." Zille was just part of a plot to prevent voters from having a real choice. "When we say that people like Zille represent ... the apartheid system, colonizers and are backward, we mean this. When they can't defeat them [opponents], they must arrest them and lock them up," he explained.

Shortly before the elections, Zille insisted that Zuma should have his day in court. "Zuma has not proven his innocence," she said. "He has not been acquitted. He has merely been let off the hook by the NPA."

"Why would the NPA withdraw the case in April, just two weeks before a general election? The unseemly haste can only be politically motivated," said Zille.

"Cannot open Jacob Zuma jpeg. File corrupt." Error message

But Zille was battling against forces larger and more powerful than her own. If God was on the side of the ANC, the universe was punting for Zuma. At the beginning of 2009, Vosloorus sangoma Sweetness Tau predicted that Jacob Zuma stood a good chance of becoming president. "There is a high possibility that Jacob Zuma may ultimately become the president of SA, although his legal woes may continue to threaten to derail his plans," she said. "But because he [Zuma] has been through this before and he has the support of his ancestors, he will survive with few scars."

Astrologer Roger Fidler, asked by *The Star* what the year promised, made the astounding prediction that Zuma would be busy during the general elections. "Zuma's astrological chart shows that April will be an important month in his life. It shows that he will be more active in this period."

Um, ja, okay.

"The last time I saw the DA campaigning outside my local Spar I gave them a wide berth. They feel a bit like Jehovah's Witnesses to me, sympathetic though I am to Helen Zille's brand of self-righteous white-madam politics. That's the only role available for white people in South African politics today, unless you assume the Alec Erwin position and have a special tripartite-alliance bolt installed through your brain." Shaun de Waal

Political toddlers

"Racist … colonialist … imperialist." Julius Malema on Helen Zille. Later he also declared, "Helen Zille is a political toddler." Takes one to know one, presumably

As it turned out, Zuma was fairly active in April, so much so that he won the election and took office in a ceremony in front of the Union Buildings, just as Julius Malema had predicted he would.

South Africans, so grateful that the world had not come to an end, gave him a rapturous welcome. And Zille of all politicians managed to miscalculate the national mood.

In response to the howls of protest against her all-male cabinet, Zille wrote a long letter in which she pointed out that the ANC and its alliance partners did not exactly boast a sterling record when it came to the promotion of women. After all, none of them had ever had a female leader. Besides, Jacob Zuma's own record with women was hardly one to be proud of. "Zuma is a self-confessed womanizer with deeply sexist views who put all his wives at risk by having unprotected sex with an HIV-positive woman," Zille wrote.

It was one sentence. One little sentence. But one that even Zille would come to regret.

> "Jacob Zuma. President of South Africa. To run a country like this you need the energy of a nightclub, the power of a Yamaha, the carrying capacity of a big handbag, the imagination of a computer game and the ability to enthrall like the Cirque du Soleil." David J. Smith

Even before the retort, there was trouble.

COSATU for one was not impressed, calling the appointments an "insult to women and blacks". They were based "rather on cronyism"—something about which they themselves knew nothing.

Former *Mail & Guardian* editor Ferial Haffajee complained: "Rather than a thumbs-up, Zille's given a middle-finger-up to women leaders in the composition of her leadership at the sphere in which she exercises real power."

"The scaly Godzille was in a pigsty-rolling mood this week," sniffed the *Sunday Times* as it deemed Zille Mampara of the Week. The paper was not impressed with her "'70s Nat-looking cabinet"—which sounds like something made from imbuia and bought from Morkels—or her "frolicking" in "the gutters of thoughtlessness".

The ANCYL in the Western Cape dubbed the DA the "Devil Alliance" and issued a statement declaring that "the dawn of the worst new era has come to the province of the Western Cape and its people". They were incensed that Zille did not feel "disgusted" or "ashamed" by her cabinet. Nonetheless, it did not surprise them that Zille "acted so racist when appointing her cabinet" as her office was full of white people when she was MEC.

"As the ANC Youth League in the province we shall not rest until racism and sexism is uprooted in the provincial government led by the GodZille. An intensified programme of action will be rolled out soon to exert pressure on this racist provincial government to change and be representative of sectors of the province.

"We call upon all those people of the province who have fought for non-racialism, non-sexism and democracy in their lives to join hands with us in the fight against apartheid of the Western Cape government. We are not going to rest till the racist and apartheid regime of the Western Cape is overthrown."

"The sooner DA leader Helen Zille acknowledges that Joe Seremane has a better chance of being a president than she does, the better. If there's one thing the majority of black people in this country fear more than a white man as a president, it's a white woman. Yes Madam! No Madam! Sorry Madam! Yo yo yo—Eish!" David Kau

Zuma-hate and Platonic love

"Lads, when she says it's Platonic, she doesn't in fact mean she's shagging Cape Town's new philosopher-mayor Dan Plato." Chris Roper on the ANCYL's reaction to Helen Zille's all-male cabinet

In the light of all this criticism, Zille must have thought that the reference to Zuma in what was otherwise a considered and logical response, was perfectly legitimate under the circumstances.

She must have been surprised by the reaction, which was swift and filled with the self-righteous fire of outrage. First, ANC spokeswoman Jessie Duarte got theatrical, declaring that Zille's comments were an "unprecedented example of Zuma-hate". Patrick Craven of COSATU huffed, "Rather than try to enter into a genuine debate on the representivity of her cabinet, she has tried to deflect attention from these serious allegations with a disgraceful, and totally irrelevant, slur against President Jacob Zuma."

ANC secretary-general Gwede Mantashe said that Zille was now public enemy no 1. "She has elevated her role from that of opposition to that of the enemy—an offer from the DA that we must accept," he warned.

Youth Communist League national secretary Buti Manamela said that Zille wanted to turn the Western Cape into Orania. Zille, he said, was "a front of extremely right-wing" elements "running" the opposition party. "She is merely a token," he said, and added that it was "quite unfortunate" that Zille had resorted to "infantile rhetorical mud slinging" when challenged on her all-male cabinet.

ANC Youth League spokesman Floyd 'Rocket Scientist' Shivambu had theories of his own. "Zille has appointed an all-male cabinet of useless people, [the] majority of whom are her boyfriends and concubines so that she can continue to sleep around with them, yet she claims to have the moral authority to question our president," he thundered, and promised to take "militant action" against "the fake racist girl who was dropped on her head as a child".

Later Floyd denied that "sleeping around" meant "having sex" with more than one person. "No, we never said she is going to have sex with them," he said. "We are saying that she is sleeping around with them. We have our own interpretation of that [and] people can give their own interpretation. We stand by that statement and we are not going to change it, we stand by that one hundred percent."

Asked if he wasn't worried about being sued for defamation, he said: "We are not afraid of any legal action. We are not afraid of anything. We are going to defend and stand by each and every word we have said here as the ANCYL—that Zille is sleeping around, she is appointing people that she wants to be sleeping with—we stand by that particular view."

> "It seems that, except for beauty, talent, education, intelligence and style, DA leader Helen Zille is an exact carbon copy of ANCYL-biters leader Julius Malema."
> Chris Roper

Kebby Maphatsoe of the MK Veterans Association had similar beliefs about Zille. "Just recently, she appointed half her sex boys into the Western Cape provincial cabinet to keep them close enough to satisfy her well-evolved wild whore libido," he informed the public. He also accused Zille of being a "racist longing for the apartheid past" and threatened to make the Western Cape ungovernable unless she retracted her statement. Should Helen Zille not refrain from this anti-African and racist behaviour, we are not going to hesitate, but craft and launch a political programme aimed at rendering the Western Cape ungovernable," he warned. The MKMVA then attempted to present a list of demands to Zille, but was greeted by Housing MEC Bonginkosi Madikizela. Dismissing him as one of Zille's boyfriends, they told him to "voetsek".

> "Her continuous attacks on President Jacob Zuma attest to the deep hatred and disregard of black people." The Western Cape ANCYL offers an insightful analysis of Helen Zille

Reflecting on statements by the ANCYL, Chris Roper thought that perhaps referring to Zille as a "fake racist girl" was not the best way to establish one's feminist credentials:

"Telling the world that you're going to bliksem her if she doesn't learn her place, is not really the way to get women … to embrace you as defenders of freedom." He also wondered about the ANCYL's apparent lack of ability to spell, specifically in its reference to the fact that "will never be a Mickey-mouse republic like [Zille] wants to portray it".

"Not that I insist on correct spelling in a country where English is only one of eleven official languages," he reflected, "but in an official communication to the world, one that you expect to be taken seriously, can't you make it look less like the petulant spewings of a sugar-maddened child?"

> "Pity I won't c Man U lift the trophy. I'm sitting in a long mtg wt my friend, Helen Zille. We'v really kissed n made up, literally." Home Affairs deputy minister and ex ANCYL president Malusi Gigaba updates his Facebook status

For his part, Andrew Donaldson was convinced that the "anaulstic bluster of the ANCYL and the MK Veterans in response to "Mrs Fuss Pants" could be ascribed to sexual pathologies. "Broadly speaking, both are hopeless Zillephiliacs. The merest mention of the Western Cape premier is enough to compel them to commit unseemly acts with themselves in public, the likes of which haven't been seen since Sodom and Gomorrah."

Donaldson suggested an ice-cold bath for Maphatsoe, "followed perhaps by the strategic deployment of stinging nettles down the front of [his] customized stud-muffin posing pouch". As for Shivambu, Donaldson suggested a "Jou Ma se Oedipus" T-shirt and a stint in a padded cell.

To punish Zille for her insult about Zuma, the ANC decided not to allow the DA to chair any of Parliament's portfolio committees. "It is a question of relations being serviced. There must be mutual respect between the parties," said African National Congress secretary-general Gwede Mantashe, as he announced the party nominations for the positions. "They have taken a position that is hostile. You first manage the hostility, then you build a relationship." He accused Zille of showing "a total disrespect to the office of the President of the republic … We must have very thin skins to that. It cannot be allowed to continue".[4]

---

[4] Never mind that Mantashe had stood by while Julius Malema and Jacob Zuma disrespected the office of the President when they referred to its then incumbent as a dead snake, but hey, if you can't be an unabashed hypocrite, then what's the point of getting into politics in the first place?

"His unforgivable cheap comment about Zuma wearing 'leopard skin and monkey tails' is a grave insult to indigenous Africans. Donaldson is a neo-liberal English-speaking DA type of garbage that should pack his bags and go back to the UK where he will find 'barbarians' more civilized than him." Vince Masuku, Midrand, letter to the *Sunday Times*, responding to an article by Andrew Donaldson

Zumamania

"I didn't feel like the proverbial pork sausage in a mosque." Helen Zille after her first meeting with the extended cabinet, which included all provincial premiers

"When Julius Malema and Blade Nzimande and Zwelinzima Vavi insulted Mbeki, was that not unpatriotic and un-African?" wondered Max du Preez. He quoted James Myburgh, editor of Politicsweb, who wrote that the ANC alliance "appears to be trying to teach her [Zille], and South Africa, a lesson. This is that from now on everyone should grovel before the feet of the new big man".

"The difference," argued du Preez, "is that Mbeki took on his critics himself; Zuma uses his fox terriers to do it while the grandfatherly smile never leaves his face."

Barney Pityana thought that Zuma's was a pyrrhic victory. The ANC under Zuma, he said, was driving South Africa towards a totalitarian state "where the will of the party prevails and subordinates all other opinions to its own will. We must act. With our finger in the dike we can hold back the prospect of Zumamania."

But Zumamania was spreading like wildfire. The newly minted president was a superstar. When he visited Maponya Mall in Soweto during May 2009, one shopper speculated as to his whereabouts. "Maybe he has gone to the movies to watch Wolverine," he suggested. "He does not need to watch Wolverine. He is the wolverine," said another.

As for Zille, when asked how she felt after the elections, she said: "I know I'm going to be man alone."

Well, he seems nice

"He has talked a lot, but he has done squat! Sweet Fanny Adams!" Llewellyn Kriel on Jacob Zuma's first hundred days in office

Zuma biographer Jeremy Gordin once argued that so many people disliked Zuma—who had otherwise been depicted as a charming, intelligent and astute political operator—because he was not a saint. "Just as we don't like change," he wrote, "we don't like deviations from our national myth. It's frightening and makes us dislike those whom we hold responsible."

Still, despite JZ's featuring role in a thousand jokes and countless nightmares, it seemed South Africans were warming to him. Even the media were being nice for once. "As president, he is turning out to be much better than my, admittedly low, expectations," Tim Cohen reflected in the pages of *Business Day*.

As it turned out, Zuma's first hundred days had passed much as they have done for years in South Africa, marked as they were by service delivery protests, cabinet ministers expressing their cultural identity by buying 7-series BMWs and S-class Mercedes-Benzes, and dodgy characters getting let off the hook. The sky had not fallen in, and given that many South Africans had told their Facebook friends that they were planning to buy tickets for Sydney when the NPA dropped their case against Zuma, everyone was pleasantly surprised.

Everyone seemed to agree that Zuma was, well, *nice*.

Even Helen Zille thought Zuma "affable, humble and approachable", even if she was still convinced his relationships with questionable individuals was going to cause trouble down the line. "The personal tone of the presidency is open and friendly,' she added. Patricia de Lille gave Zuma 6 out of 10, saying "in many ways we still have the same Government and the same ANC and so not much has changed, except that there is a President that smiles and dances".

Bantu Holomisa said Zuma was on the right track. "He seems not to have forgotten that it is people who voted him to office. He is in touch with them."

Not that Zuma had actually *done* anything, people agreed, but he did make for a refreshing change from the Mbeki era, and that was nice. Also, the fact that he had inherited a global recession prompted some to feel rather sorry for him. After all, it wasn't his fault.

The media, said Kriel, had fallen "for this heap of rancid codswallop like dazed denizens of the mosh pit at a Metallica concert".

"For heaven's sake, Zuma has got to be the president who has done least to deserve such blind adoration since the golden calf caused the Israelites to fall down in worship to their self-made idol.

"Zuma has had a rather ordinary first 100 days as fearless leader of a fear-filled nation," he concluded acidly. "I suppose that's as good as can be expected from a sworn communist who doesn't see the contradiction in asking his supporters to bring him a machine gun and asking God to bless Africa."

"The Sword of Damocles of prosecution has been over his head and will always follow him, but it does not feature much at the moment," said one international diplomat. "Now we want to see how well he can run a country."

Time will tell.

"She, the racist little girl, must remember that Zuma is her boss. Helen Zille must give report to Zuma about the Western Cape ... the racist girl has not won ... all of them must call President Zuma, president." Julius Malema demonstrates his own commitment to non-sexism after Zille was taken to task for not having women in her Western Cape cabinet

Chapter 15

Last, but alas, least: Zimbabwe is mine, mine, mine!

"This Gorgon's imagination and creativity can only be matched by his gargantuan ego. His Hitlerian streak is the stuff of horror movies." Hogarth, on awarding Robert Mugabe the title of Mampara for Life

"What kind of *muthi* is Mugabe using?" wondered Makroty Sokana in a letter to *The Citizen*. "The entire world is afraid of him. Mugabe has pulled all the tricks and strings from his bag of nefarious tools to illegally hold on to power. I appeal to the United Nations and George Bush to give uncle Bob an ultimatum. Please remove that murdering buffoon from power now."

But the murdering buffoon shows no sign of going anywhere. The irrepressible Uncle Bob has survived elections that not even his own party could rig, a so-called unity government with his chief political rival, international sanctions and a troublesome prostate, and he is still going strong.

"The land reform exercise is irreversible. Those who have sought relief from outside Zimbabwe should know that land acquisition is through legal means and for that reason, the noises they make will simply frustrate them more." Robert Mugabe, September 2009

Zimbabwe has been circling the plughole for so long, it appears to defy all known laws of the universe, gravity included. In a similarly scientific vein, Hogarth observed that modern science "had yet to come up with a method to gauge exactly how ineffective the Southern African Development Community has been in its efforts to broker an agreement between Zimbo president Bob Mugabe and prime minister-designate Morgan Tsvangirai".

SADC had ruled that Mugabe and Tsvangirai should "share" the ministry of home affairs, which manages the police and the electoral process. "Whether the parties agree or not, that is the position of the summit," SADC declared.

"Well, the parties disagree—and what is the SADC's position now?" wondered Hogarth. "Why, somewhere between Irrelevant and Useless, two of the more interesting destinations in Mamparaland."

> "He makes sure he doesn't stay in South Africa for more than a day and brings his own official vehicle—a big black Mercedes—and driver. He doesn't trust South African security services and suspects they can easily be bought by overseas agents to kill him." A Zimbabwean official, on why President Robert Mugabe brought his own bodyguards to South Africa to attend a SADC summit

"They make you really, really feel the pain before you die"

> "We've been throttled, abused, tortured and killed and these leaders still want to pamper Mugabe's ambition to die in power. I find it strange that they don't see anything wrong with Mugabe at all." Former MDC MP Job Sikhala

Hogarth's comments were made in the wake of elections that many had hoped would lead to some kind of resolution to nearly nine years of chaos and despair. On balance, they seem to have done little to end Zimbabwe's agony.

Back in April 2008, hopes were high that change might finally arrive. Zimbabwean immigrants in South Africa even said that they would return if things started looking up, prompting David Kay to observe: "This means all those highly qualified Zimbabwean teachers, engineers, accountants and war veterans working in South Africa will be going back home, if they remember where the hole in the fence they came through is."

Fred Khumalo was less sanguine. "The long and short of it is that by being docile and not voting, the Zimbabweans will get the government they deserve a few days from today," he wrote.

"Your vote is your bullet," a Zimbabwean soldier told a crowd of prospective voters ahead of the presidential 'elections'.

Stories of torture and murder abounded. One dead MDC supporter was paraded around town at the back of a bakkie, his killers crowing "We have killed the dog."

An MDC official explained: "Better's body was found first. They found the other two four days later. They were stabbed with knives and screwdrivers. Their eyes were gouged out and their faces burned … There's a pattern. They torture you. They make you really, really feel the pain before you die."

"No. I wouldn't describe that as a crisis. There is a normal electoral process according to the laws of Zimbabwe." Thabo Mbeki's response to the farcical Zimbabwean election run-off

The final round

"We've been betrayed by these leaders in the region and the continent who see no evil and speak no evil about each other." Former MDC MP Job Sikhala criticizes SADC's softly-softly approach with Robert Mugabe

In a turnaround of events that surprised everybody, it turned out that ZANU-PF was not able to rig their own election. The MDC scored a comfortable victory, while the presidential election was so close that—conveniently—a run-off would be needed to determine the winner.

Initially, Tsvangirai indicated that he would not participate in the presidential run-off in order to avoid further bloodshed. Later, when he changed his mind, he said, "A run-off election could finally knock out the dictator for good. I am ready and the people are ready for the final round."

When Tsvangirai sought protection in the Dutch embassy during the lead-up to the presidential run-off elections, government mouthpiece *The Herald* crowed that he was a "lost child". "His constituency is in Europe and he will be elected the best Euro-American puppet of the country while having tea and Dutch cheese in the Dutch Embassy in Harare."

"This makes wonder, whoever comes up with such phrases: rainbow and miracle nation; jewel of Africa; Harare the Sunshine City. For when things fail, then the white man becomes the survival kit that we should depend on."

Later, *The Herald* suggested that if Mugabe's biographer Heidi Holland needed three psychologists to understand Mugabe, Morgan Tsvangirai was an "open book".

"He does not only suffer from foot and mouth disease, but he also moves around with an open mouth and a closed mind.

"Zimbabweans and his Western handlers can read him like an open book, for it is that simple with a trackless and content free person, a lesson that some in Zimbabwe still have to grasp ... Tsvangirai's pranks can fool the uninitiated, but not all Zimbabweans are as dumb as he is. Zimbabweans have had enough of his theatrics and the nonsense he frequently exposes us to."

> "They want to undermine the African Union and [South African] President Mbeki's [mediation] efforts because they are racist, because they think only white people think better. It's an insult to African leaders." Deputy Zimbabwean Information Minister Bright Matonga, who isn't, uses the race card

ZANU-PF's continued targeting of the MDC triggered a chorus of international disapproval. Lord Malloch-Brown, a UK Foreign Office minister, said that Mugabe was no longer the legitimate ruler of Zimbabwe. "Our objectives are to get in every forum possible a recognition that today President Mugabe no longer remains the proper rightful leader of the country," he said. "He has no claim under his own constitution for the presidency ... we do not accept the status quo, we do not expect the international community to accept the status quo."

In typically limp-wristed fashion, the African Union said the violence was a matter of "grave concern", but failed to offer any actual solutions.

Even Julius Malema described the election as a "joke" and said that Zimbabwe had reached a political "cul-de-sac".

"The conditions on the ground in Zimbabwe were never conducive to a free and fair election, and the credibility of this election is seriously wanting," Malema said. "To recognize its outcome would be a betrayal of not only our own values, but also of the aspirations of the people of Zimbabwe ... What was meant to be a presidential run-off election deteriorated into a joke of the worst order."

In the midst of the brouhaha, one Zuzu McBerth Mdluli—presumably his parents were fans of Shakespeare, and whoever typed up his birth certificate wasn't—wrote to *The Times* to inform readers that Mugabe was "suffering" for Zimbabwe. "What is happening in Zimbabwe is a lesson that the colonizers hope South Africa is learning from; that is: don't upset the apple cart as Mugabe has done, lest you suffer the same fate," wrote Mdluli. "The supporters of Mugabe that your reader wonders about are those that are not influenced by the trends of the day. They know that Mugabe, and Zimbabwe, suffers for their emancipation. For that they remain true to their leader and I say all power to them."

> "Behaving like spoilt brats will never deliver any solution, but will serve to advance the agenda of those who do not want to see Zimbabwe succeed." Julius Malema, who knows all about behaving like a spoilt brat, on ZANU-PF and the MDC

Phakeme Khumalo was mystified by Mugabe supporters. "What are pro-Mugabe advocates hoping to gain by worshipping him? Why would anyone vote for him? I find myself forced to ask two questions: who are the people willing to vote for Mugabe, and are they literate? It should be noted that by literate, I mean sane."

The Australians were fascinated by events in Zimbabwe, with exposés on the situation there a weekly feature.

Sydney satirist Aaron Timms imagined what Mugabe would say about his glasses. "As many of you know, in recent months I have changed my glasses, switching from the over-sized, Jiang Zemin-style bifocals I favoured through the '80s and '90s to a pair of sexy, Left Bank intellectual-style black rims. This is the great irony of Zimbabwe's relationship with the West: they refuse to sell us basic commodities, yet they are happy to keep our country flush with designer spectacles.

"The double standard is atrocious. In the years ahead, the Government will continue to expose the West for the filthy colonialists they are, primarily by ensuring that all our ministers are kitted out in natty Italian suits. Armani, Versace, Zegna, Pal Zileri: these are our strongest allies in the struggle against oppression."

> "... our border officials are too incompetent to successfully stop a drunk camel carrying a dead suicide bomber from walking across Beitbridge." Cartoonist Jeremy Nell comments on the vast numbers of illegal Zimbabwean immigrants streaming into South Africa

Our commander-in-chief and hero

"No mealie meal". ZANU-PF wish list inviting corporations to donate caviar and champagne to celebrate his 85th birthday. At the time, seven million Zimbabweans survived on international food aid

Time passed by. The presidential elections were eventually held for a second time, and Kgalema Motlanthe claimed that South Africa's policy of quiet diplomacy would be vindicated by the formation of an "inclusive and democratic" unity government in which Tsvangirai was due to be sworn in as prime minister.

Mugabe and ZANU-PF continued to buy time, retaining control of the armed forces, the police and the central bank, which was still under the control of Gideon Gono 'rrhoea'.

On the occasion of Mugabe's 85th birthday, the Defence Ministry placed a newspaper ad cynical enough to convince the most bitter and twisted satirist that he was out of a job and it would be sensible to throw himself off the nearest cliff at the earliest opportunity.

"Like a mighty crocodile,[1] you have remained resilient, focused and resolute against all odds and stood by the principles of our liberation struggle as well as the sovereignty of our beloved motherland, Zimbabwe," the ad read. "We indeed salute you our commander-in-chief and hero, and further pray that the Almighty God grant you many more years. We should never forget that 50 of the 85 years, Comrade Mugabe has been in the trenches slaving so that you and me could live a life of dignity."

Misheck Sibanda—who, granted, was paid to keep his nose firmly affixed to the presidential posterior—also praised Uncle Bob's "visionary leadership, selfless dedication to the ideals of national unity, sovereignty and empowerment of the indigenous majority. Mugabe, said Sibanda, had provided an "enduring legacy that should inspire both current and future generations".

As, indeed, it no doubt will.

Harare street vendor Brian Chibwe, asked what he thought of the occasions, summed it up most succinctly when he said: "The best birthday present he could give us is to retire."

---

[1] One wonders what southern Africa's other *groot krokodil* would have thought of this. The reference to Mugabe as a "mighty crocodile" brings to mind the tale of Whitey, a 3.5m crocodile in Australia who, like Mugabe, terrorized tourists but, unlike Uncle Bob, died in November 2008 after ingesting 25 plastic shopping bags, a plastic wine cooler bag and a rubber float. If only.

"Some African countries have done worse things and when I go to the AU meeting next week [in Egypt], I am going to challenge some leaders to point out when we have had worse elections. I would like some African leaders who are making these statements to point at me and we would see if those fingers would be cleaner than mine." Robert Mugabe, who may actually have a point. Sort of. Although it still doesn't let him off the hook

Melancholera

"I have to say that I am deeply, deeply distressed that we should be found not on the side of the ones who are suffering." Archibishop Emeritus Desmond Tutu, in an interview with the BBC

Not even a cholera epidemic could dampen the enthusiasm of ZANU-PF for their blighted cause. Amid calls for Mugabe to step down once and for all, one of his ministers accused the West of "contaminating" Zimbabwe. At a funeral featuring placards reading "Brown's cholera", Mugabe claimed that the cholera epidemic—which by then had claimed nearly 800 lives—was over. "Britain wants military intervention because of cholera," he said, adding that the World Health Organization was helping out. "Now there is no cholera, there is no cause for war."

After Condolleeza Rice criticized the failure of other African leaders to force Mugabe to step down, Uncle Bob said he did not know of any African leader who would be brave enough to topple him.

As Zimbabwe's central bank released a $10 billion note in mid December 2008, Mugabe told the annual ZANU-PF conference, "I will never, never, never, never surrender. Zimbabwe is mine, I am a Zimbabwean. Zimbabwe for Zimbabweans. Zimbabwe never for the British, Britain for the British."

Apparently oblivious to the fact that he had lost the last election, he told the conference that he would remain in power until "his people decide to change him". He also said that claims by the UN that more than 1,100 Zimbabweans had died of cholera were a "pack of lies" and merely an excuse for a war with the British. "I won't be intimidated," he said. "Even if I am threatened with beheading, I believe this and nothing will ever move me from it: Zimbabwe belongs to us, not the British."

"We have always said it—African leaders fear Mugabe for some reason, and for anyone to expect anything from them is wishful thinking. We just give our fate to the gods." Zimbabwean primary school teacher Tinashe Zulu

British prime minister Gordon Brown called Mugabe's government a "blood-stained regime" for its role in allowing preventable deaths and urged the international community to tell Uncle Bob: "enough is enough". His comments were echoed by the Archbishop of York, Ugandan-born John Sentamu, who wrote that the time had come for Mugabe to answer for his crimes against humanity in The Hague.

"The time to remove them from power has come."

After US Assistant Secretary of State for African Affairs, Jendayi Frazer, said that the American government no longer supported a government that included Mugabe, Uncle Bob dismissed Bush as "stupid". "Let him keep his comments to himself," said Mugabe. "They are undeserved, irrelevant, quite stupid and foolish." He also declared: These are the last kicks of a dying horse. We obviously are not going to pay attention to a sunset administration. Zimbabwe's fate lies in the hands of Zimbabweans."

As for Frazer, she was a "little girl" who was out of touch. "She thinks that Africans are idiots, little kids who cannot think for themselves," he said, a viewpoint which—based on the state of his land—was not unreasonable.

UN human rights expert Jean Ziegler—who back in 2002 had said that Mugabe had history and morality on his side—did not mince his words when it came to the Zimbabwean situation. "This mad dictator is practically under the protection of the South African government," Ziegler said in December 2008. "There needs to be pressure from international public opinion on South Africa."

Mugabe, he added, was a "head of state who has lost all sense of reality", and "the horror which is currently unfolding in Zimbabwe is completely intolerable".

Naturally, such comments had no impact whatsoever, as South Africa gave Uncle Bob a R300 million Christmas present in the form of food aid. "We are satisfied that the aid will reach the intended recipients in a non-partisan manner," said spokesperson Thabo Masebe, who added that South Africa "remains committed to the establishment of an inclusive government".

Sure.

"They rally behind fellow leaders against the West and go on about imperialism and nothing is mentioned about bettering the lives of people back home." Effie Ncube of the Matabeleland Constitutional Reform Agenda, on SADC's reluctance to force Robert Mugabe to accept change

To be fair, not every African leader was so enamoured of Mugabe. Raila Odinga of Kenya—who was evidently not a member of the liberation old boys' club—told delegates at Davos in January 2009: "There are the remnants of the past era, the dinosaurs, and Mugabe belongs to that group."

He criticized SADC for their "kid gloves" approach with Mugabe, saying, "The others do not have the courage to come up and tell Mr Mugabe that the time to leave has come."

The solution was to give Mugabe a "golden handshake" in order to persuade him to leave office.

COSATU's Zwelanzima Vavi also professed to be frustrated by the apparent lack of substantive change in Zimbabwe many months after the elections. "We are not quite excited by our current government led by Comrade Motlanthe's take on the issue. It is disappointing to say the least," he said.

"He needs to tell Mugabe in his face that we are withdrawing our acceptance of him as the President of Zimbabwe and that his government has no legitimacy, and that alone will signify to Mugabe that the party is over."

"Mugabe still retains all executive power almost a year after losing national elections, and this morning SADC leaders hailed the achievement as inspiring, reassuring and 'kick-ass'." Hayibo.com

Grace full of it

"Her explosive response and her determination to confiscate his film can only suggest, to even the most neutral observer, that she had something to hide, or that she has an ego that makes Paris Hilton and Lindsay Lohan look like shy, blushing maidens." Barry Ronge on Grace Mugabe

The party was still in full swing for Grace Mugabe, however. Not long after the news of Zimbabwe's cholera epidemic had reached the world, Mrs Mugabe took time out of her hectic shopping schedule to beat up a photographer who took shots of her as she emerged from the Kowloon Shangri-La hotel. This was where she and her husband were spending $92,000 of Zimbabwe's foreign reserves on a holiday in Hong Kong. Richard Jones, who was on assignment for the London *Sunday Times*, said that she had ordered her bodyguards to attack him. While he wrestled with them, Mrs Mugabe started punching him.

"The bodyguard grabbed Mr Jones, wrestled with him, attempted to take his camera. He then held him while Mrs Mugabe struck him in the face repeatedly," said a journalist who witnessed the assault.

"I was in complete shock; she was totally enraged," said Jones, who claimed that he had suffered nine cuts to his face inflicted by Mrs Mugabe's diamond rings. "My face is still swollen from all the blows, and I have bruising as well."

Barry Ronge wrote, "For me, that high-heeled mugging was her Marie Antoinette 'Let them eat cake!' moment, but sadly, her expensively coiffed (and monstrously swollen) head will probably stay on her puffed-up shoulders."

The Hong Kong government elected not to pursue the matter. Jones was furious. "I think it's a disgrace for the Hong Kong government to allow a person to walk on a street in Hong Kong, punch a member of the media, and walk free from it. This is a town where the freedom of the media is a strong tradition," he said.

"This cancer on the face of the planet and his loathsome wife are the symbol of all that is evil and wrong with the continent of Africa." Michael Trapido on Robert and Grace Mugabe

Unjustified and cruel: sanctions

"The fact that fuel coupons are seen as a stronger currency than the official Zim dollar bears testimony to a nation in agony." Andrew McNulty, *Financial Mail*

Grace was forced to shop in Hong Kong in the first place thanks to targeted sanctions that prevented Mugabe and his cronies from browsing in Harrods or accessing the funds they'd stashed in Swiss bank accounts. Naturally, this was a particular bone of contention. "We believe that these illegal sanctions are not only unjustified and cruel, but they have also contributed deeply to the suffering and the poverty-induced polarization of the people of Zimbabwe," Mugabe said.

Donors were simply punishing Zimbabwe for his noble land-reform programme: "Our condemnation, our isolation is because my government took the necessary measures to create conditions for equal opportunities, for decolonization, for creating conditions in which our people could regain their lost resources," he said, deftly ignoring calls by the UN to free political prisoners and guarantee human rights.

"We are therefore ready and more than willing in playing our part and contributing towards the rebuilding of the global economy." Cue the violins.

Prior to the visit of an EU delegation in September 2009, state media again harped on about the sanctions issue, quoting an information ministry official who said that Zimbabwe would demand that the EU admit that sanctions were "wrong".

"Are they here on a public relations exercise or are they here because they realized they erred in imposing sanctions?"

Former MDC MP Job Sikhala said that sanctions should only be removed once Mugabe dies. "Mugabe must die isolated if he doesn't want to reform," Sikhala averred. "People can reform—even the evil Satan had the capacity to reform. So the ball is in Mugabe's court. If he fails to change he must be ostracized until his very last day on this universe."

> "There are no sanctions against Zimbabwe. The issue is that Mugabe has been denied access to civilized communities and I hope they will still deny him that opportunity until he has reformed himself." Former MDC MP Job Sikhala

"We have not invited these bloody whites"

> "They can go and hang a thousand times, they have no basis, they have no claim on Zimbabwe politics at all." Zimbabwean government spokesman George Charamba comments on international concern over the presidential run-off elections

The sanctions issue can be linked to Mugabe's calculated obsession with the British and, by extension, the West. It was a sore point. "What is Zimbabwe to Britain?" he asked the crowd at the launch of a food-subsidy programme. "The answer has not been provided, but we know what they want. It's regime change, so the resources of our country can come under their control."

At the time, inflation in Zimbabwe had passed two million percent.

At the funeral of Susan Tsvangirai, who was killed in a car accident, he attempted a more conciliatory note: "When we fight each other as brothers, it has nothing to do with the British. Zimbabwe is for Zimbabweans. We should be prepared to die for it, defend it and refuse to be divided by the British." he said. "We should refuse the sanctions. We should tell them to remove the sanctions so that we improve the lives of our people. All we want is friendship," Mugabe added. "We don't want masters. No more masters. Those who would want to be our friends and partners are welcome. Those who think the road to friendship can become the road to domination should stay away."

> "Zimbabwe has a history and heritage and it will never be afraid. Zimbabwe is not for sale and Zimbabwe will never be a colony again." Robert Mugabe, during the opening of a trade fair in Bulawayo

"Let everyone in the inclusive government and the country generally know that our nation will never prosper through foreign handouts," he said at another funeral, that of former deputy president Joseph Msika. In a pointed reference to his new best friends from China, he told the crowd: "The West seeks to divide us and disturb our peace. If they do not want to deal with us why should we continue to want their help?

"Zimbabwe need not be tied to any one corner of the world, least of all, to a corner of former imperialist and racist colonizers. We are not part of western Europe and the United States."

He was perplexed by Britain's announcement that it would repatriate hundreds of its elderly citizens still living in Zimbabwe. "They are free here. They are quite comfortable. It's queer, strange thinking by the British. We don't understand," he said.

Even after reports that he had been rushed to a Dubai hospital under mysterious circumstances, he still had the strength to rant about an impending EU visit, telling ZANU-PF's youth wing in September 2009: "Who said the British and the Americans should rule over others? That's why we say: down with you. We have not invited these bloody whites. They want to poke their nose into our own affairs. Refuse that."

It was all so terribly ironic. Mamphele Ramphele for one saw in the installation of Robert Mugabe as president of Zimbabwe at the end of June the "symbolism of British colonialism writ large".

"Unfortunately, many of our leaders cast themselves in the roles of the very colonial masters they replaced. Their revolutionary fire for freedom from oppression has too often turned into a passion for emulating the same oppressors and their methods. Such emulation is both in symbolic and material terms. It is a tragic indicator of the deep-seated yearning to be the master just like the one he replaced—more British than the British."

Robert Mugabe flies to England to see the Queen. Over a cup of tea, he brings up his plans for his country. "Your Majesty, can we turn Zimbabwe into a kingdom, in order to increase its force in the world market?"

The Queen shakes her head and replies: "One needs a king for a kingdom, Mr Mugabe and unfortunately you are most certainly not a king."

Not to be dissuaded, Bob asks: "Would it be possible to transform Zimbabwe into an empire then?"

"No, you silly chap," snorts the Queen, "for an empire you need an emperor, and you are most certainly not an emperor."

Bob thinks for a moment and then asks if it is possible to turn Zimbabwe into a principality.

The Queen replies: "For a principality, you need a prince, and you Mr Mugabe, are definitely not a prince." Pausing for a sip of tea, she adds: "I don't mean to appear rude but having met you, I think Zimbabwe is perfectly suited as a country"

Plus ça change

"I have had enough, haven't I?" Robert Mugabe, in apparent reference to the difficulty of forming a unity government

Nearly a year after the elections that were meant to bring some kind of relief to Zimbabwe's suffering people, the MDC and ZANU-PF were still trying to reach some kind of agreement over the unity government—and Thabo Mbeki was still ensconced as mediator. Frustrated, Tsvangirai wrote to President Kgalema Motlanthe, in his capacity as SADC chairman, asking that the regional body replace Mbeki because his relationship with the MDC was now in an "irretrievable state".

Tsvangirai said: "The negotiations have been hampered by the attitude and position of the facilitator, Mbeki. He does not appear to understand how desperate the problem in Zimbabwe is, and the solutions he proposes are too small. He is not serving to bring the parties together because he does not understand what needs to be done.

"In addition, his partisan support of ZANU-PF, to the detriment of genuine dialogue, has made it impossible for the MDC to continue negotiating under his facilitation."

At the same time, the MDC was reported to be angry about a letter written to Tsvangirai by Mbeki last week, in which the latter accused the MDC of undermining African leaders.

The media reported that Mbeki had taken issue with the MDC's statement accusing SADC leaders of being "cowards" for failing to tell Zimbabwean president Robert Mugabe to give in to the opposition's demands.

Mbeki, demonstrating that he had lost none of his facility with the subtle use of the race card, wrote: "It may be that, for whatever reason, you consider our region and continent as being of little consequence to the future of Zimbabwe, believing that others far away, in western Europe and North America, are of greater importance."

In contrast, Botswana's foreign minister, Phandu Skelemani, said that because the talks had produced so little in the way of results, his government was now prepared to allow Tsvangirai to operate "a democratic resistance movement" from within Zimbabwe's western neighbour, which was already home to many thousands of Tsvangirai's countrymen.

> "Mad Bob has even … oh, forget that twit … he is not even worth kakking on after a serious Biryani." Comment by 'Sanjay', Dispatch blogs

Tsvangirai later made himself unpopular with his supporters by telling them that Mugabe was an "indispensable, irreplaceable" part of Zimbabwe's 'transitional solution'. In an interview with the *Daily Telegraph*, Tsvangirai appealed to the half a million Zimbabwean exiles in Britain to return home and help rebuild their shattered nation.

"It is a workable relationship, surprisingly," he said of his meetings with the old crocodile. "Yes, I am actually surprised. Who would have thought that sworn opponents like us could sit down and talk about what's good for Zimbabwe? It's an extraordinary experience."

Citing the reining in of inflation from a world-record 500 billion percent to three,

Tsvangirai said that he needed to re-establish Zimbabwe's relations with the outside world: "We must be part of the community of nations again and not a pariah state."

> "Southern African leaders say they have been greatly inspired by the way in which Robert Mugabe has reinvented the concept of an election. 'It's brilliant,' said one head of state. 'You can lose at the polls and still retain complete control. It really gives us hope for the future when our people get wise to this sweet little racket we've been running.'" Hayibo.com

Well, as they say, *plus ça change, plus c'est la même chose.* Mugabe still retains his grip on power even as the fragile unity government threatens to disintegrate at any moment. ZANU-PF continues to target MDC supporters, and the South African government continues to soft-soap the situation. "President Mugabe is of an advanced age. It is not very helpful to devote all our efforts to dealing with him as an individual," deputy president Kgalema Motlanthe told parliament, attempting to justify why sanctions against Mugabe and his cronies should be dropped.

In September 2009, *Sunday Times* editor Mondli Makhanya reflected that Mugabe had managed to outlast all of the leaders who were in power when Zimbabwe first descended into chaos: Kabila, Nujoma, Mogae, Chiluba, Mbeki, Bush and Blair—all of them yesterday's men. "At the rate he is going," he mused, "he may even outlast the crop of leaders governing our region and those running-dog interested powers abroad."

Let us be honest with ourselves: all prayers and exhortations to higher powers aside, all fantasies about snipers and quail's eggs doctored with arsenic, all conviction that we all know exactly where he does belong, somewhere without air conditioning of any sort—Uncle Bob isn't going anywhere. We're stuck with him.

> "I wish someone would put me in a ring with Robert Mugabe … I could take him in the first round! I would knock him out with one left jab and change history by liberating the Zimbabweans. Failing this, why not hire a hitman to destroy Bob? He could do it with a clear conscience! … I am so furious about the kids who die there every day and the rest of the world does nothing to end his regime." Letter to the *Daily Sun*

> "Robert Mugabe is a doos." Title of Facebook group